HATUNQOLLA: A VIEW OF INCA RULE

FROM THE LAKE TITICACA REGION

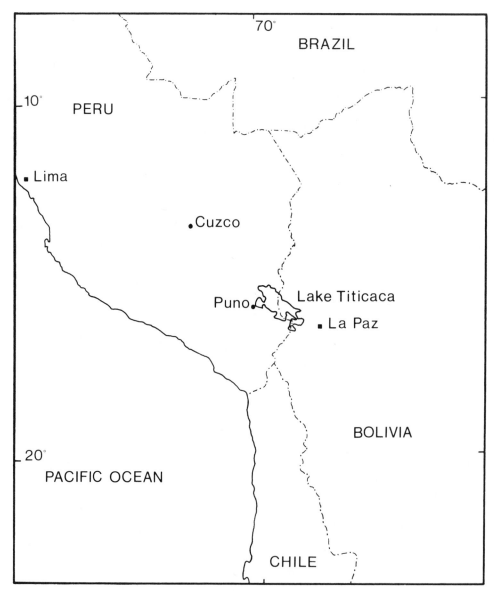

Modern Political Boundaries in the Lake Titicaca Region

Hatunqolla:
A View of Inca Rule from the Lake Titicaca Region

by Catherine J. Julien

UNIVERSITY OF CALIFORNIA PRESS

Berkeley • Los Angeles • London

UNIVERSITY OF CALIFORNIA PUBLICATIONS IN ANTHROPOLOGY

Editorial Board: Brian Fagan, Nelson Graburn,
Michael Jochim, Marc Swartz, B. J. Williams

Volume 15

Issue Date: June 1983

UNIVERSITY OF CALIFORNIA PRESS
BERKELEY AND LOS ANGELES
CALIFORNIA

UNIVERSITY OF CALIFORNIA PRESS, LTD.
LONDON, ENGLAND

ISBN 0-520-09682-7
LIBRARY OF CONGRESS CATALOG CARD NUMBER 83-3477

Library of Congress Cataloging in Publication Data

Julien, Catherine J.
   Hatunqolla, a view of Inca rule from the Lake
Titicaca region.

   (University of California publications in anthropology; v. 15)
   Bibliography: p.
   1. Incas--Politics and government. 2. Hatunqolla (Peru)
--Antiquities. 3. Colla Indians--Antiquities.
4. Indians of South America--Peru--Politics and government. 5. Indians of South America--Peru--Antiquities.
6. Peru--Antiquities. I. Title. II. Series.
F3429.P65J84 1983   985'.01   83-3477
ISBN 0-520-09682-7

Yten mandamos que ayga otro cuzco en quito y otro en tumi y
otro en guanoco y otro en hatun colla y otro en los charcas
y la cauesa que fuese el cuzco . . .

Felipe Guaman Poma de Ayala

Contents

List of Maps

List of Tables

Foreword

The present work was originally submitted as a doctoral dissertation to the Department of Anthropology at the University of California, Berkeley, in June of 1978 (Julien, 1978).

The dissertation project, a study of Inca rule in the Lake Titicaca region, was chosen in part because I was already familiar with the archaeology of Cuzco, the capital of the Inca empire. In the course of several field seasons in Cuzco, I had studied Cuzco-Inca style ceramics on the basis of a group of burial lots from the fortress of Sacsahuaman overlooking Cuzco (Julien, ms.). A knowledge of the imperial ceramic style aroused my curiosity about relationships between that style and other local styles. It was also necessary preparation for the study of a provincial Inca ceramic style. The Lake Titicaca region, moreover, was an interesting place from which to view the material expression of contact with Cuzco, since contact between the two areas is known to have antedated the Inca empire by at least two millennia.

The project involved both archaeological and historical components. The historical component of the study included such topics as provincial boundaries, ethnicity, language and imperial administration. The focus of the archaeological portion of the work was the site of Hatunqolla, known historically to have been an Inca provincial administrative center. Both parts of the study were presented in the dissertation, and each seemed to be independent of the other to a high degree.

This revision was undertaken two years after submission of the dissertation. Increased reflection upon the findings of my fieldwork permitted me to see more clearly the inter-relationship between the archaeological and historical studies. Both Part One and Part Three have been largely rewritten to make the presentation of my findings more coherent. Other changes have been purely editorial. For example, many end-of-chapter notes have been omitted or incorporated into the text.

The analysis of Hatunqolla ceramics has not been altered except to make minor editorial changes. As in the original, it was written to be read in two ways. For each phase there is a description of all analyzed material. Basic observations are made which are then gathered together in a summary section. If an abbreviated presentation of the analysis is desired, the reader is instructed to read the consecutive summary sections. In each, reference has been made to the illustrations, so that a consistent understanding of the ceramic sequence can be achieved in this way.

The chief objective of the archaeological work undertaken at Hatunqolla was to establish a ceramic sequence which would provide a precise relative chronology for the period of Inca rule in the area. Excavation in a well-stratified refuse deposit (Pit 1/1A, pls. 2-5) yielded a sample of just over 17,000 pottery fragments. [1] The fragments were treated as pieces of whole vessels, and the original shapes were recon-structed on paper as far as permitted by the size and condi-tion of the fragments. Patterns of decoration for whole vessels were established in similar fashion. Once the vessel shapes and the decoration associated with them were defined,

---

[1] All archaeological materials collected during the course of the project were formally deposited with the Centro de Investi-gación y Restauración de Bienes Monumentales (CIRBM), Instituto Nacional de Cultura, in Puno. Bone materials were deposited at the Museo Nacional de Arquelogia y Antropologia in Lima. Com-plete inventories of all materials collected were filed in the CIRBM offices in Puno, Cuzco and Lima in November and December of 1976.

virtually all of the excavated ceramics could be attributed
to vessel class. Changes in vessel classes from level to
level could then be studied qualitatively, and statements
made regarding the degree and kind of Inca influence reflected
in each. The natural layers of the deposit, as well as observations made about changes in vessel class, were the basis
for defining four phases of a relative chronology.

   Quantitative observations were also made in the course of
the study, though the analysis itself does not rely on quantitative supports. Observations about the relative quantities
of fragments from particular vessel classes, where significant,
have been included in the ceramic descriptions and summaries.
Two quantitative observations are of general significance to
the use of the Hatunqolla sequence. One is that a jar with
vertical handles (pp. 173-175) was represented in each level
by 30-50 percent of the total number of ceramic fragments.
The second observation is that somewhat less material was used
to define Phase 1 than was used to define the other phases.
Additional work with Phase 1 refuse at Hatunqolla should result
in some expansion of the definition of Phase 1.

   One of the advantages of a qualitative analysis such as
the one presented here is its precision. Style changes allow
a period as short as the occupation of Inca Hatunqolla to be
divided into phases. The picture of changing Inca influence
traceable in the Hatunqolla refuse has important implications
for future studies of Inca ceramics in the Cuzco area. No
excavation in Cuzco has yet produced a ceramic chronology
sufficiently precise to show a pattern of change. Hints from
the changes observed at Hatunqolla provide the first clues
that such a pattern should be sought.

   Another advantage to the kind of analysis presented here
is that it gives significance to small lots of ceramic material
and even to individual pieces. For example, once the relative
chronology had been established using stratified refuse at
Hatunqolla, it became possible to relate other units of archaeological material in terms of stylistic contemporaneity. A
single lot of pottery from a burial found on the slope of Cerro

Azoguini in the city of Puno proved to relate stylistically to
Hatunqolla Phase 3.

At the same time, there are interesting differences between
the Azoguini burial and the refuse at Hatunqolla. The contents
of a refuse deposit reflect the consumption habits of the living group responsible for its deposition. We can recognize a
distinctive pattern in it even before we can explain what the
pattern signifies in cultural terms. A pattern of this kind
has been termed an "association pattern" by Dorothy Menzel
(1976, p. 221). The Azoguini burial had a different association pattern from that of the Phase 3 refuse excavated at
Hatunqolla, and I interpret the difference to mean that the
individual buried at Azoguini had a different status under
Inca rule than the contemporary household represented by the
refuse sample studies at Hatunqolla (Julien, 1981, p. 139).

The Hatunqolla sequence can be used as a local reference
standard, but it does not represent a complete or even substantially complete inventory of ceramic materials in use at
Hatunqolla during it pre-hispanic occupation. Research was
focused on a particular refuse deposit where conditions for
the establishment of a relative chronology were met. Additional work at Hatunqolla will expand our documentation of the
ceramic inventory at the site.

The Hatunqolla sequence can also be tied to the reference
standard for Peruvian relative chronology, the master sequence
defined for the Ica valley (Rowe, 1962). The Late Horizon is
defined as beginning with the Inca conquest of Ica. On the
basis of historical traditions, it appears that the Incas
established their settlement at Hatunqolla before they conquered Ica (see pp. 244-249). If so, part of the occupation
deposit at Hatunqolla dates to the period preceding the late
Horizon, namely the Late Intermediate Period. Phase 3 at
Hatunqolla should certainly date to the Late Horizon, but the
question of whether any part of Phases 1 and 2 does also must
await a finer relative chronology for Inca ceramics.

Acknowledgments

The work undertaken at Hatunqolla brought me into contact with many people and institutions. Even though the list is long, the success of the project greatly depended on support and and counsel received from many sources and I wish to put the contributions made to the project on record.

Field work was funded by a Fulbright-Hays Study Abroad Program Award and a National Science Foundation Dissertation Supplement. These awards made an excavation project possible. Marcia Koth de Paredes and her staff at the Fulbright office in Lima deserve special thanks for their hospitality and for attending to many matters concerning the project.

The excavation was conducted with an archaeological permit granted by the Comisión Técnica of the Centro de Investigación y Restauración de Bienes Monumentales (CIRBM) of the Instituto Nacional de Cultura (Acuerdo 03/10.4.75). Many people in the CIRBM offices in Lima, Cuzco and Puno facilitated the fielding of the project in compliance with Peruvian regulations, and their aid is gratefully acknowledged.

Two and a half months were spent actively excavating, from November 1975 to January 1976. The CIRBM supervisor of the project, Mario Núñez M., was an integral member of the project and collaborated actively in both the survey and excavation at Hatunqolla and Sillustani. Three other people participated on a full time basis in the active field work: Ruben Orellana N., an undergraduate anthropology student from the University of Cuzco, and Aristides Tisnado P. and Ricardo Quispe Q. of the rugmaker's cooperative at Hatunqolla. The field archaeology

was a team effort, and both the abilities and spirit of the
people involved were important to the success of the project.

While some laboratory activities were carried out in the
field, most of the preparation of materials for analysis was
done in Puno. Two people participated in artifact description
and analysis, including drawing some specimens: Ruben Orellana
N. and Ada González M., undergraduate students in anthropology
from the University of Cuzco. Two colleagues who visited
during the survey and analysis period also donated some of
their time to work on the project: Tom Lennon of the University of Colorado and Anne Fetizon of the University of Paris.
The participation of these people greatly advanced the pace
of work in this phase.

Many other people contributed indirectly to the project
with logistical support and counsel: Luis Barreda M., Guido
Calderón, Abel Muñiz, Jorge Flores O., Cesar Correa, Julia
Rea, Nyelko Vukovich, Peter Allen, Ramón León, Ariel Cordero,
Gen. Jorge Matallana and Walter Tapia B. A number of archae-
ologists looked at the Hatunqolla material and made useful
comments, including Luis Lumbreras, Hugo Ludeña, Rolando
Paredes, Elias Mujica, Alfredo Valencia and José Gonzáles.

Living alone and abroad requires another kind of support,
equally essential to the execution of this project and requir-
ing the same kind of acknowledgment. I would like to thank
the families of Antonio and Catalina Mayta, Ricardo Quispe,
Mario Núñez, Mario Tapia and all my friends in Barrio Azoguini.
In particular I would like to thank Elizabeth and Rosanna Kuon
Arce, the entire Paredes Eyzaguirre family and my compadres
Walter Tapia B. and Luisa Pérez de Tapia and their respective
families for welcoming me in out of the cold so many times.

At Berkeley a number of people provided counsel or help
during the composition and preparation of the thesis. John H.
Rowe, chairman of my thesis committee, gave his time freely
for consultation during all phases of the project. He was a
particular source of inspiration for the historical study contained in the first part of the thesis. As issues concerning
the nature of Inca provincial administration were raised,

he restudied sources and brought new material to light to
spark my full consideation of the issues. My attempts to
follow the pace of scholarship he set also enhanced the final
result. The other two members of my committee were Crawford H.
Greenewalt and William S. Simmons. Both graciously read the
dissertation and offered a number of insightful comments.
Lawrence E. Dawson helped materially with comments on ceramic
technology, and with his usual encouragement. George R. Miller
permitted me to use unpublished information on the Cuzco-Inca
style for comparison with my materials. Rebecca E. Villegas
donated time to help proofread. The Department of Anthropology
provided a small grant to defray the expenses of illustration,
and Gerry Moos helped in the administration and reporting of
the NSF grant.

My progress in revising the dissertation and preparing
it for camera-ready submission was furthered by a number of
people. Patricia J. Lyon read portions of the manuscript and
offered many helpful editorial comments. She and John H.
Rowe deserve my special thanks as well for their hospitality,
extended to me on several occasions after I left Berkeley
so that I might more efficiently work with the University of
California Press on preparation of the camera-ready copy for
publication. Finally, I wish to acknowledge my gratitude to
Rose Anne White of the University of California Press for her
personal and abiding attention to the many details involved
in readying the final manuscript for publication.

To all of you, thank you for your cooperation, counsel,
support and help.

Spelling of Native Names

In general all native names will be spelled according to the phonemic orthography recommended by John H. Rowe (1950), except for place names common in the literature and the names given to the naciones, or nations, as the Spanish called them. These names are given in Hispanicized spelling so that they can be more easily located on maps and in the literature. Two exceptions to this practice are the names Qolla (Colla in Hispanicized spelling) and Hatunqolla (Hatuncolla or Atuncolla).

The same name may sometimes be spelled differently. For example, 'urqosuyu has been spelled phonemically where I have supplied the term (cf. Maps 2 and 3 and Table 2). To follow a particular usage it has been spelled urcusuyu in the case of Urcusuyu Polychrome (p. 234), the name for a particular mode of ceramic decoration, and as urcosuyo when reference is made to the Corregimiento of Urcosuyo (cf. Map 1 and Table 2), a Spanish colonial administrative province.

INTRODUCTION

The archaeological study of empire poses an intriguing problem, perhaps because the archaeological signs of political organization often cannot be interpreted until considerable archaeological work has been done. If written records were being kept, or a reliable oral tradition is available, archaeological inquiry into political organization can begin at once within a framework that from the outset both raises and answers questions. In the Andean area, the written record was begun very near the time of the last Andean empire; it was begun by the Europeans who invaded Peru in 1532. In the study of the last Andean empire, organized by the Incas and centered at Cuzco, both written sources and archaeological remains can be used to address questions about the nature and degree of centralized control.

In the present study, both kinds of evidence are used to explore the Inca administration of the Lake Titicaca region to the south of Cuzco, focusing on an important provincial capital at the site of Hatunqolla. Hatunqolla, located about 26 km. from the modern town of Puno on the north end of Lake Titicaca (pl. 1) was the residence of the Qolla dynasty in antiquity. This dynasty put up considerable resistance to the

Inca conquest and provided the leadership for at least one
serious rebellion. Hatunqolla, then, should be an interesting
place from which to examine the nature and degree of Inca
control.

The project designed to approach this problem was affected
by several important constraints. First of all, no extensive
documents have appeared which concern the Inca province whose
capital was Hatunqolla. Since it was a matter of practical
necessity for the Spanish administrators to collect information
on the workings of the Inca empire, a tremendous store of
administrative records useful in studies of Inca rule awaits
discovery in archives. Recently there has been a significant
advance in the publication of these administrative records,
including a body of documentation for another Lake Titicaca
province (the Lupaca province) to the southeast of Hatunqolla.
Information about the organization of the Lupaca province
coupled with scattered references about other parts of the
Lake Titicaca region and general information on the workings
of the Inca empire are therefore the contribution written
sources make to the present study.

A second constraint was the need to establish a sequence
of archaeological materials so that material remains could
be interpreted in a historical framework. The archaeology
of the Lake Titicaca region for the time of the Inca empire
is still in its early stages, and some basic chronological
groundwork needed to be laid. First priority was given to
defining a sequence based on ceramic materials excavated
from refuse at Hatunqolla. Study of these materials left

little time to devote to other archaeological research.

Finally, to study the effects of Inca control it was
eminently desirable to identify material remains corresponding both to the time of Inca control, and before that, to
the time of Qolla autonomy. The choice of Hatunqolla as the
focus of archaeological study was based on historical sources
which referred to the site as a center of Inca provincial
administration and as the capital of the earlier Qolla
dynasty. The modern town of Hatunqolla has been clearly
identified as the Inca administrative center by earlier
investigators who have found abundant evidence for the Inca
presence in surface ceramic materials. However, numerous
test excavations conducted at Hatunqolla revealed that
nowhere at the site was there any evidence of an occupation
prior to the time the Incas exerted control over the area.
Any hopes of obtaining stratified archaeological materials
at Hatunqolla corresponding to the era of local autonomy were
therefore abandoned; locating stratified materials corresponding precisely to the time prior to the founding of Hatunqolla
would have required considerable additional archaeological
fieldwork. Surface materials which on stylistic grounds
were thought to precede the Hatunqolla materials were found
during archaeological reconnaissance in the area, so the
deficiency was rectified in part.

Because of these operating constraints, it was not
possible to devote much time to using archaeological evidence
to check inferences from historical sources or vice versa.

The archaeological evidence turned out mainly to supplement
the conclusions reached in the historical part of the study,
providing additional information on the nature and degree of
Inca influence at Hatunqolla.

For this reason the study is organized in two parts,
the first examining the information contained in historical
sources, and the second analyzing archaeological data from
excavations and reconnaissance in and around Hatunqolla.

Three aspects of the political and cultural organization
of the Lake Titicaca region under the Inca empire were
examined using written sources. The boundaries of Inca
provinces can be roughly delineated by carefully tracing
early Spanish colonial boundaries backward in time to their
non-Spanish origins (Chapter I). A considerable body of
information about the population of the region in the 16th
Century can also be compiled. The region was crosscut by
language and other cultural boundaries. Early writers were
aware of differences in the local population but did a poor
job of ethnographic reporting on the distribution of these
differences. Recently published documents shed new light
on the distribution of languages and other features which
characterize the ethnic division of the local population
(Chapter II). No specific description of the Inca administration of the province controlled from Hatunqolla exists, but
there is enough information on Inca provincial administration
in general to reconstruct its outlines for this province.
Since local people were involved in the administration of
the Inca tribute system, the nature and degree of Inca

control can be profitably examined in this context. Inca
control is also apparent from a study of Inca relocation
policies, which resulted in major movements of people within
and between provinces (Chapter III). From this general
discussion of boundaries, people and institutions in the Lake
Titicaca region, a picture of the Inca province controlled
from Hatunqolla emerges. It is useful as a set of parameters
within which archaeological interpretation can best be
framed.

The second part of the study reports on archaeological
exploration conducted in the vicinity of the modern town of
Hatunqolla. Two aspects of the archaeological study are
presented in detail: the survey and excavations effected in
the Hatunqolla area are reported and a more detailed discussion of the ceramic sequence defined on the basis of excavated refuse from Hatunqolla follows. Standing architecture at
Hatunqolla appears to be of recent date and there was
neither time nor sufficient resources to permit an extensive
clearing effort. Therefore, a program of limited refuse
excavation designed to address the problem of chronology was
adopted. In the course of this work a domestic structure was
unearthed which could be related to the time when Hatunqolla
was under Cuzco authority (Chapter IV). The most important
result of the excavations was the establishment of a
detailed ceramic sequence for the occupation of Hatunqolla,
corresponding to the time from the foundation of Hatunqolla
until its abandonment, probably in the first decades after
the European arrival. Three successive ceramic style phases

were defined which cover this interval (Chapter V).

Both archaeological and historical evidence suggest
that the Incas were active in this region and that the tie
between Hatunqolla and Cuzco was a strong one. However,
each method was used independently in arriving at these
conclusions. There are two areas in which the archaeological
and historical results can be coordinated, largely determined
by the nature of the archaeological research undertaken.

One is the use of historical information to provide
absolute dates to bracket the ceramic phases. The refuse
used to define the three ceramic phases which correspond to
the period Hatunqolla was occupied prior to its abandonment
in the years following the Spanish conquest was deposited
over a period of about 75-110 years.

The second use of historical information was as a means
of explaining the progressive "Incaization" of material
remains near the capital. The ceramic study can be used to
cogently argue that the founding of Hatunqolla coincided with
the beginnings of strong influence on the local ceramic
tradition (the Sillustani tradition) by the Cuzco-Inca style
of the Inca capital. Moreover, the ways in which the Cuzco-
Inca style penetrated the Sillustani tradition, and the
steps followed in this process, can be precisely documented
with Hatunqolla ceramic materials. Contact with Cuzco
resulted in some very fine local imitations of Cuzco-Inca
pottery. Still, the local potters did not fully perceive
the "grammar" of the Cuzco-Inca style. The greatest effect
of the foreign style on the local tradition was as a source

of ideas, particularly in the period of initial borrowing
from Cuzco. The penetration of Cuzco-Inca influence is an
important matter as it appears that the degree of this
influence found in Hatunqolla ceramic material was greater
than on any other provincial Inca style studied to date.
Still, the local Sillustani tradition remained vigorous
during the time of strong Cuzco-Inca influence, and a considerable florescence of local innovation unrelated to the
Cuzco-Inca style is evident.

There is an interesting parallel between Inca influence
on pottery and the influence of Inca construction techniques
on burial towers of the local tradition (chullpas).
Sillustani, the probable necropolis of the Qolla dynasty resident at Hatunqolla, is where the largest number of chullpas
built in Cuzco style masonry in the Lake Titicaca region can
be found. The mode of burial associated with chullpas was
entirely local and unlike Inca practice. The use of fancy
Cuzco stone masonry is usually restricted to constructions
associated with the Incas. Its use in chullpa construction
is a further example of the Incaization of material remains
associated with Hatunqolla.

The Incaization is a reflection of some kind of identity
with Inca rule, probably fostered by the concentration of
Inca activity in Hatunqolla. However, it is hard to recon-
cile this material expression of identity with the reputation
the Qollas had as rebels. Written sources document several
attempts by the people of the Lake Titicaca region, and
particularly by members of the Qolla dynasty, to seek

their independence from Inca rule. Before the Inca conquest

the Qolla dynasty appears to have had imperial ambitions of

its own, and when a rebellion against the Inca government

was declared, the rebels did not challenge the authority of

the Inca emperor, but rather tried to usurp it. The strong

identity of these same people with the material symbols of

Inca authority, principally seen in ceramic remains and stone-

work, may not have been so much an expression of solidarity

with Inca imperial goals as a reflection of local imperial

ambitions.

1

INCA PROVINCIAL BOUNDARIES
IN THE LAKE TITICACA REGION

Tawantinsuyu was the name given by the Incas to their empire. It means "four quarters," and refers to the division of the empire into four parts. Each part, or _suyu_, was traversed by an important road linking that quarter with the imperial capital at Cuzco. The southern quarter of the empire was named Qollasuyu after the Qollas, following the Inca custom of naming each quarter after an important local group. Beyond the division into quarters, the empire was further divided into provinces. In the Qollasuyu quarter, the Inca provincial division can be traced at least as far south as Lipes and Chichas in what is now southern Bolivia.[1]

Reconstructing Inca provincial territories in the Lake Titicaca region can be attempted using Spanish administrative records from the later 16th Century. These records provide enough information to document the continuity between late Inca and early Spanish colonial era boundaries in this region. The case for establishing Inca provincial boundaries in the Qollasuyu quarter rests on determining which of two territorial divisions made during the period from 1565 to 1585 is closer to the Inca provincial division.

Continuity in boundaries is evident despite the more
than 30 year lapse which occurred between the time of the
Spanish invasion in 1532 and the establishment of the two
territorial divisions mentioned above. Both territorial
divisions were established after 1565 for different Spanish
colonial administrative ends. One, the corregimiento division, was intended to serve as the basis for rural administration under the Spanish regime. The other, the capitanía
division, was set up to facilitate mine labor recruitment.
Both divisions are similar to one another, but by checking
them against territorial information collected in the years
just following the Spanish invasion, it is possible to
connect the capitanía division more closely with a division
that in all probability was the Inca provincial division.
This argument is involved, but it is worth presenting in
some detail.

The corregimiento division was established before the
capitanía one. Corregimientos were based on encomienda
grants. Encomienda grants were made by the Spanish Crown to
reward particular individuals for their services. Each grant
consisted of a specific group of people subject to a particular native leader or kuraka.[2] Corregimientos, then, were
indirectly based on native political organization. The
encomienda grants of this time were made for two lifetimes.
Each grant was called by either the name of the people whose
services were granted or by a place name. During the same
period the corregimiento division was made, dispersely
settled people were being resettled in nucleated settlements,

many of which have continued to be inhabited until the
present day. The districts of these towns and particular
encomienda territories were often equivalent, so that it is
possible by locating these modern towns to map the
corregimiento territories (Map 1).

Attempts were made to establish corregimientos before
1565 (Rowe, 1957, pp. 161-162; Montesinos, 1906, tomo XIV,
p. 15), but only after 1565 were these establishments
successful (Maúrtua, 1906, tomo 1, p. 75). The first
detailed listing of corregimientos available for study is a
document drafted by Cristóbal de Miranda in 1583 (Miranda,
1906 and 1925). The Miranda document was based on the
1571-1573 tribute assessment of Francisco de Toledo (Toledo,
1975). The published tribute assessment lists only encomiendas, but does not indicate their grouping into corregimientos. At some point between 1571-1573 and 1583, the
corregimiento boundaries were established.

Before 1565 the only bounded territories in the Spanish
colonial administration were the districts of cities, but
since these districts were far larger than Inca provincial
territories, their limits are not likely to provide much
detail about Inca provincial boundaries. At the same time,
the lack of boundaries established by the Spanish colonial
administration before 1565 ensures that the only precedent
for bounding the corregimientos were Inca provincial boundaries or other local ones. The corregimientos do approximate Inca provincial boundaries, it will be argued, but not
as closely as the capitanía division.

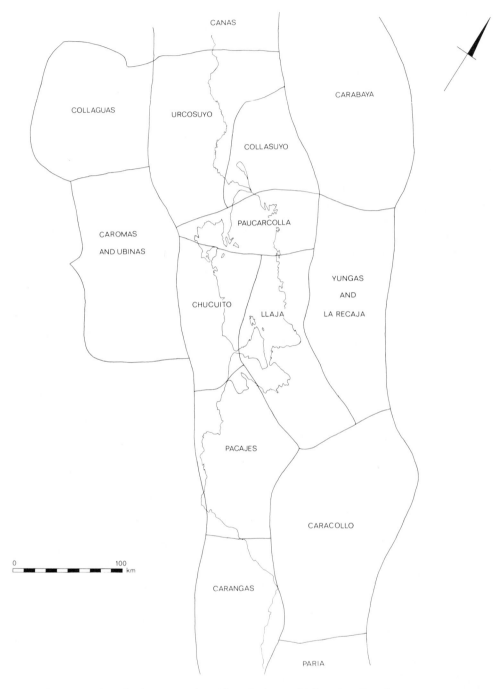

MAP 1. Corregimientos in the Lake Titicaca Region.

The capitanía division was created for the purposes of recruiting labor for the silver mines at Potosí. Potosí is located in the southern half of the Qollasuyu quarter, and quotas of men from the surrounding highland areas were assigned to work in the mines there owing to the nearly uniform high altitude of their territory, a necessary pre-adaptation to the extreme high altitude of Potosí, and their nearness to the mines (Capoche, 1959, p. 135). Territories, similar in size to the corregimientos, were the focus of labor recruitment. These territories, called capitanías, were defined with reference to native groups, referred to by the term naciones or nations in the written sources. Since the naciones or groups within them had been awarded in encomienda, the capitanías could also be defined in terms of encomienda grants. A list of the encomiendas in each capitanía dating to 1585 has survived (Capoche, 1959, pp. 136-139), and the capitanías can also be approximately mapped (Map 2). This list may date to the preceding decade when capitanías were first established.

While naciones served as the basis for the capitanías, only in rare cases do the capitanías coincide with individual naciones. Much more usual is the lumping of naciones into a single capitanía, or the splitting of a nación into more than one capitanía. Each capitanía is headed by a single indivi-dual, or capitán, whose affiliation with a particular nación is given in the 1585 list.

Not only are the capitanías similar in size to the corregimientos, but in a number of cases there is a one to

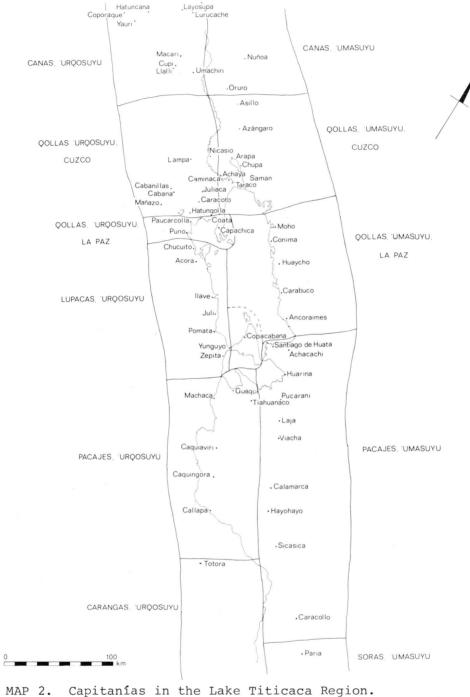

MAP 2.   Capitanías in the Lake Titicaca Region.

one correspondence between them.   In the case of the Lupaca
territory, the capitanía and the corregimiento territories
are identical (cf. Maps 1 and 2).   Other capitanías and
corregimientos substantially overlap and differ mainly at
their boundaries.   It will be argued here that the relationship between the two territorial divisions is that they are
both based to some extent on Inca provincial boundaries and
that the capitanía division is closer to the Inca provincial
division than is the corregimiento division.

At first glance, it is clear that the capitanía division
is making use of some kind of local territories, as the units
are composed of naciones.   Early Spanish sources, from the
period before 1560, help to document the existence of boundaries between the naciones in the early years following the
European arrival.

One of these sources was written by Cieza de León, a
Spaniard who travelled from Cuzco to La Paz in 1549 (1924).
Although he gives very few place names, the boundaries he
mentions are a closer reflection of the capitanía division
than the corregimiento one.   Heading along the Qollasuyu road
from Cuzco, Cieza passed through Urcos and then Quiquijana,
both Inca <u>tambos</u> or road stations (1924, cap. XCVII, p. 283).
He noted that a nación called the Caviñas lived in the
Quiquijana area.   The first Canchis town is further down the
road.   The corregimiento boundary is elsewhere, and it was
closer to Cuzco.   The places in the Corregimiento of Canchis
included the Villa de Leytosa in the valley of Andaguaylas
la Pequeña (Andahuaylillas) and San Clemente de la Laguna de

Vicos, evidently in the area of Urcos (Miranda, 1906, pp.
200-201). Andahuaylillas is even closer to Cuzco than Urcos,
so the Corregimiento of Canas and Canchis included considerable
territory on the Cuzco side of Urcos that was not part of
the Canchis nación in Cieza's time. Other evidence provided
by Cieza can be used to establish the antiquity of capitanía
boundaries in the Qollasuyu quarter in similar cases where
they differ from the corregimiento boundaries.[3]

Another check on which territorial division is the
earlier one is provided by the ordenanzas de tambos or road
station ordinances issued by Vaca de Castro in 1543 (Vaca
de Castro, 1908). The ordenanzas list Llalli as part of
Canas territory (Vaca de Castro, 1908, p. 432). Llalli was
part of the capitanía territory which included the nación of
Canas, but it was not part of the Corregimiento of Canas and
Canchis. Instead, Llalli was included in the Corregimiento
of Urcosuyo, a corregimiento that was composed mainly of
Qollas (see Map 1)(Miranda, 1906, p. 195).

The ordenanzas contain another kind of evidence for the
antiquity of the capitanía division. They suggest the equa-
tion of some of the capitanías with entire Inca provinces.

The ordenanzas document the course of the Inca royal
road through the Qollasuyu quarter and list the road stations,
in order, along it. These road stations were staffed by
people who also served encomenderos. Since the ordenanzas
give the name of the encomendero or encomenderos who had to
staff each road station, it is possible to reconstruct the
early encomienda situation, at least in part. The

ordenanzas were issued in 1543, not long after the death of
Francisco Pizarro (in 1541), the author of the earliest
grants. In several cases grants vacated before 1543 had not
been reassigned, and the original holder's name appears in
the ordenanzas. For example, there is a reference to Diego
de Almagro, co-director of the invasion of Peru (Vaca de
Castro, 1908, p. 437). If Almagro's grant had passed to his
son after his death in 1538, the course it would have taken
as grants were awarded then for two lifetimes, it would have
reverted to the Crown after his son's death in 1542 (Means,
1932, pp. 67, 80). This grant was not reassigned, however.
Another grant which apparently remained vacant was the grant
Francisco Pizarro awarded himself in the southern Lake
Titicaca basin (Vaca de Castro, 1908, pp. 436-437). This
evidence suggests that the grant situation may have remained
somewhat static since before the time of Francisco Pizarro's
death.

By studying the list of Spaniards who received very
early grants in conjunction with the capitanía lists, a
pattern emerges (see Table 1). Francisco made a number of
large grants to single individuals, including himself, his
brother Gonzalo, Francisco de Carvajal (a member of his
original raiding party) and the Spanish Crown. These large
grants are territorially similar to a number of capitanías.
Pizarro granted the territory which corresponds to the
Lupaca capitanía to the Crown. He awarded himself the territory which corresponds to the two Pacajes capitanías. To
his brother Gonzalo, he apparently awarded the same territory

TABLE 1

Early Encomienda Grants
in the Lake Titicaca Region

Tambo	Encomendero	Nación
Ayaviri	Villacastín	Qolla, 'Umasuyu[1]
Pupuja	----	----
Chuquicache	----	Qolla, 'Umasuyu[2]
Huancané	Francisco Hernández	----
Moho	Francisco de Carvajal	Qolla, 'Umasuyu
Guaycho	Francisco de Carvajal	Qolla, 'Umasuyu
Carabuco	Francisco de Carvajal	Qolla, 'Umasuyu
Achacache	Francisco Pizarro	Pacajes, 'Umasuyu
Guarina	Francisco Pizarro	Pacajes, 'Umasuyu
Pucarani	Francisco Pizarro	Pacajes, 'Umasuyu
Llaja	Francisco Pizarro	Pacajes, 'Umasuyu
Viacha	Francisco Pizarro	Pacajes, 'Umasuyu
Calamarca	Francisco Pizarro	Pacajes, 'Umasuyu
Hayohayo	Antonio Altamirano	Pacajes, 'Umasuyu
Sicasica	Antonio Altamirano Gabriel de Rojas*	----
Caracollo	Manjares	Pacajes, 'Urqosuyu
Paria	Pedro del Barco	Soras, 'Umasuyu
Guanachuspa	Alonso Riquelme*	----
Chayanta	Gonzalo Pizarro	Charca, 'Umasuyu
Pocoata	Gonzalo Pizarro	----
Macha	Gonzalo Pizarro	Caracara, 'Urqosuyu
Caracara	Gonzalo Pizarro	Caracara, 'Urqosuyu
Moromoro	Gonzalo Pizarro	Caracara, 'Urqosuyu
Pucará	Gonzalo Pizarro	----
Nicasio	Francisco Maldonado	Qolla, 'Urqosuyu
Camata	Hernando Bachicao	----
Caracoto	Anton Ruiz	Qolla, 'Urqosuyu
Paucarcolla	Capitán Guevara*	Qolla, 'Urqosuyu
Puno	Macuelas	Qolla, 'Urqosuyu

(Table 1, cont.)

Tambo	Encomendero	Nación
Chucuito	Crown	Lupaca, 'Urqosuyu
Acora	Crown	Lupaca, 'Urqosuyu
Ilave	Crown	Lupaca, 'Urqosuyu
Juli	Crown	Lupaca, 'Urqosuyu
Pomata	Crown	Lupaca, 'Urqosuyu
Zepita	Crown	Lupaca, 'Urqosuyu
Machaca	Francisco Pizarro	Pacajes, 'Urqosuyu
Caquiaviri	Francisco Pizarro	Pacajes, 'Urqosuyu
Caquingora	Francisco Pizarro	Pacajes, 'Urqosuyu
Callapa	Antonio Altamirano	Pacajes, 'Urqosuyu
Totora	Francisco de Retamoso Lope de Mendieta	Carangas, 'Urqosuyu
Choquecota	Lope de Mendieta	Carangas, 'Urqosuyu
Corque	----	Carangas, 'Urqosuyu
Andamarca	----	Carangas, 'Urqosuyu
Churimarca	----	----
Aullaga	Pedro de Inojosa	Asanaques/Quillacas, 'Urqosuyu
donde Aldana	Hernando de Aldana	----

*Encomendero from a nearby encomienda.

---

[1]Listed as Ayaviri Chichero in Capoche (1959, p. 136).

[2]Chuquicache was a territory that included Pupuja, Caquizana, Achaya, Saman, Pusi and Caminaca (Maúrtua, 1906, tomo 1, p. 76 and 195-196).

TABLE 2

Comparison of Corregimientos and Naciones
in the Lake Titicaca Region

Corregimiento	Encomendero	Nación
Urcosuyo		
Macarí	----	Cana, 'Urqosuyu
Omachiri	----	Cana, 'Urqosuyu
Llalli	----	Cana, 'Urqosuyu
Ayaviri and Cupi	Villacastín	Qolla, 'Umasuyu[1]
Vilacache	----	Qolla, 'Urqosuyu
Nuñoa	----	Cana, 'Umasuyu
Oruro	----	Cana, 'Umasuyu
Pucará	Gonzalo Pizarro	----
Sangasara	Setiel	----
Juliaca	Hernando Bachicao	Qolla, 'Urqosuyu
Lampa	----	Qolla, 'Urqosuyu
Mañazo and Vilque	----	Qolla, 'Urqosuyu
Cabanillas	----	Qolla, 'Urqosuyu
Cabana	Capitán Perançures	Qolla, 'Urqosuyu
Caracoto	Anton Ruiz	Qolla, 'Urqosuyu
Hatunqolla	Delgado	Qolla, 'Urqosuyu
Collasuyo		
Asillo	----	Qolla, 'Umasuyu
Asángaro	----	Qolla, 'Umasuyu
Arapa	----	Qolla, 'Umasuyu
Chupa	----	Qolla, 'Umasuyu
Caquizana	----	Qolla, 'Umasuyu
Caminaca	----	Qolla, 'Umasuyu
Saman	----	Qolla, 'Umasuyu
Taraco	----	Qolla, 'Umasuyu
Pusi	----	
Paucarcolla		
Huancané	Francisco Hernández	----
Vilque	----	----

(Table 2, cont.)

Corregimiento	Encomendero	Nación
Paucarcolla, cont.		
Moho and Conima	Francisco de Carvajal	Qolla, 'Umasuyu
Coata	----	Qolla, 'Urqosuyu
Capachica	----	Qolla, 'Urqosuyu
Paucarcolla	----	Qolla, 'Urqosuyu
Puno	Maçuelas	Qolla, 'Urqosuyu
Chucuito		
Chucuito	Crown	Lupaca, 'Urqosuyu
Acora	Crown	Lupaca, 'Urqosuyu
Ilave	Crown	Lupaca, 'Urqosuyu
Juli	Crown	Lupaca, 'Urqosuyu
Pomata	Crown	Lupaca, 'Urqosuyu
Yunguyo	Crown	Lupaca, 'Urqosuyu
Zepita	Crown	Lupaca, 'Urqosuyu
Llaja		
Guaycho	Francisco de Carvajal	Qolla, 'Umasuyu
Guangasco	----	Qolla, 'Umasuyu
Carabuco	Francisco de Carvajal	Qolla, 'Umasuyu
Ancoraimes	----	Qolla, 'Umasuyu
Achacache	Francisco Pizarro	Pacajes, 'Umasuyu
Copacabana	----	----
Guarina	Francisco Pizarro	Pacajes, 'Umasuyu
Pucarani	Francisco Pizarro	Pacajes, 'Umasuyu
Llaja	Francisco Pizarro	Pacajes, 'Umasuyu
Chuquiabo	----	----
Pacajes		
Guaqui	----	Pacajes, 'Urqosuyu
Tiahuanaco	----	Pacajes, 'Urqosuyu

(Table 2, cont.)

Corregimiento	Encomendero	Nación
Pacajes, cont.		
Machaca la Grande	Francisco Pizarro	Pacajes, 'Urqosuyu
Machaca la Grande	Francisco Pizarro	Pacajes, 'Urqosuyu
Viacha	Francisco Pizarro	Pacajes, 'Urqosuyu
Caquiaviri	Francisco Pizarro	Pacajes, 'Umasuyu
Caquingora	Francisco Pizarro	Pacajes, 'Urqosuyu
Callapa	Antonio Altamirano	Pacajes, 'Urqosuyu

_____

[1]Listed as Ayaviri Chichero in Capoche (1959, p. 136).

as that occupied by the capitanía of Caracara and part or all of the capitanía of Charcas. To Francisco de Carvajal, he gave part of the capitanía of the Qollas of 'Umasuyu, the portion which fell within the limits of the La Paz city district (Vaca de Castro, 1908, p. 437).

The consistency of fit for a number of these large grants with the capitanías suggests that the capitanías were based on a territorial organization that existed at the time Pizarro made his grants. This fit is not nearly as good using the corregimiento boundaries (see Table 2). For example, the grant given to Francisco de Carvajal is split between two corregimientos: Paucarcolla and Llaja. The corregimiento of Llaja included a number of places, specifically Guarina, Pucarani and Llaja, which were part of the capitanía of Pacajes of 'Umasuyu and part of the large grant Francisco Pizarro awarded himself.

Another clue to the antiquity of the capitanía division is the assignment of each capitanía to either 'Urqosuyu or 'Umasuyu. The Qollasuyu quarter was divided into two parts. If a line is drawn from Cuzco to La Plata (modern Sucre), bisecting Lake Titicaca, the territory north of this line corresponds to the division of Qollasuyu known as 'Umasuyu, and the territory south to the division known as 'Urqosuyu. The evidence for this division is found in the capitanía lists: each capitanía was listed as either 'Urqosuyu or 'Umasuyu except the capitanía of Condes, probably because it was not part of Qollasuyu (Capoche, 1959, p. 139). The mapping of the capitanías makes the division in halves

obvious (see Maps 2 and 3).

The names 'Urqosuyu and 'Umasuyu were also given to

different branches of the Inca road of Qollasuyu (Map 3).

The Qollasuyu road forked in Ayaviri.   The branch following

the southern shore of Lake Titicaca was known as 'Urqosuyu,

while the road following the northern shore was called

'Umasuyu.   The two branches joined again before or upon

reaching the road station at Caracollo, to continue on to

La Plata (Sucre)(Vaca de Castro, 1908, pp. 432-433, 436,

438).

The exact nature of the boundary between the two halves

cannot be determined.   Natural topographic features or the

road system may have been used as the physical basis for

this boundary, or it may have been based on other principles

(Bouysse-Cassagne, 1978).

The 'Umasuyu-'Urqosuyu division is a very significant

one, and where single naciones are split into parts, this

division is responsible.   The naciones of Canas, Canchis,

Qollas and Pacajes are split into two parts by the division

into 'Umasuyu and 'Urqosuyu territories.   The division of

the entire Qollasuyu quarter into halves was certainly not

Spanish in origin.   Division into halves was a feature of

Andean social organization, at least in Inca times and

afterward (Murra, 1968, pp. 117-118).   Many smaller social

units were organized into saya divisions, called Hanansaya

and Hurinsaya in the southern half of the Inca empire.

Cuzco itself was divided in this way.[4]   The names <u>hanan</u> and

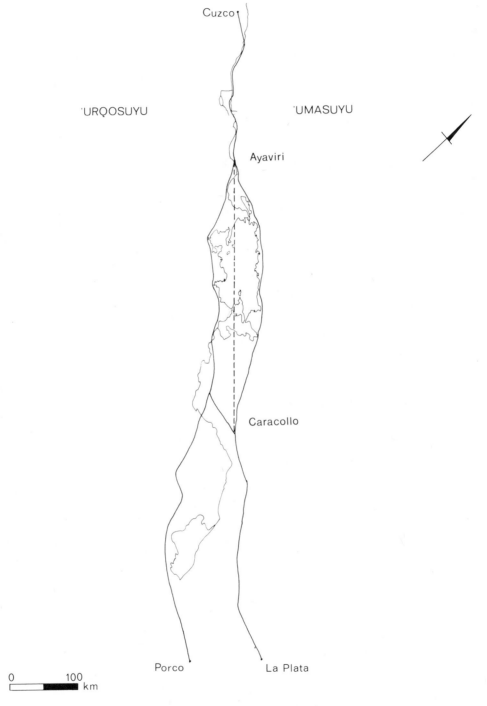

MAP 3. Roads in the Lake Titicaca Region.

hurin meant higher and lower in the physiographical sense,
but also referred to higher and lower status (Capoche, 1959,
p. 140; Cobo, 1964, tomo 92, lib. 12, cap. XXIV, p. 112).
'Urqosuyu and 'Umasuyu were also hierarchically ordered,
and 'Urqosuyu was accorded higher prestige. The author of
the capitanía lists, Luis Capoche, devotes an aside to
explaining what 'Urqosuyu and 'Umasuyu meant. 'Urqosuyu
people had the reputation of being masculine and strong,
according to Capoche, while 'Umasuyu people were feminine
and "not worth much." People from 'Urqosuyu had higher
prestige than 'Umasuyu people, and the Inka always let them
be at his right side in public places (Capoche, 1959, p.
140). Capoche also noted that 'Umasuyu people lived down on
the flat lands near the water. 'Uma meant water, and 'urqo
meant hill, so there may have been a physiographical aspect
to the division.[5] While some of the 'Urqosuyu towns are in
the flat lands and some of the 'Umasuyu towns are in the
uplands, the physiographical aspect of the definition of
'Urqosuyu and 'Umasuyu given above is another parallelism
with the division into Hanansaya and Hurinsaya.

   The division into 'Urqosuyu and 'Umasuyu is a major
feature of the capitanía division, while the corregimiento
one does not respect it (see Table 2).[6] If both territorial
divisions were based on an earlier division which respected
the 'Umasuyu/'Urqosuyu division, then clearly the capitanía
division is the more conservative one.

   If the capitanía division reflects a native territorial
division in existence at the time Pizarro distributed

encomiendas, then its most probable antecedent was the Inca
provincial division. There are a couple of lines of
evidence to support this idea.

For one thing, the capitanías did not correspond
exactly with the naciones of Qollasuyu. The capitanías
which coincide with the large grants made by Pizarro include
one case where an entire nación and capitanía was granted
(Lupacas); one case where part of a nación, but an entire
capitanía was awarded (Qollas of 'Umasuyu, district of La
Paz) and one case where a nación was given in one large
grant but was divided into two capitanías (Pacajes)(Vaca de
Castro, 1908, pp. 433-438). The remaining capitanías
include three cases where two or more naciones were grouped
together, one case where only part of a nación was included
and three cases where naciones made up the entire capitanía.
Splitting naciones and lumping them together indicates a
political organization with authority over all the groups.
This authority was held only by the Inca government in the
years before the Spanish invasion.

The establishment of another set of territories similar
to the corregimiento division is also an indication that
the capitanía boundaries were modelled after the Inca
provincial division. If territories of appropriate size
based on native leadership were all that was required for
Potosí recruitment, then the corregimientos could have
served. Inca provinces were centers of labor recruitment
for the Inca government (see Chp. III), and a possible reason

for reviving this particular territorial division was to revive the ties which had served the recruitment purposes of the Inca government decades earlier.

It is not surprising that the first Spanish administrative territories were modelled after the Inca provincial division. Pizarro's grants were made long before the Inca domain had been fully explored and must have utilized native political boundaries. Moreover, political boundaries in the Inca empire were well defined. A special class of imperial civil servants was charged with setting up stone boundary markers, and severe sanctions were applied against those who tampered with them (Guaman Poma de Ayala, 1936, pp. 352-353; Betanzos, 1924, p. 150). The Spanish administrators had no trouble with this kind of boundary, as stone boundary markers were used to mark territories by the Spanish government long into the Spanish colonial era.[7]

Using the capitanía division as a guide, it is possible to reconstruct the following Inca provinces in the Lake Titicaca region:

Qolla province of 'Urqosuyu

Qolla province of 'Umasuyu

Lupaca province of 'Umasuyu

Copacabana province[8]

Pacajes province of 'Urqosuyu

Pacajes province of 'Umasuyu

The list of Inca provinces is tentative, because even though these territories can be argued to have existed at the time of the European arrival, they may have been combined or split, creating a larger or smaller number of provinces. For example, it is possible that the two halves of Pacajes formed a single Inca province since Francisco Pizarro awarded himself both halves. It is also possible that the city district boundary between La Paz and Cuzco divided the Qolla provinces into four and not two provinces, as reconstructed above. The Qolla territory of 'Umasuyu within the district of La Paz was awarded to a single Spaniard (see Table 1 and Map 2), suggesting that the boundary had a non-Spanish precedent. Moreover, there was a settlement of potters and tapestry weavers near Huancané on the north side of Lake Titicaca. It may have been composed of people from only that part of the Qolla territory of 'Umasuyu which lay within the district of Cuzco (Murra, 1978b, pp. 418-420). This section of the boundary between the city districts of Cuzco and La Paz probably existed during the later Inca empire. If it was an Inca provincial boundary, Hatunqolla may have been the capital of one of four Qolla provinces.

Notes to Chapter I

[1]
Rowe, 1946, p. 162 and map 3, facing p. 184; Guaman

Poma de Ayala, 1936, pp. 983-984; Cobo, lib. 12, cap. XXII,

1964, tomo 92, p. 107; Cieza de León, 1924, cap. XCII, p.

272; Acosta, 1940, lib. 6, cap. 13, pp. 296-297; González

Holguín, 1952, p. 333; Pizarro, 1944, p. 179; Garcilaso de

la Vega, 1959, lib. 2, cap. XI, pp. 162-163.

[2]Rowe, 1957, pp. 159-161. My use of the word kuraka

requires some explanation. It refers to native political

authorities in the Spanish colonial era, but to officers in

the decimal administration during the time of the Inca empire

(Cobo, 1964, tomo 92, lib. 12, cap. XXVI, p. 115; see Chp. III).

[3]For example, the boundaries Cieza observed between Canas

and Canchis (1924, cap. XCVIII, p. 285), Canas and Qollas

(1924, cap. XCVIII, p. 285) and between Pacajes and the

province of Paria (1924, cap. CVI, p. 304; cf. Vaca de Castro,

1908, p. 434)are more in accordance with the capitanía

division than with the corregimiento one.

[4]Molina, 1943, p. 35; Segovia, 1943, p. 33; Castro y

Ortega Morejón, 1974, p. 94; Acosta, 1940, p. 296; Cobo,

1964, tomo 92, lib. 12, cap. XXIV, p. 112; Matienzo, 1967,
pt. 1, cap. VI, pp. 20-21.

[5]Capoche, 1959, p. 140; Bertonio, 1879b, tomo I, p. 27
{Vma}; González Holguín, 1952, p. 357 {Vrcco}.

[6]One area where the capitanía division may not follow
the 'Urqosuyu/'Umasuyu division is the area around Guaqui
and Tiahuanaco.   Both these encomienda grants are listed as
Pacajes of 'Urqosuyu in Capoche (1959, p. 136).   These two
encomiendas were also part of a corregimiento on the
'Urqosuyu side of the line (Miranda, 1906, p. 186).   However,
in a document recording the reassignment of the Pacajes
territories, formerly held by Francisco Pizarro, in 1549,
Tiahuanaco and Guaqui are listed as encomiendas in 'Umasuyu
(Loredo, 1958, pp. 205-208).   The Potosí assignment list for
1690 also preserves an 'Umasuyu assignment, even though the
earlier list does not (Sánchez Albornóz, 1973, pp. 96-131).

[7]For example, in the composiciones de tierras (sales of
excess lands) in the 18th Century, chain surveys were
carried out and stone boundary markers were set up or
renewed as necessary.   Some examples of this kind of activity
in the Lake Titicaca region are a survey in Vilque (Archivo
Nacional del Perú, Derecho Indígena, legajo 21, cuaderno 550,
año 1793), one in Capachica (Archivo Nacional del Perú,
Derecho Indígena, legajo 21, cuaderno 551, año 1798-1804)
and one in Azángaro (Archivo Nacional del Perú, Derecho
Indígena, cuaderno 574, año 1802).

[8]Copacabana may have been a separate province. In the
capitanía lists it was included in the Lupaca capitanía,
though it was noted that it did not belong to that province
(Capoche, 1959, p. 136). Under the Incas, the Copacabana
peninsula was settled with foreigners from all over the
empire; its original inhabitants were relocated in Yunguyo
(Ramos Gavilán, 1976, p. 43; see note 5 to Chp. III). Since
Copacabana was not part of the Lupaca province, its
assignment to either 'Urqosuyu or 'Umasuyu is also uncertain.

2

THE NATIVE INHABITANTS OF
THE LAKE TITICACA REGION

The Inca provincial division utilized existing
organization in the Lake Titicaca region, just as the
Spanish administration did some years later. The Inca provinces were based loosely on what the Spanish called naciones
or nations. The naciones observed by early European writers
had endured a century or more of Inca rule. The organization
that early European writers observed, then, may have been an
artifact of Inca administration, leaving the question of
earlier political organization open.

Earlier political organization may well have had
something to do with the bounded provinces the Incas established, and there is some information available which bears
on the subject. If political boundaries divided the area,
it was also unified by a common identity which can be
detected by references to dress, since a common form of
headdress and the head deformation associated with it characterized the entire region. The identity expressed by dress
may only have characterized the cultural majority, known as
the Aymara in the 16th Century and later times. Language,
occupation and wealth served to divide the native population

of the area along lines very unlike the Inca provincial
division.   The evidence for local boundaries will be taken
up in this chapter.

EARLIER POLITICAL ORGANIZATION

The naciones have been interpreted as "Aymara kingdoms"
in recent times (Lumbreras, 1974, pp. 200-201; Murra, 1968,
p. 115).   This term evokes an image of the political organization of the Lake Titicaca region at the time of the Inca
conquest, approximately 100 years before the European arrival
in 1532.   At that time, when the region was not governed by
a foreign authority, hereditary dynasties are presumed to
have controlled the area.   Aymara was the name given by
early European writers to both the majority language and the
cultural majority in the area, and so the term Aymara kingdoms associates hereditary dynasties with the cultural
majority.

The subject of political organization is difficult to
address because of the scarcity of references to it in the
written sources, but there is some information to support the
existence of hereditary dynasties in at least one part of the
Lake Titicaca region.   Precisely for the Hatunqolla area
there is evidence for a hereditary dynasty in control of a
larger territory.   A special case has to be made that this
kind of political organization existed before the Inca conquest, since members of the local elites served as officers
in the Inca provincial administration and since office was
hereditary (see Chp. III).   These officeholders would have

resembled hereditary dynasties to European writers, and they
may have behaved like hereditary dynasties after Inca
provincial administration came to an end; however, the
antiquity of each dynasty needs to be established before it
can be known whether or not it had pre-Inca origins.

Four local lords were mentioned by early writers. They
are Zapana (also called Chuchi Qhapaq or Qolla Qhapaq) of
Hatunqolla, Qari of Chucuito, Humalla from somewhere in
Lupaca territory and a lord of Azángaro.[1] All four had some
following in either the Qolla or Lupaca territories (see
Map 2). The names may be lineage or dynasty names, as the
name Qari and possibly Zapana were the names of Spanish
colonial era descendents of these local lords (Diez de San
Miguel, 1964, p. 13; Cordero and others, 1971, pp. 64-65).

Of the four lords mentioned, only one, the lord of
Hatunqolla, appears to have been a dynastic leader who controlled a larger territory before the Inca conquest. The
name Chuchi Qhapaq or Qolla Qhapaq is often used when referring to the lord of Hatunqolla before and during the time of
the Inca conquest of the Lake Titicaca region (Sarmiento de
Gamboa, 1906, cap. 36, pp. 75-77, cap. 40, pp. 81-83, cap.
41, p. 83). Qhapaq means hereditary king (González Holguín,
1952, pp. 134-135). It was used by Inca informants to refer
to a limited number of hereditary dynasties similar to the
Inca dynasty. It was used only in reference to several
dynasties in the Cuzco area, the dynasty of Chimor on the
North Coast, the dynasty of Cajamarca, the dynasty of the
Cañares and the dynasty with its seat at Hatunqolla in the

Lake Titicaca region (Sarmiento de Gamboa, 1906, cap. 19, p.
49, cap. 25, p. 58, cap. 37, pp. 75-76, cap. 38, p. 79, cap.
44, p. 87). In the case of the dynasty of Chimor, sources
independent of the Inca tradition can be used to establish
both the existence of a hereditary dynasty and a considerable
territorial domain under its control (Rowe, 1948, pp. 29,
39-41). All of the dynasties labelled by the term Qhapaq
were obstacles to the Inca conquest, and it is likely that
from an Inca point of view each group was similar not only
in terms of having hereditary rulers, but also in being a
political power of some importance.

Apart from the status of the Hatunqolla lord accorded by
Inca informants, there are other indices of the importance of
the Qolla dynasty. The earliest reference to the Qolla
dynasty, early in terms of Inca dynastic succession which
serves as a chronological scale in the historical accounts
for the years before the Spanish invasion, is found in the
account of Cieza de León. As noted earlier (Chp. I), Cieza
travelled through the Lake Titicaca region in 1549. He
recorded not only more information about the area than other
writers, but also obtained some of it from local sources
(Cieza de León, 1967, cap. IV, p. 7). Cieza describes
Zapana as the "tyrant" of Hatunqolla who had begun a
campaign of territorial aggrandizement at the time of the
first Inka, Manqo Qhapaq (1967, cap. VIII, p. 25). Qari,
the Lupaca lord, was mentioned by Cieza, but without reference to a contemporary Inca ruler. Qari was said to have
come from Coquimbo and to have founded a number of towns in

Lupaca territory (Cieza de León, 1967, cap. IV, pp. 6-7, cap.
XLI, pp. 138-139). Since Qari's activities were said to have
prompted the Hatunqolla lord to ask Wiraqocha 'Inka's aid to
defeat this upstart, the first Qari appears to have lived
during the reign of Wiraqocha 'Inka, the eighth Inka (Cieza
de León, 1967, cap. XLI, pp. 138-139, and 1924, cap. C, p.
290). For the other two lords, Humalla and the lord of
Azángaro, no information is available other than that they
participated in a general rebellion which probably occurred
following the death of Pachakuti, the ninth Inka (Cieza de
León, 1967, cap. IV, p. 7, cap. VIII, p. 25, cap. XLI, pp.
138-141, cap. LIII, p. 178).

Another document which spotlights the lord of Hatunqolla
is the account of Juan de Santa Cruz Pachacuti, a native of
the Canas/Canchis area just north of Qolla territory. His
account contains a song, sung by the Hatunqolla lord on the
occasion of the marriage and coronation of Wiraqocha 'Inka
(Pachacuti Yamqui Salcamaygua, 1924, p. 175). The song
implicitly compares the prestige of the two rulers:

    You are king of Cuzco

    I am king of Qolla

    We will drink

    We will eat

    We will talk

    Let everyone be silent

    I sit in silver

    You sit in gold

    You worship Wiraqocha Pachayachic {the creator god}

I worship the sun

Etc.

Even though the author was not from Cuzco, the song appears
to have a bias for Cuzco prestige indicators, as the lord of
Hatunqolla is deliberately portrayed as a person of less
stature than Wiraqocha by comparing indices of prestige.[2]
Even from a Cuzco point of view, however, the importance of
the Hatunqolla lord is still clearly evident.

A history of the Incas recorded from Inca informants by
Sarmiento de Gamboa indicates the territorial worth of the
Hatunqolla lord at the time the Inca ruler Pachakuti defeated
him in battle. When the Hatunqolla lord was captured,
Pachakuti went directly to Hatunqolla and waited until repre-
sentatives of the towns obedient to this lord came to declare
their allegiance to Pachakuti (Sarmiento de Gamboa, 1906,
cap. 37, p. 76). While it is obvious in Sarmiento's account
that Thupa 'Inka, the 10th Inka, militarily conquered some of
the southern Lake Titicaca basin, a large piece of territory
was annexed to the Inca empire when the Hatunqolla lord fell.
It cannot be certain that the entire region was controlled
by this lord, since some people may have submitted because
they were afraid to stand alone after a very powerful lord
was defeated. Still, the importance of the lord of
Hatunqolla is clear.

The lord of Hatunqolla was an important figure before the
Inca conquest, and there is a clue to the size of the
territory he controlled in the reconstruction of Inca provinces given in the last chapter (p. 28). The provinces were

identified by the names of several naciones. The provinces
identified as Qolla (see Map 2) cover a large territory,
one that may have been subject to the lord of Hatunqolla at
the time the area was annexed to the Inca empire. If the
story recorded by Cieza de León that Qari usurped Qolla
territory during the rule of Wiraqocha 'Inka was true, and
not just a biased point of view obtained from Hatunqolla
sources, then Lupaca territory may have been part of the
Hatunqolla lord's domain as well. If the story was true,
then the Incas may have been responsible for legitimizing
Qari and the territory he usurped (Cieza de León, 1924, cap.
C, p. 290, and 1967, cap. XLI, pp. 140-141, cap. XLII, p.
144).

The political picture resulting from a consideration of
the information contained in written sources in light of the
reconstruction of Inca provinces differs from the view of
the area as a series of "Aymara kingdoms." As yet there is
no information about the political organization of the southern Lake Titicaca basin. In the remaining region surrounding Lake Titicaca there was only one local lord identified
as a hereditary ruler in control of a large territory by the
Incas. This lord, the lord of Hatunqolla, appears to have
controlled a territory of considreable size, covering the
entire Lake Titicaca region excepting Pacajes territory and
perhaps Lupaca territory. The kind of control exercized by
this lord is not clear. If the account of Cieza de León
is correct, the Hatunqolla lord undertook military campaigns
which enlarged his territory. Whether the territory he

conquered was administered or owed only symbolic allegiance
leaves unanswered the question of whether this lord had
organized an empire or not.

QOLLA IDENTIFICATION BY HEADDRESS

The word Qolla has so far been used only in reference to
the territory labelled Qolla in the capitanía division from
which the Inca provinces were reconstructed (Chp. I). The
word Qolla had a much broader meaning for Cieza de León, who
described a "Qolla" territory which included the Qolla,
Lupaca and Pacajes provinces, from Ayaviri in the north to
Caracollo in the south. Caracollo is a common place name in
the area, but Cieza clearly lists the town along the Inca
royal road heading south in what was Pacajes province,
following Hayohayo and Sicasica (Cieza de León, 1924, cap.
XCIX, p. 287, cap. CVI, p. 304). This boundary is exactly
the southeastern limit of Pacajes territory. Cieza never
uses the names Lupacas or Pacajes in his writing.

What Cieza probably recorded were the limits of some kind
of larger identity. The quality of early ethnographic reporting is not such as to allow precise definition of this
identity, but some material evidence is available, particularly for headdress and the head deformation associated with
it. Similarities in men's headdress are found within the
area Cieza identifies as Qolla. A number of scattered
references in the early written accounts allow this larger
Qolla identity to be defined.

The most signal item of Qolla dress was men's headdress,
consisting of a tall brimless hat which narrowed at the top.
The illustrated work of Guaman Poma de Ayala shows four kinds
of headdress for the Qollasuyu quarter, one of which fits
this description (1936, pp. 147, 153, 169, 243, 270, 277,
293, 324, 364, 366, 384). Heads were deformed in conformance
with this shape. This kind of headdress was worn in the
entire Lake Titicaca region, from the northern Lake Titicaca
basin to the southeastern limits of the Pacajes provinces
(Map 2). The evidence is not pictorial, but comes from
descriptions of either the headdress itself or the kind of
head deformation associated with it. Head deformation of
the Qolla type was also practiced in Lupaca territory.
Braided wool was wrapped around an infant's head for more
than a year after birth (Diez de San Miguel, 1964, p. 224).
People in Pacajes territory wore the Qolla hat, but yellow in
color to distinguish them from others who wore hats of the
same shape (Jiménez de la Espada, 1885, tomo II, p. 59).

Some evidence exists that this kind of headdress was
not used outside the boundaries of the Lake Titicaca region,
except in the case of neighboring Collaguas province (see
Map 1). By 1586 native headdress in Collaguas province had
already been changed for the Spanish hat, but people in that
region were reported to have worn the Qolla hat before the
change. Head deformation is described for both Collaguas
province and for the Cabanas province further south, and from
the description, it is evident that the Collaguas practiced
the Qolla type of head deformation, while the Cabanas

practiced a different kind. The Cabanas wore a wide, squat

hat to match their style of head deformation. The author of

the information on head deformation in Collaguas and Cabanas

specifically associates the kind of head deformation prac-

ticed in Qollaguas with the Qolla type of hat, as does Cieza

de León (Jiménez de la Espada, 1885, tomo II, pp. 40-41;

Cieza de León, 1924, cap. C, p. 290). The Collaguas, then,

participated in the identity defined by headdress as Qolla.

North of Qolla territory, the different naciones wore

headbands of different sorts or hats of a style different

from the Qolla hat. The nación closest to Cuzco in the

north, the Canas, used a large, wide hat (Cieza de León,

1924, cap. XCVIII, p. 285). The Canchis, Caviñas and

Chumbivilcas all wore headbands (Jiménez de la Espada, 1885,

tomo II, pp. 14, 13, 22, 25, 29, 32, 35). Less information

is available for the area south of Pacajes. Men of the

province of Paria, the next province south of Pacajes, wore

a small woolen bonnet (Cieza de León, 1924, cap. CVI, p.

304). All the descriptions of the Qolla hat emphasize its

height as a distinguishing feature, so this bonnet was

not the same as the Qolla hat.

The origin of the identity evoked by the visual symbol

of headdress is not clear. The Incas encouraged the use of

headdress as a means of identification (Cieza de León, 1967,

cap. XXIII, pp. 78-79; Jiménez de la Espada, 1885, tomo II,

p. 45). In general gatherings, people were identifiable on

sight. Even colonists sent by the Incas to distant provinces

were expected to continue their native dress styles, though

observing many other customs in the new province.[3] Sanctions
were applied to people who wore the headdress of another
group (Cobo, 1964, tomo 92, lib. 12, cap. XXIV, p. 113).
Dress may have figured in the drawing of provincial boundaries, and one witness in Pacajes listed dress as one of
the criteria for demarcating Inca provinces (Jiménez de la
Espada, 1885, tomo II, p. 72). Despite Inca encouragement
of the wearing of native headdress, the Qolla headdress with
its accompanying head deformation almost certainly had a
local and not an Inca origin.

The evidence for headdress corresponds rather neatly to
the area Cieza identified as Qolla. Although the area was
not unified politically at the time of the Inca conquest
and it was divided into a number of provinces by the Incas,
the Qolla identity symbolized by dress survived into the
early Spanish colonial era.

LANGUAGE

The area was also united by a common language, called
Aymara, though three other languages are known to have
coexisted with it, called Puquina, Uruquilla and
Quechua, the Inca language. The distribution of these languages can be plotted from a document which lists languages
parish priests needed to learn to work in specific parishes
(Bouysse-Cassagne, 1975, pp. 314-317). Unfortunately, the
document does not include the district of Cuzco and there is
little information on the distribution of languages in the
northern Lake Titicaca basin. There may also have been

parishes in the area covered by the ecclesiastical document
mentioned above where only a few speakers of a language
resided or multilingualism was widespread, so that even if a
language was spoken in a particular parish it may not have
been necessary for parish work and so was not included on
the list. Still, the partial distribution of languages
recorded in this document and other evidence for language
distribution calls attention to the considerably different
distribution of languages from that found in modern times.
The modern distribution clearly cannot be presumed to
reflect the past situation in any detail.

Aymara

Aymara was the language spoken over the largest area,
by the largest number of people until at least the 17th
Century. Ludovico Bertonio, a Jesuit who compiled the earliest published grammar and vocabulary of the Aymara language,
reported in 1603 that Aymara was the dominant language in the
area from about 30 miles south of Cuzco to what is now
southern Bolivia (Bertonio, 1879a, p. 10). He described its
distribution by reference to naciones, including Canas,
Canchis, Qollas, Collaguas, Lupacas, Pacajes, Carangas,
Charcas and others. At present Quechua has replaced Aymara
in the area south of Cuzco, as far south as the town of Puno,
and in some areas at the southern end of the distribution
described by Bertonio. The Quechua language clearly gained
ground after the area was in Spanish hands, though it was

spoken in scattered enclaves in the area as will be
discussed in a moment.

Some differences were noted between Aymara speaking
regions, but all dialects of Aymara were said to be mutually
intelligible. The dialect of the Pacajes region had the
reputation of being the most elegant (Bertonio, 1879a, p.
11). The dialects of Charcas and Yamparaes were said to be
intelligible to all Aymara speakers but were singled out as
being somewhat different from the other dialects (Pizarro,
1944, p. 94).

Puquina

The distribution of Puquina overlaps with the
distribution of Aymara. The ecclesiastical document mentioned earlier listed a number of parishes where Puquina was
spoken (Bouysse-Cassagne, 1975, pp. 314-317):

<u>Qolla province of 'Urqosuyu (Map 2)</u>

    Paucarcolla

    Coata

    Capachica

<u>Qolla province of 'Umasuyu (Map 2)</u>

    Huancané

    Moho

    Conima

    Carabuco

    Ancoraimes

<u>Larecaja province (Map 1)</u>

Mocomoco

Camata

Ambaná

<u>Pacajes province of 'Umasuyu (Map 2)</u>

Achacache

Guarina

<u>Asanaques and Quillacas province of 'Urqosuyu</u> (Capoche, 1959, p. 137)

Puna

Except for Puna, located in what is now southern Bolivia, the areas where Puquina was spoken are near Lake Titicaca, particularly along the north shore of the lake and the inland region behind it. This distribution was noted by Reginaldo de Lizárraga, who reported that the majority of the population of Omasuyu (Qolla province of 'Umasuyu, within the city district of La Paz; see Map 2) were Puquinas or speakers of the Puquina language (1909, lib. I, cap. LXXXIX, p. 542). The ecclesiastical document did not include any parishes in the Lupaca province, though other sources indicate that it was spoken in Juli (see Map 2)(Ramírez, 1936, p. 48). It was also said to have been spoken in Chuquiabo (modern La Paz, near Laja; see Map 2)(Jiménez de la Espada, 1885, tomo II, p. 69).

Puquina may be extinct, except for a curious survival in the Charassani area, located near Mocomoco, where Puquina was spoken in the 16th Century (Miranda, 1906, p. 185). Apparently a Puquina lexicon is combined with a Quechua

grammar in a special language used only by curers during
their curing rituals and passed from father to son (Stark,
1972, pp. 199-201).

Uruquilla

The distribution of Uruquilla also overlaps with the
distribution of Aymara. It was a requirement for parish
work in the following parishes (Bouysse-Cassagne, 1975, pp.
314-317, 321):

Lupaca province of 'Urqosuyu (Map 2)

    Zepita

Asanaques and Quillacas province of 'Urqosuyu (Capoche,
1959, p. 137)

    Aullagas

    Uruquillas

Soras and Charcas province of 'Umasuyu (Capoche, 1959,
p. 137)

    Paria

Lipes province (Miranda, 1906, pp. 181-182)

    Lipes

Except for Zepita, the areas where Uruquilla was spoken
are in the far south, in the region of Lake Poopó beyond the
southern limits of Pacajes territory. The Uruquilla speakers
in Zepita were probably a group known as the Uruquilla of
Huchusuma, who were settled on an island in the Desaguadero
River near its source at the southern end of Lake Titicaca
(Toledo, 1975, p. 79; Calancha and Torres, 1972, tomo 1,
lib. I, cap. I, p. 113).

The distribution of Uruquilla suggests that this language can be identified with the Uru-Chipaya language spoken in the same area in the 20th Century.[4]

Quechua

Quechua, the Inca language, was a required language for parish priests in the following parishes (Bouysse-Cassagne, 1975, pp. 314-317):

Qolla province of 'Urqosuyu (Map 2)

    Paucarcolla

Qolla province of 'Umasuyu (Map 2)

    Ancoraimes

    Carabuco

Larecaja province (Map 1)

    Mocomoco

    Camata

    Ambaná

    Hilabaya

Copacabana province (Map 2)

    Copacabana

Pacajes province of 'Umasuyu (Map 2)

    Chuquiabo (modern La Paz)[5]

Cochabamba province[6]

    San Miguel de Titipaya

Mizque province (Miranda, 1906, pp. 175-176)

    Pocona

    Mizque

Yamparaes province (Miranda, 1906, pp. 177-178)

Condes de Aravate

Pacha

Conima province (Miranda, 1906, p. 174)

Tarabuco

The distribution of the Inca language suggests scattered enclaves of Quechua speakers. An enclave distribution may be a reflection of Inca relocation policies, which resulted in the movement of fair numbers of people from one part of the empire to another (see Chp. III). The places listed above are probably where people whose home territory was Quechua speaking were relocated. Early writers were told that the Incas tried to impose their language on the area they conquered, but the above distribution suggests they were not very successful in the Lake Titicaca region (Cieza de León, 1967, cap. XXIV, pp. 84-85). The Inca language was also said to have been used as an administrative language, and the local elites were expected to know it. Children of kurakas in Inca times were taken to Cuzco and educated in the Inca language, and the kurakas who took goods produced as tribute to Cuzco spent considerable time in the capital (Segovia, 1943, p. 33; Cieza de León, 1967, cap. XVIII, p. 56, cap. XIV, p. 44; Cobo, 1964, tomo 92, lib. 12, cap. XIII, p. 110, cap. XXX, p. 125). If local elites spoke the language, it may have spread locally because of the prestige associated with it.

ETHNICITY

The subject of ethnicity has already been taken up in
part, because both language and dress served as a means of
ethnic identification. Since the cultural diversity found
in the region in the 16th Century impressed early writers,
there is a wealth of references to aspects of ethnicity.
These references are often confusing, and one of the biggest
sources of confusion is caused by the imprecise use of names.
For example, the word "Aymara" variously referred to a language, the cultural majority and a tribute classification,
even though there were people who spoke Aymara who were not
members of the cultural majority and who were not assessed
as Aymara. This confusion can be sorted out in part because,
with the help of the ecclesiastical document mentioned
earlier, it is possible to determine when language corresponds with other aspects of ethnicity and when it does not.
Moreover, the publication of the tribute assessment or tasa
of Viceroy Toledo, levied in 1571-1573, also contributes a
great deal to understanding the relationship of occupation
and wealth to ethnicity (Toledo, 1975).

The tasa of Toledo classifies the entire population of
the Lake Titicaca region into two groups: Aymara and Uru.
People classified as Uru were taxed at half the rate of
those classified as Aymara. People classified as Uru were
located in a majority of the encomiendas listed in the tasa.
It is clear from the tasa that some of the people classified
as Uru spoke Puquina, while others spoke Aymara. Moreover,
some people classified as Aymara spoke Puquina. For example,

in Capachica Puquina was the only language required of
parish priests, but the people of this parish were classified as both Uru and Aymara for tax purposes (Toledo, 1975,
p. 62; Bouysse-Cassagne, 1975, p. 316).   The distribution of
people in two tax categories does not correspond in any meaningful way with the distribution of languages in the area.

People classified as Uru in the later 16th Century were
a lower status group considerably poorer than the cultural
majority in the Lake Titicaca region.   It was for this reason that they were taxed at half the usual rate.   The Urus
lived mainly by fishing and were settled on reed islands in
the lake or near the lake shore.[7]   People classified as
Aymara were cultivators and herders (Cieza de León, 1924,
caps. XCIX, C, CI, CII, CIII).   It is reasonable to suppose
that the occupation of the Urus did not generate as much
wealth as farming and herding, and that this occupational
difference may have been an important aspect of the ethnic
division.

The tasa of Toledo provides a clue to the impoverished
condition of the Urus.   People in the Uru category were never
taxed in animals or wool, unlike the Aymara taxpayers who
contributed heavily from their herds (Toledo, 1975; Diez de
San Miguel, 1964, p. 59).   This lack of animals may have
reflected the poverty of those classified as Uru or even
some sort of persecution rather than any disdain for
livestock, meat or wool on the part of the Urus.

The Urus ate meat, in fact they were said to raid the
herds of lakeside villages, killing and eating animals raw

with amazing speed, perhaps to avoid being caught with the
evidence (Vellard, 1960, p. 33; Calancha, 1638, tomo I, p.
353). Similar incidents occurred during the Inca empire,
as there is an account of an Inca attempt to resettle the
Urus on solid land which failed because the surrounding
people complained bitterly about the livestock thievery that
resulted from having Urus as their neighbors (Toledo, cited
by Vellard, 1960, pp. 32-33).

Despite their lack of access to herd animals, the Urus
were weavers (Diez de San Miguel, 1964, pp. 45, 62, 109;
Matienzo, 1967, lib. II, cap. 14, p. 276). Labor on woolen
clothing was the second most frequently assessed item to be
provided by people in the Uru tax category; the wool had to
be provided to them (Toledo, 1975). The Urus themselves wore
very little clothing, and it was made of reeds (Calancha,
1638, tomo I, pp. 650-651; Morúa, 1946, lib. III, cap. XX,
p. 214; Toledo, cited by Vellard, 1960, p. 33). Their
condition of poverty is again obvious, rather than a lack
of skill or interest in weaving woolen clothing.

Some Urus were said to own land, although land ownership
was not common (Toledo, 1975; Morúa, 1946, p. 214). In the
tasa of Toledo, people in the Uru tax category who paid
tribute in freeze dried potatoes, called chuñu, probably
owned land. The distribution of those taxed in chuñu is
interesting. They lived in the following places: Yaye
(near Guarina); Guarina and Tiahuanaco (Pacajes province of
'Umasuyu); Capachica, Puno, Paucarcolla and Coata (Qolla
of 'Urqosuyu); and Arapa, Saman, Taraco and Achaya (Qolla of

'Umasuyu)(Toledo, 1975; see Map 2). All of the places in

Qolla territory are very close to each other, and it can be

concluded that the Urus of this area were somewhat different,

at least in occupation, from most other Urus and appear

to have been materially better off.

Material well-being and occupation that would generate

certain kinds of tribute were considerations in the classi-

fication found in the tasa of Toledo. A similar classifica-

tion may have characterized the Inca tribute system in this

area. The same underlying differences between those classi-

fied as Uru and those classified as Aymara are illustrated

by the attempt to settle Urus on dry land which failed

because of livestock theft. The classification itself is

repeated in a late Inca census, recorded in a 1567 visita

or administrative survey of the Lupaca province (Diez de San

Miguel, 1964). In this census, recorded on a khipu or knot

record, the native inhabitants of Lupaca territory were

classified only as Aymara and Uru, despite the fact that

there were Puquina and Uruquilla speakers in the area (Diez

de San Miguel, 1964, pp. 64-66). Another indication that

the Incas classified the population into these two groups

and that the classification was based on wealth and occupa-

tion was a petition Toledo received while setting the tasa

of the Lupaca province. A group of wealthy Urus, living

near Zepita, owned animals. They petitioned to be reclassi-

fied as Aymara and were taxed in herd animals and wool

unlike other people classified as Uru (Toledo, 1975, pp.

32-33). Since reclassification effectively doubled their

tax, under the Spanish colonial administration it would have
been against their interests to ask for such a change.   If
the Spanish tribute system had borrowed the fundamental
classification from Inca practice, then perhaps they
expected some kind of gain from a change in status.   In any
event, the request illustrates that the classification was
not considered immutable by those classified.

Although the Urus were given separate tribute status
apparently on the basis of well-being and occupation, they
were also regarded as barbaric and uncivilized by the
native inhabitants of the area and Spanish administrators
alike.   The word uru was used as a pejorative, and unsavory
phrases were concocted in the Inca language which referred to
Uru behavior (González Holguín, 1952, p. 356).   In the descriptions of the Urus, the barbarity of their existence is
emphasized (Calancha, 1638, tomo I, pp. 353, 650-651).   The
Incas tried to organize the Urus into what they considered
an orderly existence.   Resettlement on dry land was mentioned earlier, and it may have been attempted more than once
and more successfully than the mentioned attempt.   Wayna
Qhapaq, the eleventh Inka, issued ordinances to govern the
Urus and assigned certain fishing areas to each Uru settlement (see note 7).   The Incas did not teach the Urus the
ritual practices associated with the state religious cult,
and this omission from a basic element of Inca rule indicates
that from an Inca point of view the Urus were uncivilized
(Jiménez de la Espada, 1885, tomo II, p. 55; Sarmiento de

Gamboa, 1906, cap. 59, p. 105; Cabello Valboa, 1951, pt. 3,
cap. 21, p. 362).

The Urus may not have been the only minority.
Differences in occupation, wealth and status between two
other groups, referred to as the Puquinas and the Choquelas,
may also indicate minority status.

References to the Puquinas are particularly problematic,
since the referent may be to Puquina speakers and not a
group as separate from the cultural majority like the Urus.
Martín de Morúa, who served as a parish priest in Capachica
in the late 16th or early 17th Century, classified the population into Qolla, Puquina and Uru. Qolla presumably referred to the cultural majority or Aymara group. Since in
Capachica the Urus presumably spoke Puquina (Toledo, 1975,
p. 62; Bouysse-Cassagne, 1975, p. 316), Morúa probably did
not refer to Puquina speakers with his use of the term
Puquina. Lizárraga noted that Puquinas owned large camelid
herds, referring to people in the Qolla province of 'Umasuyu
within the limits of the city district of La Paz (Lizárraga,
1909, lib. I, cap. LXXXVI, p. 540, cap. LXXXVI, p. 542).
Morúa noted that, of the Qollas and Puquinas, some raised
livestock while others lived near the lake among the Urus
(Morúa, 1946, lib. III, cap. XX, p. 214). There is a small
amount of evidence that the people referred to as Puquinas
utilized lake resources. Guaman Poma de Ayala said that both
the Puquinas and the Urus made sacrifices of fish and other
foodstuffs to the lake (1936, p. 271). This reference may

have been to speakers of Puquina and Uruquilla and not to
culturally separate minorities, however.

A few references to a group called the Choquelas suggest
that hunters living in the highlands away from Lake Titicaca
may have formed some kind of cultural minority. The
Choquelas were described as wild people who lived on the
highland plains and supported themselves by vicuña hunting
(Bertonio, 1879b, pt. 1, p. 107, pt. 2, p. 89; Matienzo,
1967, lib. II, cap. 14, p. 276). They were also said to have
no kurakas (Bertonio, 1879b, pt. 2, p. 290). Their hunting
occupation would necessarily have kept them away from centers
of population and probably also somewhat out of control. In
1574 there was a group accounted as Ayllu Chuquila Cazadores
(group of Choquela hunters) in the district of Chucuito
(Gutiérrez Flores, 1964, p. 312), indicating that these
people may have formed an occupationally specialized unit
in the Inca tribute system (see Chp. 3). Other references
to people who were hunters can be found, including the mention of a group of Urus who hunted vicuña and guanaco in the
province of Lipes in what is now southern Bolivia (Jiménez
de la Espada, 1885, tomo II, App. III, p. XXIII). Since
occupation was clearly one of the reasons for the classification of the Urus as a cultural minority, it may again have
served to set hunters apart.

INHABITANTS OF THE QOLLA PROVINCE OF 'URQOSUYU

As in most of the region surrounding Lake Titicaca, the
Qolla province of 'Urqosuyu contained people who spoke
Aymara, Puquina and Quechua and who were classified on the
basis of wealth into Aymara and Uru categories.

Information on the distribution of languages covers only
the part of the province within the city district of La Paz,
but Aymara was the general language of the area, and it was
probably spoken everywhere. There was a concentration of
Puquina in the Capachica area, where it was the only language parish priests needed to know in the 16th Century.
There were Puquina speakers in Paucarcolla, only 10 km. from
Hatunqolla, and so it is quite possible Puquina was spoken
on the Cuzco side of the La Paz/Cuzco boundary. The Inca
language was spoken in Paucarcolla. This site may have been
a provincial capital in its own right, or just a town subor-
dinate to the provincial capital at Hatunqolla. If the
presence of the Inca language in Paucarcolla was related to
Inca activities there, then it was probably spoken in
Hatunqolla as well. The presence of numerous foreign colonists from Quechua speaking areas might also account for the
language in Paucarcolla, and it might be expected that it
would be spoken anywhere in the province where foreign
colonists were numerous.

People classified as both Aymara and Uru were found in
all parts of the Qolla province of 'Umasuyu except in Coata
where only people classified as Uru resided. In this area,
at the foot of the Capachica Peninsula, and in the area of

Paucarcolla and Puno as well, people classified as Uru were
expected to provide chuñu (freeze dried potatoes) in the
tribute assessment of 1571-1573 (Toledo, 1975). These people
probably had access to enough land to produce a surplus. Not
all of those classified as Urus were required to provide
fish, however. Only people near Lake Titicaca (Puno, Coata
Capachica, Caracoto, Paucarcolla), Lake Umayo (Hatunqolla,
Mañazo), or up the Ramis River (Nicasio) were assessed in
fish. There were people classified as Uru in other parts of
the province (Cabana, Lampa), but their assessment does not
provide any clues to their subsistence.

Notes to Chapter II

[1]Pachacuti Yamqui Salcamaygua, 1924, p. 175; Cieza de León, 1924, cap. C, p. 290, cap. CII, p. 295, cap. CIV, pp. 298-299, and 1967, cap. IV, pp. 6-7, cap. VIII, p. 25, cap. XLI, cap. XLII, cap. XLIII, cap. LIII, p. 78; Sarmiento de Gamboa, 1906, cap. 36, pp. 75-77, cap. 40, pp. 81-83, cap. 41, p. 83.

[2]One of the indices of prestige was the height of stools important people sat on, and the material they were made from (Rowe, 1946, p. 258; Guaman Poma de Ayala, 1936, pp. 14, 369, 398). Gold was a metal of higher prestige than silver (Rowe, 1946, pp. 246, 247-248, 261). The other index of prestige is the reference to the deity each ruler worshipped; the creator god had authority over the sun in Inca religion (Rowe, 1960, p. 422; Molina, 1943, p. 19).

[3]Garcilaso de la Vega, 1959, pt. I, lib. V, cap. IX, p. 84; Cobo, 1964, tomo 92, lib. 12, cap. XXVI, p. 117; Acosta, 1940, lib. 6, cap. 16, p. 302.

[4]The distribution of Uruquilla is of some interest because it offers a possible solution to the confusion extant about the existence of an Uru language. The Uru and

Uru-Chipaya languages, thought to be associated with the
Urus, have been recorded in the Lake Poopó region and among
the inhabitants of several islands in the Desaguadero River.
This distribution suggests that the so-called Uru language
is Uruquilla. For a review of the controversy and a discussion of the distribution of Uru and Uru-Chipaya, see La
Barre, 1941, pp. 496-499, and Chamberlain, 1910, p. 418.
These authors both believed that Uru and Puquina were two
separate languages, a situation that also agrees with the
16th Century historical evidence.

[5]The La Paz area may have been outside the limits of
the Pacajes province of 'Urqosuyu, to the northeast.

[6]San Miguel de Titipaya is in the Cochabamba Valley.
This valley was originally populated by people known as the
Cotas and Chuis, but these people were moved to Pocona by
Wayna Qhapaq, the eleventh Inka, and people from the adja-
cent highlands were relocated there to produce maize for the
Inca army (Morales, 1977, p. 25). This province was unlike
the others on the list, in that it did not have a native
population.

[7]Information on the Urus is scattered among the written
sources. See especially, Morúa, 1946, lib. III, cap. VIII,
p. 184, cap. XX, p. 214; Jiménez de la Espada, 1885, tomo II,
p. 55; Calancha and Torres, 1972, tomo 1, lib. 1, cap. 1,
pp. 110-116, cap. XVIII, p. 293; Diez de San Miguel, 1964,
pp. 140, 196; Matienzo, 1967, pt. I, cap. 11, p. 41; Cobo,
1964, tomo 92, lib. 2, cap. 4, p. 15; Vellard, 1960, pp. 29-41.

3

INCA PROVINCIAL ADMINISTRATION
IN THE LAKE TITICACA REGION

Because the particular concern of the present study is
the nature and degree of Inca control in the Lake
Titicaca region, two aspects of Inca administration
receive particular attention in this chapter: the administration of tribute, and population movement. In both cases,
the effects of Inca control can be documented using 16th
Century written records, either because the new colonial
regime made particular inquiries about the matter or because
the effects of Inca control endured despite the collapse of
the Inca government.

The following discussion focuses on the Lake Titicaca
region provinces; it is not a general summary (see Rowe,
1946, pp. 260-273). In recent years a number of new source
materials have been published which greatly aid in the reconstruction of Inca administration in particular provinces.
For the Lake Titicaca region, a very valuable source is the
visita of Chucuito, an administrative survey conducted by
the Spanish administration for its own purposes in the territory of the former Lupaca province (Diez de San Miguel,
1964). Unfortunately, no similarly detailed documentation
for any of the Qolla provinces has been found.

In addition to the Chucuito visita, general accounts of
Inca administration and documents pertaining to the administration of other provinces have been used in historical reconstruction. If Inca administration was intended to be
uniform and equitable, then it should be possible to general-
ize details about the administration of one province to
another. This method can be applied when documentary sources
exist for both provinces, and traces of Inca administration
in one province can be detected in the other. Of course,
accounts which describe the same aspect of Inca administration
in general outline may be used to confirm these uniformities.

TRIBUTE ADMINISTRATION

The Inca government was supported by a continuous flow of
goods and services from all parts of the empire. While
direct appropriation of land and movable property was practiced by the Inca government chiefly at the time a new territory was annexed to the empire, the ongoing administration of
the provinces was intended to function without any further
direct appropriations. All contributions were to be made in
labor, even if the end result was the production of goods.[1]

Tribute exaction was organized around a labor assignment.
The assignment for one province, the province of Huánuco in
the north-central highlands, has been published (Helmer,
1955-1956, pp. 40-41; Mori and Malpartida, 1967, pp. 290-304).
The labor services assigned to the tributary population of
Huánuco are similar to a list of services found in two
general accounts of Inca administration (Morúa, 1946, lib. 3,

cap. LXVII, pp. 332-334; Falcón, 1867, pp. 466-468). Of course, the kinds of labor service varied somewhat, probably depending on the particular resources of a province, but certain services could be performed in virtually any province, and so there was some similarity in what was exacted.

Some of the goods and services could be more efficiently extracted if the tributaries who generated them did so on a permanent basis (Ortíz de Zúñiga, 1967, pp. 239-240; Santillán, 1968, tomo III, p. 509). Part of the tributary population was reserved to perform these tasks. The remainder formed a pool subject to recruitment on a more temporary basis.

Permanently assigned tributaries were no longer subject to recruitment. They may have served the government directly, and they were more closely identified with it (Julien, 1978, pp. 52-53, 57, 68). Their assignments were passed along to their descendents, and if their line was extinguished they were replaced by other tributaries from their province of origin (Ortíz de Zúñiga, 1967, pp. 239-240; Diez de San Miguel, 1964, pp. 106-107). For this reason, they continued to be accounted with the tributaries of their home province. For example, the Huánuco labor assignment included all of the tributary population of the Huánuco province, including tributaries under permanent assignment (Mori and Malpartida, 1967, pp. 290-304).

Both the group of tributaries in the general pool and the group under permanent assignment were organized into decimal units. Units ranging in size from 5 to 10,000

tributaries were mentioned in the early written accounts
(see Table 3).[2]

TABLE 3

Inca Decimal Units

Unit Name	Number of Tributaries
hunu	10,000
piska waranqa	5,000
waranqa	1,000
piska pachaka	500
pachaka	100
piska chunka	50
chunka	10
----	5

Several writers described a hierarchical organization of
decimal units, each headed by an officer. Officers who
staffed the recruitment organization were said to have been
chosen from the local elites, while those who headed decimal
units assigned to permanent service were of more common
descent (Falcón, 1867, p. 463; Cobo, 1964, tomo 92, lib. 12,
cap. XXV, p. 115; Cabello Valboa, 1951, pt. 3, cap. 19, p.
348; Guaman Poma de Ayala, 1936, p. 330). Inheritance of
office characterized the decimal hierarchy above the level
of the pachaka (100) but may have also included this unit
(Falcón, 1867, pp. 463-464; Ortíz de Zúñiga, 1967, p. 25).
Both groups of decimal officers were coordinated in a single

provincial administration under the direction of a governor appointed from the Cuzco nobility.[3]

An organization like the one just described was probably found in each province incorporated into the tribute system. Traces of it can be documented in several parts of the Inca empire. In the Lake Titicaca region information about its application is scarce. Information contained in the Chucuito visita, however, can be used to show that the Lupaca province was organized like other Inca provinces (Julien, 1982).

One of the chief objectives of the Chucuito visita was to record information about the kurakas of Chucuito and about the demands for goods and services they imposed on the people subject to them. Though more than 30 years had passed since the Spanish invasion, it is still possible to establish a connection between the kurakas of 1567 and the kurakas who staffed the recruitment organization in the later Inca empire. The connection is possible by examining information provided by the kurakas in light of a khipu or knot record said to be the last Inca census of the province (Diez de San Miguel, 1964, pp. 64-66).

The khipu was organized around a number of political divisions still in existence in 1567, and therefore establishes their antiquity. In 1567 the Lupaca province was organized around seven towns (Diez de San Miguel, 1964, pp. 14, 27, 37). Each town and the district belonging to it was further divided into two parts, or sayas, called Hanansaya and Hurinsaya (see pp. 24-25). One town, Juli, was further subdivided, but since the subdivisions were affiliated with

either Hanansaya or Hurinsaya, the original division was
preserved (Diez de San Miguel, 1964, p. 119). Saya division
was also respected at the provincial level. The two kurakas
who headed the major sayas of Chucuito also served as the
heads of their respective saya divisions for the entire
province (Diez de San Miguel, 1964, pp. 13, 27).

Both of these kurakas had a copy of the khipu census.
One khipu was read into the record. The census entries
from this khipu are duplicated in Table 4 in the same order
as they were recorded. Totals in the far right column and
at the bottom of the other columns were supplied for the purposes of analysis. The other khipu, brought forward to
corroborate the first, differed by only two tributaries
(Diez de San Miguel, 1964, pp. 64, 75). The entry for
Hanansaya of Pomata had two more tributaries in the second
khipu.

Thirteen entries were recorded in the khipu, each
representing either a saya of one of the Lupaca towns or an
entire town, except for the entry for Sama, a pacific coastal
valley.[4]

The tributary counts contained in the khipu census
provide key information about the decimal organization of the
Lupaca province (see Table 4). The total number of tributaries, 20,280, approximates two hunu (units of 10,000). Since
a breakdown into Hanansaya and Hurinsaya is reported for all
but two of the Lupaca towns in the province proper, it is
possible to estimate the number of tributaries in Hanansaya
and Hurinsaya. A total of 10,214 tributaries can be

TABLE 4

Categories of the Last Inca Census of Chucuito

Lupaca Province	Aymara	Uru	Other	Total
Hanansaya, Chucuito	1,233	500		1,733
Hurinsaya, Chucuito	1,384	347		1,731
Hanansaya, Acora	1,221	440		1,661
Hurinsaya, Acora	1,207	378		1,585
Hanansaya/Hurinsaya, Ilave	1,470	1,070		2,540
Hanansaya/Chanbilla, Juli	1,438	158	153	1,749
Hurinsaya, Juli	1,804	256		2,060
Hanansaya, Pomata	1,663	110	20	1,793
Hurinsaya, Pomata	1,341	183		1,524
Hanansaya/Hurinsaya, Yunguyo	1,039	381		1,420
Hanansaya, Zepita	1,112	186		1,298
Hurinsaya, Zepita	866	120		986
Pacific Coastal Valley				
Hanansaya/Hurinsaya, Sama			200	
TOTALS	15,778	4,129	373	22,280

TOTAL HANANSAYA*: 10,214

TOTAL HURINSAYA*: 9,866

---

*Totals for Ilave and Yunguyo were halved to approximate saya division totals. Sama was not included in these totals.

estimated for Hanansaya and 9,866 for Hurinsaya.   Each
provincial saya contained approximately a hunu of tributaries.
The two kurakas who headed the Hanansaya and Hurinsaya
divisions of the Lupaca province appear to have been hunu
officers.   From the text of the visita, it is possible to
trace these positions back to the time of the Inca empire
(Diez de San Miguel, 1964, pp. 22, 34).

In addition to hunu units, the tributary counts reveal
the existence of other decimal units.   As noted before, the
heads of Hanansaya and Hurinsaya of the Lupaca province were
also heads of Hanansaya and Hurinsaya of Chucuito town.
Subject to each were 17 ayllus[5] in the district of Chucuito
(Diez de San Miguel, 1964, pp. 14, 27).   Each saya contained
just over 1700 tributaries, as recorded in the khipu census
(Table 4)(Diez de San Miguel, 1964, p. 64), and so, if
decimal units were represented, each saya in Chucuito town
consisted of 17 pachakas (units of 100).

Furthermore, a breakdown of these 17 ayllus was given
for both sayas of Chucuito town.   In each case, ten ayllus
were composed of Aymara tributaries, five were composed of
Uru tributaries, and of the two remaining, one was an ayllu
of silver workers and the other an ayllu of potters (see
Table 5)(Diez de San Miguel, 1964, pp. 14, 27).   This distribution suggests that each saya was composed of a waranqa
(unit of 1,000), a piska pachaka (500) of Uru and a pachaka
(100) each of potters and silversmiths.

Less information about the other Lupaca towns was
collected by the administrators of the visita.   It is clear

TABLE 5

Ayllus Subject to Qari and Kusi

	Number of Ayllus				Number of Tributaries	
	Aymara	Uru	Potters	Silversmiths	Total	Actual Total	Ideal Total
Qari (Hanansaya of Chucuito)	10	5	1	1	17	1733	1700
Kusi (Hurinsaya of Chucuito)	10	5	1	1	17	1731	1700

that few if any of the towns had an organization exactly
parallel to that of Chucuito. Even so, the points of similarity and contrast between the organization of Chucuito and
the organization of the other towns are of interest, and they
suggest that the khipu accounting followed certain organizing
principles.

An organizing principle that immediately comes to mind
is size, since the entries of the khipu census approximate
each other in the number of tributaries they contain. Even
more closely approximate, however, is the number of Aymara
tributaries in each. That the number of Aymara tributaries
was more important in the accounting than the total number
is indicated by the lumping of Hanansaya and Hurinsaya together in a single entry in some cases and splitting them in
others. For example, if the total number was the determining
factor, then it might be expected that Ilave would be accounted by two entries, rather than one, since a smaller number
of tributaries in Zepita was accounted by two entries.
The total number of tributaries in Ilave was expanded by the
number of Uru tributaries there. The number of Aymara tributaries is about the same in Ilave as the number in other
khipu entires, and so the focus was on the number of Aymara.

This focus is not surprising, because this group was
probably more important from the point of view of imperial
administration than any other. Political control of the area
was in their hands at the time of the Inca conquest. Moreover,
the chief subsistence activities of this group, herding and

cultivation, appear to have generated more wealth than the
fishing occupation associated with the Urus (see Chp. II).

If the number of Aymara tributaries was a significant
factor, then the size of each entry suggests that a waranqa
of Aymara tributaries was the minimum set for each unit. The
number of tributaries classified as Aymara tends to fall
between 1,000 and 1,500 in each entry, but in only one case
(Hurinsaya, Zepita) does it fall below 1,000. A waranqa was
clearly the largest decimal unit contained in any of the
khipu entries, and so, waranqa office was the highest office
in each unit. The information available for Chucuito indicates that the heads of the two sayas of Chucuito town were
also waranqa officers. A moment ago it was noted that these
same two individuals were both heads of the saya divisions at
the provincial level and hunu officers. In the ideal decimal
system, one decimal officer in each group of ten was also
officer of the unit represented by all ten (Santillán, 1968,
tomo III, p. 382; Castro and Ortega Morejón, 1974, p. 94;
Cobo, 1964, tomo 92, lib. 12, cap. XXV, p. 114). Hunu
officers were also waranqa officers. Conveniently, waranqa
office was the highest office in either saya in Chucuito.
By this line of reasoning, the heads of Hanansaya and
Hurinsaya of the Lupaca province were waranqa officers in
Chucuito town. If these two individuals were waranqa officers, they each were at the same time head of a larger group
in Chucuito town: their respective sayas. The saya divisions
of Chucuito town, then, appear to have been another level
in the administration, one not organized along decimal lines.

If the organization of the other Lupaca towns was similar
to Chucuito's, the following reconstruction is plausible.
In each saya, or in each town when it was accounted by a
single khipu entry, a waranqa officer headed an administrative unit composed of a waranqa and a number of additional
pachakas. In the case of Hurinsaya of Juli or Hanansaya of
Pomata, the Aymara group may have been organized into two
waranqas.

The reconstruction of Inca administration obtained from
the organization of the khipu census and information in the
Chucuito visita is illuminating. Instead of a straightfor-
ward nested hierarchy of decimal units, the Lupaca organization appears to have respected certain local conditions such
as saya division and the importance of a particular group of
tributaries. A likely reason for the organization to stray
from the ideal decimal hierarchy was so that local lines of
authority could be utilized for recruitment. The organization
of the khipu census, then, suggests the lines along which
recruitment was carried out.

While the khipu contains the outline of the recruitment
organization, it offers no way of distinguishing the two
major groups of tributaries: those under permanent assignment and those still in the tributary pool. The khipu
accounted the entire tributary population of the Lupaca
province, so it included both groups.

There is some information about specialized craftsmen in
Chucuito, and these people were very likely to have been
assigned on a permanent basis. Earlier it was noted that

among the 17 ayllus of each saya in Chucuito town, there
were two ayllus of potters and silver workers. A list of
communities in each saya division was provided in the visita
(Diez de San Miguel, 1964, pp. 14, 27). In general the lists
contain a non-overlapping set of communities, with only a
few exceptions. Both the head of Hanansaya and the head of
Hurinsaya included Cupi, a community of potters, and Sunicaya,
a community of silver workers, on their lists. From their
evidence it can be inferred that an ayllu of potters from
each saya resided in Cupi and an ayllu of silver workers
resided in Sunicaya. Both Cupi and Sunicaya appear to have
been located within the district of Chucuito town because the
heads of Hanansaya and Hurinsaya listed the communities
within the boundaries of the Chucuito district before men-
tioning any far away places, and Cupi and Sunicaya are named
with this group of communities. Sunicaya has been identified
as the modern town of Platería, on the road between Chucuito
and Acora, but efforts to locate Cupi have not led to an
identification of its site (Murra, 1978b, p. 417).

The Chucuito visita does not directly link these
communities with the Inca tribute system, but evidence from
one of the Qolla provinces suggests a link. On the other
side of the lake, near Huancané, similar communities existed.
Huancané was located in the Qolla province of 'Umasuyu, on
the La Paz side of the boundary between the city districts
of Cuzco and La Paz (Toledo, 1975, p. 57). Two communities,
one a pachaka of potters called Hupi and the other a waranqa
of tapestry weavers called Millerea, were located in the

district of Huancané town in 1583, originally put there by
Wayna Qhapaq, the eleventh Inka (Murra, 1978b, p. 418). The
two communities appear to have lived side by side (Murra,
1978b, p. 420). The document containing this information was
a litigation between native authorities in Huancané and the
members of the occupationally specialized communities. The
Huancané authorities charged that the residents of the communities were from a number of places in the Qolla province of
'Umasuyu within the district of Cuzco (Murra, 1978b, pp.
418-419). In their defense, the potters said that in addition
to the various sites in what was then the district of Cuzco,
people from several places in the Qolla province of 'Umasuyu
within the district of La Paz were settled there as well
(Murra, 1978b, pp. 419-420). Regardless of the veracity of
either side's claim, the community was composed of people
from several parts of the Qolla province of 'Umasuyu, and
perhaps from all over that province.

This pattern repeats a pattern found in the Huánuco
province, where occupationally specialized communities were
also composed of people from many parts of the same province
(Helmer, 1955-1956, pp. 27-38; Julien, 1978, note 30 on p.
249). In Huánuco, half of each pachaka was assigned to
perform permanent service in the Inca tribute system (Ortíz
de Zúñiga, 1967, pp. 239-240). From the published labor
assignment of that province, it is evident that these specialized craft communities frequently contained people "from all
over the province" (Helmer, 1955-1956, pp. 40-41). By

analogy with Huánuco, the communities in Huancané, and
probably those in Chucuito, were settled in this way.

The Lupaca visita contains very little other information
about occupationally specialized communities, and no information about the percentage of the Lupaca tributary population
tied up by permanent assignment. It is possible to show
that the Lupaca province was under an assignment like the one
imposed in Huánuco by examining what the kurakas of Chucuito
said they gave to the Inca government as tribute. In inter-
views conducted with the kurakas of several Lupaca towns,
this question was asked (Diez de San Miguel, 1964, pp. 39,
80-81, 85, 92-93, 99, 106-107, 116-117). Responses to the
question are not uniform, but all of them indicate that a
variety of assignments, in addition to producing pottery
and silver work, were imposed on the Lupaca province. When
a list of what was reportedly given as tribute is compiled,
a general similarity to the Huánuco labor assignment is
evident (Julien, 1982).

It is clear that a great deal more remains to be known
about the organization and delivery of labor service in the
Lupaca province and for no other province in the Lake Titicaca
region is there a similar quantity of information about
provincial administration. Still, various aspects of the
general outline of tribute administration presented at the
beginning of this section can be documented in the area.
The decimal hierarchy in charge of recruitment can be
detected in the Lupaca province. The existence of
occupationally specialized communities, who performed their

labor service under permanent assignment, can be documented
in the Qolla province of 'Umasuyu. Moreover, a labor assignment, similar in general outline to the one published for the
Huánuco province, can be reconstructed for the Lupaca province (Julien, 1982). The Lake Titicaca provinces not unexpect-
edly reflect the general outline of tribute administration.

POPULATION MOVEMENT

A moment ago it was noted that tributaries who practiced
certain crafts in performance of their labor obligation were
relocated in specialized craft communities with other people
from their province. Relocation of people to facilitate
payment of their provincial labor obligation was only one of
a number of reasons people were moved by the Inca government.
Relocation policies, especially those connected with the
tribute system, gave shape to Inca provincial administration.
A number of them resulted in the concentration of people near
Inca administrative centers. A study of these policies is
complicated by the fragmentary nature of information about
population movement in the written sources. A partial list
of classes of relocated people can be compiled, and the evidence for population movement in the Lake Titicaca region can
be examined in its light.

One early writer, Cieza de León, was able to distinguish
several classes of relocated people. He gave a list of
three, but his information allows the identification of six
different classes of relocated people. The three he called
particular attention to were: 1) people relocated when a new

territory was organized into provinces, both for security
reasons and to aid in acculturation of the inhabitants to
their role as subjects of the empire; 2) people settled in
frontier areas to serve as garrisons; and 3) colonies sent
to underpopulated regions to bring them into production
(1967, cap. XXII, pp. 73-78). The other classes of relocated
people he mentioned were: 4) people relocated outside of
their home territories for the purposes of growing or collect-
ing certain plants unavailable at home, like maize, coca
and a variety of fruits (1967, cap. XVII, p. 55, cap. XXII,
p. 75); 5) people from the coast who were relocated near
four highland administrative centers, including Cajamarca,
Vilcas, Cuzco and Hatunqolla, to facilitate storage of goods
produced by their labor (1924, cap. LXXV, p. 232); and 6)
people who were moved from hilltop locations to more level
ground (1967, cap. XXIV, pp. 83-84). Other classes of relocated people may have gone without mention, of course. For
example, Cieza did not mention people relocated within their
provinces to facilitate payment of their labor obligation.

All of the classes of relocated people above may have
been applicable to the inhabitants of the Lake Titicaca
provinces, but several would have had a negative effect. For
example, people sent to garrison the frontiers (2) or people
relocated for the purposes of obtaining plant materials
unavailable at home (4) would have resulted in the movement
of people outside the boundaries of the Lake Titicaca provinces.   Colonies of this latter kind (4) have been well
documented for the Lupaca province (Murra, 1964, pp. 428-429).

All are located well outside the boundaries of the Lupaca
province.   Colonization of underpopulated areas (3) might
also have resulted in a negative balance.   There is no information on this subject for the Lake Titicaca region, but
there were large expanses of unpopulated territory in the
highlands adjacent to Lake Titicaca (Cieza de León, 1924,
cap. XCIX, p. 287).

Of the other policies mentioned, only two would have
involved the introduction of people from outside the
province: the relocation of people to other provinces for
security reasons or to aid in the acculturation of newly
conquered peoples (1) and the relocation of people from
coastal provinces to be nearer to the highland administrative
center where there tribute was assigned for deposit (2).[6]

The resettlement of foreigners for reason (1) above was
not only described in some detail by Cieza, but also by
Bernabé Cobo (Cobo, 1964, tomo 92, lib. 12, cap. XXIII, pp.
109-111; cf. Segovia, 1943, p. 33, and Acosta, 1940, lib. 6,
cap. 12, p. 474).   Cobo stresses both the security and the
acculturation aspect of the resettlement of these people and
locates them in administrative centers.   These people were
no longer subject to their provinces of origin, but they were
probably still accounted in the census there and may have
been replaced if their line died out just like people who
were assigned to permanent service (Diez de San Miguel, 1964,
p. 170; Cobo, 1964, tomo 92, lib. 12, cap. XXIII, p. 109).
They may have been assigned on a permanent basis and so
would have resembled other groups relocated in craft

specialized communities (Guaman Poma de Ayala, 1936, p. 338).
People from the Cuzco area and even Cuzco nobles were often
selected for this kind of relocation. It was a prominent
part of Inca population policy, and for ease of reference I
will call it the resettlement program.

The resettlement program was said to have been authored
by Pachakuti, the ninth Inka (Cieza de León, 1967, cap. XXII,
p. 77), but became an important part of organizing new
provinces under Thupa 'Inka, the tenth Inka (Sarmiento de
Gamboa, 1906, cap. 50, p. 97). Pachakuti may have used
resettlement in the organization of his conquests, but it is
possible that in his early conquests it was not a prominent
feature of provincial administration.

Since the Lake Titicaca region was annexed to the empire
fairly early, resettlement may have been effected later or
perhaps not at all. The best source of information on the
Inca administration of the Lake Titicaca region is Cieza de
León, and he does not give sufficient detail on the subject.
In his chronology of events, the area was conquered early in
the reign of Pachakuti (1967, cap. XLVIII, pp. 160-161). This
emperor settled an Inca governor, his delegates and a group
of Cuzco nobles in the area (1967, cap. LIII, p. 178). Cieza
does not discuss further relocation in the area until some
time later, following a major rebellion of the northern provinces during which the Inca governor and most of the Cuzco
nobles were executed. At the time the rebellion was quelled,
garrisons were set up for security and people were moved from
one Lake Titicaca province to another (1967, cap. LVI,

p. 184).   In his description of Hatunqolla (1924, cap. CII,
p. 295) he mentions garrisons set up at the frontiers as
security against the rise of a tyrant, perhaps in reference
to the garrisons set up following the rebellion.   He also
noted that at Hatunqolla were a large number of mitimas,
literally foreigners, who may well have been people relocated
there under the resettlement program, but might have been
there for some other reason.   Another source of information
on the subject is Cobo, who mentioned that people from
Chinchaysuyu (the northern quarter of the Inca empire) were
resettled in the area.

The information provided by Cieza and Cobo can be
checked with a small amount of information on foreigners in
specific parts of the Lake Titicaca provinces.   In the
Lupaca province a group of people from Chinchaysuyu was
located in Hurinsaya of Juli (Diez de San Miguel, 1964, pp.
65, 114).   The khipu census reported 153 tributaries from
Chinchaysuyu for that saya.   (In 1567, at least some of the
people were in Moquegua, p. 33).   People from Chinchaysuyu
were also located in the Qolla province of 'Umasuyu.   In
1573, the entire encomienda of Ancoraimes reportedly contained
only people from Chinchaysuyu (Toledo, 1975, p. 67).   At
that time there were 151 tributaries and a total of 772
people residing there.   These groups are probably among the
groups Cobo mentioned.

The modern naming of territorial divisions indicates that
other foreigners were relocated in the area.   For example,
in the Lupaca province, both Chucuito and Acora have

Inca ayllus (see note 5), and Yunguyo has a Canas ayllu.
In the Qolla province of 'Urqosuyu, there is a Chimu ayllu
in Puno and a Canchis ayllu in Caracoto. Finally, in the
Qolla province of 'Umasuyu, there is a Caquingora (Pacajes)
ayllu in Azángaro and a Canchis ayllu in Achaya.[7] It is
likely that even after more than four centuries the names
continue to reflect the names of groups resettled in the
area by the Incas. Except for the Chimu ayllu in Puno
(from the Chinchaysuyu quarter) and the Inca ayllus, the
groups mentioned are from fairly nearby provinces. If
Cieza's chronology of events can be used to interpret this
situation, these people may have been relocated following
the major rebellion Cieza described.

The other kind of relocation which involved the
introduction of foreigners into the Lake Titicaca provinces
was the relocation of tributaries from the coast in the
vicinity of Hatunqolla to be nearer the storage facility
where their tribute was to be deposited (5). No documentation exists for this class of relocated people in the
Hatunqolla area, but a very early document (1540) for
Cajamarca provides information on how the deposit of coastal
goods was organized (Espinoza Soriano, 1967, pp. 33-39). The
document is a part of the 1540 visita of Francisco Pizarro.
It lists seven population units subject to local authority,
including one unit composed of foreigners from different
highland provinces, probably settled there under the resettlement program. In addition, other foreigners who were settled
near Cajamarca but not subject to local authority were

listed. The list includes people from Guaman and Chilcho
(in Chachapoyas territory); Guambo (highlands near Cajamarca);
and from Pacasmayo, Saña, Collique, Chuspo, Cinto and Tucumé
(North Coast). This latter group of foreigners had been
relocated in Cajamarca by the Inca government. In documents
of a later date, the colony from Collique was revealed to be
a pachaka of potters who practiced their craft to satisfy
their province's labor obligation (Espinoza Soriano,
1969-1970, pp. 14-15). Since Hatunqolla was listed by Cieza
along with Cajamarca as one of four highland centers where
coastal tribute was destined, groups of coastal people may
have resided in the Hatunqolla vicinity for the same reason.
The coastal people relocated at Hatunqolla would probably
have originated from the far South Coast, if distance to
the highland center was a consideration.

   The remaining relocation policies would have resulted in
moving people within provincial boundaries. The relocation
of people in craft specialized communities, documented earlier
for the Huancané area, was one kind of movement of people
that took place within provincial boundaries. Other kinds
of relocation connected with the tribute system may also have
existed. Unconnected with the tribute system was movement
of people away from fortified hilltops (6). Cieza noted that
this policy was carried out all over the Inca empire and
specifically mentioned the Lake Titicaca region (1967, cap.
XXIV, p. 83; cf. Hyslop, 1977b). Connected with moving
people from hilltop locations was the founding of towns.
Cieza described a trip Pachakuti made along the 'Umasuyu

road (Map 3) in the northern Lake Titicaca basin (1967, cap.
LII, p. 175). At that time he concentrated the population
of the area in a number of towns in the flat lands. Concen-
trating the population was probably a major objective of
this resettlement effort, as was removing people from militarily defensible sites (Cobo, 1964, tomo 92, lib. 12, cap.
XXIV, p. 111; Cabello Valboa, 1951, pt. 3, cap. 19, p. 348).

INCA ADMINISTRATION

OF THE QOLLA PROVINCE OF 'URQOSUYU

Information from other Lake Titicaca provinces,
particularly from the Lupaca province, suggests in general
outline the organization of Inca administration in the Qolla
province of 'Urqosuyu. The Lupaca province was organized
around seven Lupaca towns, all of which were listed in the
capitanía lists (Capoche, 1959, p. 136). In the same lists,
13 towns were given for the Qolla province of 'Urqosuyu, nine
within the city district of Cuzco and four within the city
district of La Paz (see Map 2). These towns may have been
foci of recruitment, as were the Lupaca towns given in the
same lists. The seven Lupaca towns appear to have been
divided into 12 administrative divisions in the Lupaca province proper. The Qolla towns may have been divided, or even
grouped together, so that the number of subdivisions used in
accounting this province cannot be estimated. The accounting
of the Lupaca province followed saya division lines where-
ever towns were divided, and saya division was a feature of
territorial organization in the Qolla province of 'Urqosuyu,

as it continues to be to this day.[8] Other aspects of the

Lupaca organization, such as the focus on a waranqa of

tributaries classified as Aymara, may have been features of

the Qolla organization.

Similarities in what was exacted as tribute might also

be expected between these two provinces. Specialized

communities near Huancané produced pottery and tapestry

textiles for the Inca government. Both textiles and pottery

were produced as tribute in the Lupaca and Huánuco provinces

and were likely to have been extracted almost anywhere in

the empire. Similar communities probably existed in the

Qolla province of 'Urqosuyu, and other kinds of tributaries

under permanent assignment may have been settled together.

Other communities of people from outside the bounds of

the Qolla province of 'Urqosuyu were probably settled within

its limits. Some communities, for example the Canchis

community in Caracoto and the Chimu community near Puno,

were probably brought in under the resettlement program. By

analogy with Cajamarca, a highland center which like

Hatunqolla was designated for the receipt of coastal tribute,

a number of communities of coastal people were also relocated

in the area.

Besides people moved expressly to facilitate the

performance of labor service or the collection of goods pro-

duced through labor service, people were moved away from

inaccessible places and were congregated into nucleated settle-

ments. The towns of the Qolla province of 'Urqosuyu may

have been formed or enlarged in this fashion.

Notes to Chapter III

[1]Polo de Ondegardo, 1940, pp. 133, 136-137, 165, and 1916, tomo III, pp. 66-67, 88, tomo IV, p. 51; Cobo, 1964, tomo 92, lib. 12, cap. XXVII, p. 120; Falcón, 1867, pp. 461, 471-472.

[2]Falcón, 1867, pp. 463-464; Bandera, 1968, tomo III, p. 505; Cobo, 1964, tomo 92, lib. 12, cap. XXV, p. 114; Polo de Ondegardo, 1917, tomo IV, p. 51; Santillán, 1968, tomo III, p. 382.

[3]Cobo, 1964, tomo 92, lib. 12, cap. XXV, p. 114; Santillán, 1968, tomo III, pp. 382-383; Pizarro, 1944, pp. 81-82; Guaman Poma de Ayala, 1936, pp. 184, 346-347; Bandera, 1968, tomo III, p. 496.

[4]Sama has not been considered in the analysis that follows, in part because the tributaries were accounted separately from the Lupaca province proper and so could not be related to the remainder of the province.

[5]Ayllu refers to a social group; concomitant with this meaning is its reference to a particular territory. In this case, the name probably once referred to a specific group

with foreign origins, but has now lost that significance
because of the changes in the group's composition.

[6]In two areas, a complete replacement of the local population occurred. In both Copacabana and Ayaviri, the local
population was entirely replaced with foreigners. The
original inhabitants of the Copacabana Peninsula were relocated in Yunguyo and people from all over the empire were
settled on the peninsula, from as far away as Quito in the
north to Copiapó in the south (Ramos Gavilán, 1976, p. 43).
The foreigners settled on the Copacabana Peninsula formed a
special staff for the island shrines adjacent to its tip.
The inhabitants of Ayaviri were also replaced with foreigners
because the Incas almost totally annihilated them (Cieza de
León, 1967, cap. LII, pp. 173-174). In the Cochabamba Valley
further to the south the local population was entirely replaced by foreign colonists who were there to cultivate maize
for the Inca government on a large scale (Morales, 1977).
These cases involve imperial precincts, not regularly consti-
tuted provinces, and so, the objectives of this kind of
relocation were different from those of the recruitment
program.

[7]Gutiérrez Flores, 1964, pp. 309-311, 317; Romero, 1928,
pp. 280-285. John Rowe visited Pucara in 1958 and collected
names of the ayllus of that town.

[8]Cordero and others, 1971, p. 5; Romero, 1928, p. 280;
Archivo Nacional del Perú, Derecho Indígena, legajo 11,
cuaderno 265, año 1748; see pl. 1a.

4

ARCHAEOLOGICAL EXPLORATION
OF THE HATUNQOLLA AREA

Hatunqolla was known to be the center of Inca activities in the northern Lake Titicaca region. At Hatunqolla were a temple of the Inca state religion, a number of chosen women and others who served this cult, a great many buildings built by the Incas and a large quantity of storehouses for the deposit of tribute. At the time of the Spanish invasion in 1532, Hatunqolla was one of the largest and most important urban settlements in the southern Inca empire (Cieza de León, 1924, cap. CII, p. 295). Inca government business was an important part of the life that went on in Hatunqolla, and the archaeological record should reflect this situation.

The modern town of Hatunqolla sits on a hillside over-looking a broad plain (pl. 1). There are a number of initial reasons for identifying modern Hatunqolla as the site of the ancient settlement. A considerable number of finely dressed square and rectangular building stones in good Cuzco masonry style have been used in modern walls. One entire doorway of fitted stones has been reused in a modern house. Wedge shaped dressed stones of the sort used in circular burial towers (chullpas) are common as well. Such stones may have been brought from the nearby site of Sillustani where almost

all the dressed stone burial towers are round, but there are
dressed stone foundations from round burial towers in and
around Hatunqolla as well.[2] Sillustani is a less likely
source for the small square and rectangular stones, however.
These stones are more likely to represent the remains of
Inca construction at Hatunqolla itself, perhaps having been
used in the Inca temple of the state religion reportedly
built there (Cieza de León, 1924, cap. CII, p. 295).

While no standing architecture was found, the layout of
Hatunqolla itself can be argued to be ancient. Hatunqolla
is laid out on a grid plan which does not follow Spanish
canons of planning. Rather, its layout suggests Inca
planning.

The town is laid out on a grid plan determined by two
principal roads (pl. 2a and 2b). One road runs north-south
and is locally known as Inka Ñan, which literally means
"Inca road" (Cordero and others, 1971, p. 3). This road
runs south to Sillustani, and north then northeast to
Caracoto. The second principal road is perpendicular to the
first. To the east it leads to Puno, to the west to the
Hacienda Llungo and then to Cabana. The intersection of
these roads is the center of the grid. The grid consists of
two rows of long rectangular blocks, laid out along both
sides of the east-west road. The blocks do not have parallel sides but tend to fan out on either side of the north-
south road. The blocks on the east side fan out to the
north, and the blocks on the west side fan out to the
south. The intersection of the principal roads is not

exactly at the center of the grid, as there are seven blocks
east of the north-south road and only five blocks west of it.

Like Spanish towns, Inca towns had some sort of central
open space, or plaza. The modern plaza is square, but the
original plaza was probably not. The original plaza may have
included the area between the modern plaza and the principal
north-south road, as well as the space occupied by the
modern plaza. From the modern plaza to the principal north-
south road, the land is roughly level. It is covered with
very small pottery fragments uncharacteristic of the surface
of the remainder of the grid where large fragments are abundant. The small size of the fragments suggests trampling.
The land just west of the modern plaza belongs to the church,
and the only construction on it until recently was the
priest's house. This house had been in ruins for some time,
when around 1970 a building intended to house a Mother's
Club was erected nearby by CARITAS, a Catholic charity organization. This building is now the location of the rug maker's
cooperative of Hatunqolla as well as a Mother's Club and
kindergarten. No other construction in this area can be
recalled (Cordero and others, 1971, pp. 78-79).

If the ancient plaza occupied the two blocks just
indicated, its shape would have been more in conformance with
Inca canons of planning. In general, Inca plazas were quadrangles, and two of the opposite sides of the figure tended
to be shorter than the other two sides. Rectangles, trape-
zoids and other irregular quadrangles or polygons were
common (Gasparini and Margolies, 1977; Hardoy, 1964; Kubler,

1962). Since Spanish plazas were square, it is likely that
the Hatunqolla plaza was cut down to a square in accordance
with Spanish ideas about plazas.

The town plan is associated with several other features
of possible pre-Spanish date. Due north of the center of the
grid, where the ancient plaza appears to have been located,
is a trapezoidal parcel of land. An open trapezoidal court,
in addition to the plaza, is a feature of the plans of both
Huánuco Viejo and Cuzco (Morris and Thompson, 1970, p. 350,
fig. 2; Gasparini and Margolies, 1977, p. 58, fig. 49).
Also, the north-south road connects Hatunqolla with a low
hill to the north named Qolqa Chupa. Qolqa is the modern
form of the name used to refer to Inca storage houses by
early writers (Pachacuti Yamqui Salcamaygua, 1924, p. 193;
Guaman Poma de Ayala, 1936, p. 335). The hillside is ter-
raced, and has the remains of some long rectangular constructions about halfway up the slope, situated on the terraces.
In this area, a certain amount of Inca influenced ceramic
material was observed. South of Hatunqolla and to the west
of the north-south road are remains of similar structures.
The structures had walls of roughly hewn basalt or limestone,
depending on the proximity of the source of stone. A great
number of storage houses were reportedly located in the
Hatunqolla area (Cieza de León, 1924, cap. CII, p. 295).

If any doubt remained that Hatunqolla is located on the
same site as the town mentioned in the historical sources,
study of refuse at the site removed it. A remarkable quantity of ceramic material showing strong influence from the

Cuzco-Inca style of the Inca capital can be found on the
surface. A road constructed in 1971 cuts through the grid
plan of the town revealing stratified deposits with some
strata containing Cuzco related material showing no trace
of Spanish related features. Excavation of the site
revealed three distinct phases corresponding to the occupation of the site before contact with Europeans. A fourth
phase, related to an occupation in the early Spanish colonial
era, was also defined.

The chronology just mentioned was the major result of the
archaeological investigation carried out at Hatunqolla.
Since very few traces of architecture with any likelihood of
being ancient could be identified on the surface, the
research design was directed toward maximizing the information that could be obtained from refuse. Finding superimposed refuse that spanned the entire pre-Spanish occupation
of the site was the major objective behind the archaeological
investigation undertaken at Hatunqolla, and a stragegy was
designed to minimize the possibility that nothing but dis-
turbed material would be found.

The first step taken was to walk over the site to
establish its limits. The distribution of archaeological
material on the surface roughly coincided with the area of
the grid. The grid has an extension of 1.5 km. on the east-
west axis, and .5 km. on the north-south axis. Since a
division had already been effected by the grid itself, areas
for surface collection frequently corresponded to blocks in
the grid (pl. 2b). Surface collections were made in a number

of areas. If any kind of horizontal stratigraphy existed, it
was hoped that it could be detected through analysis of
surface remains from different sectors. Then, plans to excavate could be made with some forehand knowledge of what to
expect. No real horizontal stratigraphy was found. It
became apparent that, except in the case of the western side
of the site where some unusual material was collected near
the foundations of burial towers, no differences in surface
remains could be detected.

The sampling was not confined to the grid alone. Several
broad sweeps behind and in front of the town produced sample
collections of very meager quantity, and of mainly unidentifiable ceramic material (pl. 3a). Two other sites were discovered during the broad sweeps of the area behind the town
(Ale and Esturi), and surface collections from these sites
revealed them to have remains very unlike Hatunqolla material
and more like material from middens at Sillustani,thought
to be pre-Inca.

At the time the excavation program was initiated, no
material thought to date to the period before the Incas controlled the area had been identified. It was still possible
that Hatunqolla would provide a chronology extending back to
the time before the area was incorporated into the Inca
empire and one of the chief goals of the text excavation
phase was to uncover pre-Inca material. The notion that
Hatunqolla had a pre-Inca occupation was fostered by written
sources (Cieza de León, 1924, cap. IV, p. 6).

Eleven testpits of .75 x .75 meter were excavated at

Hatunqolla, and two profiles of the road cut were systemati-
cally cleaned and collected. Another testpit of 1 x 1 m.
was excavated at Sillustani in an area near a cut with
refuse material coming out of it. The Hatunqolla pits were
small, but since the object was to get enough material out of
the ground to make a decision about where to get a good stratigraphic sample, the quantity excavated in the small pits
was thought to be sufficient. Always in mind during these
excavations was the idea that the context of the refuse could
not be understood from such small excavations, but since it
was necessary to testpit extensively in order to find
undisturbed material, there was no other option.

All of the testpits were excavated following the traces
of natural stratigraphy, by means of careful trowelling. All
visible cultural material was removed, including bone, stone,
glass, metal, burned earth, charcoal and pottery, but no
screening was carried out. The nature and content of each
level were also recorded. Depth measurements were taken at
the beginning of each layer, but no profiles were drawn. The
collections from these pits were washed, marked with the site
number and pit provenience and studied for chronological
differences in their contents.

No clearing operation was ever considered. It was hoped
instead that the small testpits and cleaned road cuts would
uncover good stratified midden and that larger excavations
could be carried out adjacent to one or two of the test excavations to recover more material and to establish a context
for it. This hope was rewarded, and one of the sampled road

cuts and one of the testpits (Road Cut II and Testpit 4)
seemed to have both the quantity of material and the stratification sought. The deepest material in the road cut
appeared to be clearly related to surface materials from the
pre-Inca middens at Sillustani. It was hoped that excavation
adjacent to this road cut would reveal an occupation prior to
the time of Inca control. A good quantity of ceramics and
bone, in fairly large fragments, was also evident. Moreover,
this particular excavation had considerable depth. Six
strata could be distinguished at that time, and at least 1.5
m. of good stratified refuse was expected.

As it turned out, only the road cut yielded any
appreciable chronological depth. Testpit 4 contained well
stratified, abundant material, but this material belonged
entirely to one of the phases represented at the road cut.
The rest of the test locations were either too shallow, contained too little material, or had ambiguous stratigraphy.
Four testpits (1, 3, 6 and 9) contained less than 40 cm. of
midden divided stratigraphically into two layers. The upper
layer was recently cultivated topsoil. Two testpits had a
couple of distinguishable strata below the cultivated topsoil (2 and 11) and only one of these (2) had a stratum with
a good quantity of Cuzco related material of possible pre-
Spanish date. Four excavations contained wholly modern or
Spanish colonial era remains (Road Cut I, and Testpits 5, 7
and 10), and only one of the two testpits with colonial
remains had any appreciable stratigraphy (7). In that pit,
however, five levels were distinguished, the lowest

containing Spanish related material and no glazed ceramics,
and the upper ones containing several different style units
of glazed and non-glazed Spanish colonial ceramics. One pit
had a stratigraphy of seven layers (8), but the stratification was not as clear cut as at other locations, and the bone
content was very low.

A larger excavation was begun at the side of the sampled
road cut (Pit 1/1A). The material from this excavation and
Testpit 4 serve as the basis for the following style analysis
(pls. 3b, 4-5). It will be useful to discuss these two
excavations in some detail.

In the large excavation material was carefully excavated
by trowel and all visible material was removed at this stage.
Detailed records of associations were kept and profile drawings of the strata were made. Any material thought to be
related to the human occupation of the site was saved, including ceramics, stone, bone, metal, glass, a textile fragment,
fish scales, earth fused by fire, unfired modelled clay,
fragments of charcoal, bits of strongly colored mineral and
pieces of clay plaster. The dirt removed from this excavation was put through a quarter-inch screen to recuperate
material missed in trowelling. The uppermost layer in the
excavation contained mixed material deposited when the road
bed was excavated. It was not screened and only some material from this layer was saved. All materials were washed
and marked with both the site number and excavation level,
except for very small fragments and carbon. Fragments

selected for drawing were numbered consecutively with Roman
numerals, beginning a new numbered series for each
stratigraphic unit.

A 2 x 2 m. pit was laid out on a north-south axis near
the road cut (Pit 1/1A)(pls. 3, 4-5). It was extended to
2 x 4.2 m. on the east side following the discovery that the
2 x 2 m. pit did not contain a deposit similar to the one in
the road cut. Instead, the pit fell within the remains of a
house. The extension linked the stratigraphy revealed in
the road cut to the construction. Both a date for the house
and a context for the refuse were established.

The strata were clearly defined and very little disturbance was in evidence (pls. 4-5). The overburden from the road
excavation was easily distinguished. Underneath it was an
even layer of somewhat more compact earth (Level 1). This
layer had been in cultivation before the road was built in
1971, according to the owners of the parcel, and the presence
of roots and absence of any bone material in the first level
seemed to confirm their report.

Level 2 was far more compact. It had a very high clay
content and was slightly pinkish and light as a result. The
ceramic content of this layer was not as high as for some of
the lower ones, and there were no features such as ash lenses
to indicate the pristine condition of this deposit. However,
there was some bone, suggesting less disturbance than evident
in the case of the overburden. A four strand braid with
yarns wrapped in silver tinsel was also recovered in fairly
good condition.

Toward the bottom of Level 2, there was a greater degree of humidity in the soil. A wet clay silt at the bottom of this level covered the stones of a floor or platform (Level 2f). Very little material was contained in this silt, and no clear break with Level 2 was found.

The house itself was quite substantial and 30 cm. of wall was still standing above the level of the floor or platform. The wall uncovered in the pit formed a right angle with a nearby wall thought to have been an agricultural terrace wall (andén) like others at the site (pl. 3b). When the space was cleared between the wall in the pit and this other wall, a corner was found. The wall itself was built of roughly hewn stones of various sizes, with no discernible mortar between them. It had a width varying from 50 to 65 cm. The stones used in the corner tended to be more carefully selected. Flat rectangular stones with one roughly dressed end were preferred. All the stone used in this construction was a pinkish basalt quarried locally very near Hatunqolla, except for limestone which occurs near the surface all over the site.

The floor/platform extended nearly 2 m. along the north end of the house, and practically covered the excavating surface (pls. 4-5). Its surface was very uneven, due to the angular surfaces of the stones and to the lack of sizing. A bench, set on top of the platform, extended along part of the east wall, and possibly along the north wall as well. A house foundation excavated at a roughly contemporary site in the southern Lake Titicaca basin had a similar platform structure, interpreted by the excavator as a sleeping

platform (Rydén, 1947, pp. 192-195, map. 21, fig. 77). This
platform was on the west side of the structure. It, too,
had an uneven surface, and the excavator had some trouble
determining where the filling of the stones ended and the
floor stratum began (Rydén, 1947, p. 192). If the interpretation of this platform also applies to the platform in the
Hatunqolla structure, it lends weight to interpreting the
structure as a domicile. The refuse outside the building
also suggests such an interpretation.

Upon clearing the platform structure, it was decided not
to remove the entire platform, but rather to excavate only
one square meter in the southwest corner of the pit. The
refuse outside the wall was excavated first, keeping slightly
ahead of the excavation in the southwest corner of Pit 1 so
as to aid in correlating the strata from both excavations in
order to establish the date of the house's construction. The
lack of a definite floor and the extension of the platform
over most of Pit 1 complicated the task of determining this
date.

Outside the house a stratification of 11 distinct strata
was excavated (Pit 1A). All but two of the strata covered
the entire excavated surface. This stratification was adjacent to the road cut, and the ceramic sample was obtained
primarily from it.

The stratigraphic deposition provided some clues to the
time the house was built, and to the time it was abandoned.
Level 2 had the same character on both sides of the wall, and
it was clear that during most of the time represented by this

level the house was in ruins. The wall height could have
been somewhat higher. The present height of the wall may
have been arrived at by removing stones to facilitate modern
plowing, and the wall is suspiciously just below the plow-
line. It was perceived during the excavation that Level 3
began before the top of the wall was discovered. It is
entirely possible that Level 3 is the last refuse to be associated with the occupation of the house. The consistency of
the deposit changed abruptly at the time Level 3 was declared,
from a very light, very hard clay soil to a much darker,
softer soil. Below Level 2 the deposit had all the characteristics of undisturbed midden, such as ash lenses, carbon
in quantity, large fragments of bone, clay features and associations of large ceramic fragments. During the excavation
it appeared that no break in occupation had occurred between
Levels 3 and 11. When the ceramic materials were analyzed,
there were no apparent breaks in the style sequence in Levels
3 to 11, while a clear break between Levels 3 and 2 was
evident.

Determining when the house was built was more difficult.
During the excavation of Level 2 it appeared that the earth
within about 16 cm. from the wall, except toward its north
end, was softer than the remainder of Level 2. The soft
earth adjacent to the wall continued for a depth of about 30
cm. This earth might have been the trench dug at the time
the foundation was laid, or it might have been the remains of
packed clay plaster above the ground level at the time. The
material contained in this earth (Level 2t) was kept separate,

and when it was analyzed it was found to contain materials
from Levels 3-8. There is a good possibility that a clear
separation between this feature and the surrounding midden
was not maintained during excavation. Still, some of the
fragments found in the upper portion of this earth feature
could be joined with fragments of Levels 7-8 which were found
at some distance from the wall. It can be inferred that the
house was built at some time during or after the deposition
of Levels 7-8. Fragments which could be joined with others
from Levels 7-8 in Pit 1A were found under the stone platform
in Pit 1, further confirming the existence of this midden at
the time the house was constructed. The house was probably
occupied from about the end of the time represented
by Levels 7-8 to the beginning of the time represented by
Level 2. This occupation corresponds rather neatly to the
time represented by Phase 3, discussed in the next chapter.

Since the midden of Pit 1A provides the basis for the
ceramic sequence, its contents will be briefly described.

Level 3 was much darker and less compact than Level 2.
It contained about the same quantity of material as Level 2
for the same unit area. Level 4 was much less compact, and
again had a similar quantity of refuse. Near the south wall
a number of fragments of fused earth were recovered. Nothing
in either of these layers suggested Spanish influence.

Level 5 was declared when no more fused earth was found.
It had the same consistency as Level 4, but the quantity of
refuse was much greater. The fragments of pottery and bone

were also larger. Articulated leg bones from the hindquar-
ters of a camelid were found in this level. These bones were
adjacent to the road cut, which had probably cut through the
burial of an entire animal. The quantity of bone was
particularly good in Level 5.

Level 6 did not cover the entire excavating surface of
Pit 1A, but only the northern half. A quantity of moist pink
clay was found in this level. It was found intermixed with
earth. Wet clay was also found near the bottom of and under
the house wall, and under another fragmentary wall found in
Levels 7-8. This association suggests some connection with
the house construction, though interpretation of the feature
is difficult. Other clay features were found in Levels 7-8,
apparently unassociated with wall construction. Little
material was recovered in Level 6, probably because it was
relatively shallow. Some material from this level could be
joined with fragments from Level 7 below.

Near the beginning of Level 7 stones began to appear
which later proved to be part of another wall, though in
very bad condition (pls. 4-5). This wall was nearly flush with
the surface of the house wall foundation, but the two were
not structurally connected. The newly discovered wall had
less form. It appeared to be not as wide as the house wall,
and to curve somewhat toward the east. This wall was
entirely contained within Levels 7 and 8.

Levels 7 and 8 were a very dark color and bore every
sign of being undisturbed. Several ash lenses and clay
features were found in this level, including an ash lens

thought to be separating Levels 7 and 8. So many fragments
from one level could be united with fragments from the other,
that the two have been considered as one level in the analysis. As the fragmentary wall began to appear, it was decided
that material from one side of the wall should be separated
from material from the other. The north side of the wall
produced the most refuse (Level 7a), but some was recovered
between the fragmentary wall and the south wall of the pit
and above the fragmentary wall (Level 7b-c). Material from
above the fragmentary wall (Level 7c) was later separated
from the material south of it (Level 7b). Ash lenses of any
size containing archaeological material were treated as separate units (Levels 7_1, $7a_1$, $7b_1$). Fragments from the major
subdivisions of Levels 7 and 8 could not be united with
fragments from another. One fragment from Level 8b was
joined to a fragment from Level 10b. Since no stratum with
characteristics of Level 9 was present on the south side of
the fragmentary wall, it is possible that the Level 8b fragment should have been associated with Level 10b below it.
Some mixing between these two levels is indicated.

Level 9 was found only north of the fragmentary wall. If
the fragmentary wall was a house wall, and the refuse pattern
associated with it was similar to the pattern for the house
above, Level 9 refuse may be associated with an occupation
related to the structure. The area north of the fragmentary
wall would then have been the area outside the house, and the
area south would have been inside the house. Level 9 was
slightly more compact than Levels 7 and 8. It contained tiny

pieces of yellow chalk and pink sandstone, giving it a variegated color. The quantity of refuse in Level 9 seemed to be somewhat less per unit area than the quantity in Levels 7 and 8.

Level 10 did not have the inclusions of Level 9, and it was a lighter color. The quantity of refuse in this level was similar to that of Level 9.

Level 11 was the bottom level in the excavation, just above the limestone bedrock. It was light in color, very fine in consistency and contained very little cultural material.

The one meter excavation in the southwest corner of Pit 1 produced a stratigraphy which could be correlated to Pit 1A. The platform was built with two layers of stones set in a dark humus earth with some wet clay inclusions. This layer was apparently sterile. Below it, the stratification correlated with Levels 8, 10 and 11 of Pit 1A (Levels 8c, 10c and 11c). The quantity of material seemed to be somewhat less in the Pit 1 levels than in the corresponding levels of Pit 1A. A stone feature at the top of Level 10c may be a continuation of the fragmentary wall in Pit 1A. If the interpretation of the wall as a house wall is valid, and the refuse pattern for this house was the same as in the house above, then this interpretation would also explain why no stratum comparable to Level 9 was found in the pit in the southwest corner of Pit 1. The material in Level 9 would presumably be refuse associated with this earlier construction. Two fragments complicate this interpretation of the stratigraphy. A

fragment from Level 8c joined with another in Level 10c.
Another fragment from Level 8c joined with a fragment from
Pit 1A, Level 10b. In both cases, faulty separation of the
levels during the excavation may be to blame.

What the earlier refuse was associated with was not
determined because of limited excavation, but it is possible
that there was another structure nearby and it was associated with this refuse.   Hatunqolla preserves an Inca house
type to the present day, and the arrangement of houses also
follows an Inca plan. Houses are arranged on several sides
of a square central space, and are usually not constructed
at the same time. Remains of another wall, probably from
another house, were found in the road cut opposite the site
of the excavation. This wall was parallel to the exposed
wall of the house in Pit 1/1A, but not aligned with it (pl.
3b). Some kind of Inca plan for clustered domestic dwellings
may be indicated by the evidence, and the house in Pit 1/1A
may have been an addition to a house cluster in formation
(Rowe, 1946, p. 223; Tschopik, Harry, 1946, p. 529). If so,
this kind of plan may have been present even before the house
in Pit 1/1A was built.

The other pit used to establish the Hatunqolla chronology
was Testpit 4. The stratigraphy of this testpit was not as
carefully documented as the stratigraphy of Pit 1/1A. It was
hoped that another larger excavation could be conducted near
this testpit, but these plans had to be abandoned. Eight
strata were discerned in this excavation. No architectural
context was established for any of the material obtained.

Without doubt, modern Hatunqolla occupies the site of the ancient town. Though this site may have been abandoned during the Spanish colonial era, perhaps more than once, there is no reason to suspect that it was not the site of the colonial reduction. What is surprising is that no pre-Inca occupation was found, suggesting that the Hatunqolla referred to in the written accounts as the capital of the Qolla dynasty before the Inca conquest must have been located elsewhere.

Notes to Chapter IV

[1]Hatunqolla is situated at 15°41'7" latitude, 70°8'40"
longitude and 3822 meters above sea level (Instituto
Geográfico Militar, Carta Nacional, 1:100,000 scale, Puno
sheet, 32v).

[2]Two stone stelae were discovered in Hatunqolla, both
dating to a much earlier archaeological period (Chávez, 1975,
pp. 5 and 11; Kidder, 1943, pp. 15-16). Because no early
occupation was found at the site it is doubtful that
Hatunqolla was their original location. Another small
stele still stands in the courtyard of the Hatunqolla
municipality. It, too, was probably relocated to that place.

5

CERAMIC STYLE SEQUENCE OF
THE HATUNQOLLA AREA

The following discussion is a synopsis of the ceramic style sequence obtained at Hatunqolla using the excavated materials from Pit 1/1A and Testpit 4.[1] Material from Testpit 12 at Sillustani and surface materials from both Sillustani and Hatunqolla, as well as material from other sites in the Lake Titicaca region will be used in the analysis where such material sheds light on the problem of chronology. The present report does not include a detailed analysis of all excavated materials, but rather is a summary of the diagnostic material relevant to the problem of chronology at the site. Only the part of the site's history corresponding to the time the area was under Inca control will be discussed in any detail. On the basis of written records, discussed in the next chapter, this period lasted only about 100 years.

The object of the analysis was to uncover the rules governing the ceramic style or styles represented in the Hatunqolla refuse. In the process of learning these rules, a classification appropriate to the style became apparent. The classification may not reflect the folk classification of the ceramics when they were in use. It probably more closely

reflects a covert classification made by the potters, depending mainly on aesthetic and functional criteria, and details
of manufacture. Even this classification is elusive, due to
the nature of the archaeological record. In order to reconstruct this classification, a sufficient amount of diagnostic
material should be available for the definition of style
units. Since ceramic styles seldom occur in isolation, it is
useful to have some familiarity with other ceramic styles of
the same period. In the case of the Hatunqolla materials,
enough diagnostic fragments were found to establish the
framework of the sequence, but more material will be needed
to complete the picture. Moreover, Inca influenced ceramics
from the southern highlands are as yet poorly known. At
some future time it will hopefully be possible to add to the
style analysis presented here.

The principal method used in the reconstruction of this
ceramic classification is to establish a complete inventory
of whole vessels using information provided by fragments, and
then to identify stylistic regularities among the vessels.
The original makers of these vessels classified whole pots,
not fragments, and any classification which lumps fragments
from two different vessels into the same group or splits
fragments from the same vessel, will never allow an understanding of the original classification. A good place to
begin is with shape, as amply demonstrated in the pioneering
work of Dorothy Menzel (1976). Once a shape inventory has
been established, technological and design features associated with each shape can be studied. When a number of these

features can be associated with a particular shape, a whole
vessel can be reconstructed. Often, only a partial reconstruction of a vessel can be made with the fragmentary evidence, but even these partially reconstructed vessels are
useful in a style analysis.

Once an inventory of whole vessels has been reconstructed,
a style analysis can be carried out. Vessels in the same
style share style features or sets of features in patterned
combinations peculiar to that style. These patterned combinations are often regular and may even be completely stan-
dardized. By studying these regularities, the set of rules
governing the style can be discerned. The analysis is complete when a set of rules can be written out, like a grammar,
for a particular style.

Certain circumstances suggested the order to be followed
in the analysis of Hatunqolla ceramic materials. Because of
the differential quantity of diagnostic material in the
strata of Pit 1A, the analysis began with those containing
abundant diagnostic material. Levels 6-8 contained by far
the best material for the definition of a style unit. Levels
9-11 may represent two separate and stylistically antecedent
units, but because they contained a smaller quantity of
diagnostic material, they have been lumped together in the
present report for the purposes of description. Levels 3-5
also comprise at least one style unit, but again the quantity
of material is not large. Testpit 4 material belonged to the
same style unit and was analyzed together with the materials
from Levels 3-5.

The correlation between these style units and the excavated material used in defining the ceramic style sequence is
summarized in Table 6.

TABLE 6

Correlation between
Excavated Material and Style Units

	STYLE UNIT	DESCRIPTION
Testpit 12:		
Levels 1-6	(no phase label given)	no Inca influence
Pit 1A:		
Levels 9-11	Phase 1	some Inca influence
Levels 6-8	Phase 2	strong Inca influence
Levels 3-5	Phase 3	strong Inca influence
Testpit 4:		
Levels 1-8	Phase 3	strong Inca influence
Pit 1A:		
Level 2	Phase 4	some European influence

Because of the concentration of materials in Levels 6-8,
Phase 2 was defined first. The other materials were then
studied in relation to this baseline. Finally, the Sillustani material was examined to see to what extent the
Hatunqolla material was an outgrowth of local ceramic styles
in existence before the Inca conquest. The Sillustani
material and the four phases defined at Hatunqolla are summarized in order from earliest to latest. For Phases 1-3, the
diagnostic material is also briefly described. Three pastes,

used commonly in the manufacture of Hatunqolla ceramics, are defined in an appendix for convenience. Reference to this appendix will be made only where a particular paste is first mentioned in the text.

Following an order suggested by the Hatunqolla materials themselves, the ceramics have been organized into six major groups. The most important organizing principle was the degree and kind of influence effected by the Cuzco-Inca style, the ceramic style associated with the Inca empire and centered at the imperial capital of Cuzco. Several groups were determined utilizing this principle. A number of shapes and their decoration were imitated directly from Cuzco-Inca models (Group V). Some of the imitations are excellent, while others are much freer copies of the originals. A group of unique vessels seems to be especially related to the Cuzco-Inca imitations (VI). The area of strongest Cuzco influence on the Sillustani style is among the bowls. A bowl shape was part of the Sillustani style inventory before Cuzco-Inca influence arrived in the Lake Titicaca region. From the beginning of the style sequence at Hatunqolla, Cuzco influence allows the bowls to be separated into two groups. The Cuzco related group has a number of Cuzco-Inca style features, but entire shapes and design compositions were not borrowed (I). Some Cuzco-Inca features are also apparent in the group more closely tied to the Sillustani style (II). The other major groups have no obvious links to the Cuzco-Inca style. A utilitarian category (III) and a category of

miscellaneous shapes with little or no decoration (IV) are
the remaining major groups.

It will be apparent to the reader that there are a great
number of shapes. All the shapes that could be reconstructed
to any meaningful degree have been included in the description. For ease of reference they have been given both a
number and a descriptive title.

Not all of the vessels represented by these shapes
belong to the same style. Some of the described fragments
are unique pieces and may represent vessels of other local
styles, imports from far away, or antiques. Some of the imitation Cuzco-Inca vessels are a problem in this regard.
Until more is known about the Cuzco-Inca style of the capital
and variants of it in other parts of the empire, determining
the origins of some of the fragments recovered at Hatunqolla
will remain a problem. Where a fragment might be an import,
the possibility has been suggested in the description.
No attempt has been made to segregate other non-local material. Most of the described fragments have been illustrated,
and when further archaeological work has been done, it should
be possible to identify some of the fragments as non-local.

SUMMARY OF THE SILLUSTANI STYLE

The first point to be made about the excavated material
from Hatunqolla is that it does not represent a time earlier
than the period of strong Inca influence in the area, certainly the time of the Inca empire. Moreover, it became
apparent during the analysis that Hatunqolla material had not

been described or illustrated before, though it was directly
related to material called "Sillustani Series" by Marion
Tschopik in her 1946 report.

Tschopik's report is the best source of information on
the Sillustani style. The style was defined by members of
Harvard Project 7 who met in Chucuito August 28 to 31,
1941, to classify surface materials recovered by project
members in the Puno area. The name Sillustani was given to
one of the types defined at that time by John H. Rowe, one
of the members of the project. Rowe had already used the
name in reference to ceramic fragments in the Bingham Collection of the Peabody Museum at Yale University. The material
classified as Sillustani by members of Harvard Project 7
was thought to be pre-Inca because it exhibited no Cuzco
influence.

Three of Tschopik's four Sillustani Series types are
readily recovered from the surface at Sillustani, and
Testpit 12 contained two and possibly three of them. The
Sillustani Black and Red type does not occur in any quantity
at Sillustani. It is possible that the white of the
Sillustani Black and White on Red type was completely effaced
on the fragments classified as Sillustani Black and Red, and
that white line decoration was originally present. This type
was defined on the basis of less than six sherds from
Sillustani and was considered tentative (Tschopik, Marion,
1946, p. 27). The Sillustani Brown on Cream type has been
recovered in surface collections at the site by the author,
though it was not found in Testpit 12. The idea of

separating bowls with different colored slips into different
classes was a good one, but there was considerably more variation among the bowls than the typology allows, and bowls
were not the only Sillustani style shapes.

Arturo Ruiz Estrada, the archaeologist who directed the
cleaning and restoration of the monuments at Sillustani
financed by CORPUNO in 1971, also published illustrations of
Sillustani style ceramics (1973b). He studied surface collections from the cleaning, and also material from a 2 x 1 m.
excavation conducted in a midden on the neck of the
Sillustani peninsula, outside the bounds of the funeral tower
site proper. It was in this excavation that he recovered
stratified material from two periods, only one demonstrating
any Cuzco-Inca influence. The upper levels contained
Sillustani materials associated with Cuzco influenced material, while the lower levels contained Sillustani materials
only (1973a, p. 45). Unfortunately, the pit did not produce
a very large quantity of ceramics. The illustrations Ruiz
Estrada published are a good source of information on the
Sillustani style, though no provenience is given for the
materials shown.

Testpit 12 from Sillustani helped to establish a pre-
Inca date for some of the Sillustani material illustrated.
A good deal of the material illustrated antedates the
occupation of Hatunqolla, but some of the fragments can be
cross-dated to the Hatunqolla sequence. Since the pre-Inca
Sillustani style[2] is not the subject here, only a brief
description of it will be given, relying on materials from

Testpit 12 and published illustrations of pre-Inca Sillustani
style ceramics.

The Sillustani style consists of a variety of bowl
shapes, small bottles and large jars. Fragments of bowls are
most frequently found. These bowls are generally deep, with
direct rims and little or no curvature in the profile. The
bowls carry the bulk of the decoration. As Tschopik was
aware, the slips on bowl interiors determine subclasses of
bowls. Two classes of slips, a kaolin white and a purple or
crimson, have decorative elements associated with them. An
unslipped or light red surface also has a class of decorative
elements associated with it. The white slip, and perhaps
the purple or crimson, may even determine subclasses of
small bottles.

The most standard kind of bowl decoration is a purple or
crimson interior slip decorated with a limited number of band
designs (Tschopik, Marion, 1946, figs. 12 and 13; Ruiz
Estrada, 1973b, pls. 22 and 23). A band design frequently
seen on surface fragments and documented in the Sillustani
testpit consists of parallel lines in solution black,[3] with
faint white dots in rows between them (Tschopik, Marion,
1946, fig. 13; Ruiz Estrada, 1973b, figs. 22e-f). Either one
or two rows of dots are painted in this space, and they may
occur in bunches with open space separating one bunch from
the next. One nearly complete specimen has another narrow
band more than half the distance from the lip to the base
(Ruiz Estrada, 1973a, pls. 21f and 22c-d; fragments from
Sillustani surface). In between the upper and lower bands

are bunches of parallel black lines with rows of white dots
between them, spaced evenly around the circumference. Other
fragments with a similar decoration were recovered by Ruiz
Estrada. He illustrates other band designs on red slipped
fragments, but does not distinguish between a light red surface and a purple or crimson slip. One of the bands, consisting of parallel black lines with an undulating white line
between them, can be found on a purple slip in surface collections (Ruiz Estrada, 1973b, pl. 23b; fragments from
Sillustani surface).

The designs used on the white slipped bowls and their
arrangements are less standard (Tschopik, Marion, 1946, figs.
10a-j, m-o; Ruiz Estrada, 1973b, pls. 16-18, 19a-d). Most
fragments have a pair of stripes just below the lip, consisting of an upper black stripe and lower red stripe in most
cases, but the reverse color order in some cases. The color
order of the stripes may be associated with certain combinations of motifs on the interior. Band designs are not preva-
lent among the motifs, though motifs may be repeated in
series between bordering stripes. The motifs themselves are
not obviously representational, but few are really geometric.
Few large fragments have been found, but several show the
repetition of large motifs around the interior of the bowl,
with smaller elements used as filler. The space between
large motifs is not carefully filled, and the design composition leaves the impression of much open space. Otherwise,
bands of repeated filler motifs, perhaps two such bands on a
single bowl, are a common decorative composition (Ruiz

Estrada, 1973b, pls. 17d, i, j, 18a-c). Narrow band
composition apparently involved the use of closely spaced
narrow band designs near the bowl's lip. One theme common to
decoration with narrow band designs, or motifs in series, is
color alternation. For example, motifs in series may alternate between black and red. If a band of these motifs occurs
next to another such band, there will also be color alternation between the two bands, so that a red motif will be
placed adjacent to a black motif, etc.

The third kind of bowl decoration documented in the
Sillustani testpit is decoration on an unpigmented or light
red surface (Ruiz Estrada, 1973b, pls. 22, 23 and 26).[4] Like
the purple or crimson slipped group, these bowls are also
decorated with band designs. The one band documented for
these bowls is a narrow band consisting of two parallel lines
between which a black undulating line or a more angular line,
or zig-zag, is placed. The one fragment with excavation provenience has a white undulating line paired with a black line
in the space between parallel stripes (fragment from Level 5,
Testpit 12, Sillustani; fragments from Sillustani surface).
Other fragments have wider bands with zig-zag lines and
broken undulating white lines between the angles of the zig-
zag lines. These bowls have polished interiors, so that the
surface is a light red color, darker than the color of an
unpigmented surface. Another kind of decoration is found on
unslipped bowls with no polish, usually consisting of some
kind of broad black line motif suspended near the rim (Ruiz
Estrada, 1973b, fig. 26h).

All of the bowls described above have well smoothed and
well polished interiors, except for some bowls in the
unslipped or light red group. These bowls still have a well
smoothed interior, often with wipe marks in evidence, but the
exteriors were not well smoothed. Some exteriors are quite
lumpy, others are somewhat more even and have some polishing
marks. The pigments were applied after the surfaces were
finished in most cases. The black tends to blur around the
edges, especially when it occurs over an unpigmented surface.
It does not blur when applied over a white slip. The blurring indicates that organic constituents of the paint were
able to creep into the surrounding surface by capillary
action. The density of the black indicates that only part of
the pigment was in solution and able to spread in this manner
(see note 3).

Less can be said about the other shapes in the Sillustani
inventory because they were not as well represented in the
test excavation. One fragment of a small white slipped
bottle with a reticulated design was illustrated by Tschopik
(Marion, 1946, fig. 101). Ruiz Estrada found several such
bottles during the cleaning of Sillustani (1973b, pls. 19f-g,
20a-c, 21a). They were decorated mainly with narrow band
designs, wider versions of the same band designs, or motifs
in series with outline stripes. The design space begins
below the inflection point at the base of the neck and
extends below the point of maximum diameter of the bottle.
The inner lip may also have some small line decoration. The
bottles are characteristically very small, about 5-10 cm. in

height. Small lug handles with pierced openings occur at the
point of maximum diameter, as do spouts which extend diagonally upwards from their bases. Tiny lugs may occur opposite
each other on the outer lip.

Though some of the designs cannot be documented for the
white slipped class of bowls, many can, and this bottle shape
appears to be decoratively matched to the bowl group. No
fragments from small bottles decorated with purple slip have
turned up at Sillustani, but some whole vessels which appear
to be Sillustani style are decorated in this manner (Puno
Municipal Museum). Even fragments of the white bottles are
extremely rare, however.

There are several jars represented among the excavated
materials from Sillustani, but fragments from these jars
rarely offer much information for shape. Fragments of large
jars with either black line decoration on an unpigmented surface, a purple slip, large strap handles, or a purple slipped
inner rim and an unpigmented exterior were also found (fragments from Levels 3-5, Testpit 12, Sillustani). At the site,
fragments were found of a large jar with a wide neck, a very
thick lip and an appliqué fillet at the base of the neck
(Tschopik, Marion, 1946, figs. 28e-f; fragments from
Sillustani surface). The fillet has punctations on its surface. Ruiz Estrada recovered a number of very large neck
fragments (Ruiz Estrada, 1973b, pls. 28a-g, 50). The known
examples were not decorated except for the fillet, and an
occasional incised tab extending from the lip. One of these
necks has a short spout extending upward from near the neck

base (Ruiz Estrada, 1973b, pl. 50). Fragments of jars like
these were found in a road cut near the site of Testpit 12.

Another kind of large jar with a taller, narrower neck
was also recovered from Sillustani during the cleaning operation (Ruiz Estrada, 1973b, pls. 47, 51, 52, 54). These jars
are greater than 40 cm. in height. Many have neck decoration
in black line motifs. One such jar also has a decorative
appliqué fillet and a pair of small lugs on the outer lip.
Another jar has solid black motifs near the shoulder. The
bodies of the jars often exhibit fire clouding. Two jars
with no black decoration may have a light red slip in some
areas. These jars have strap handles, either at the point of
maximum body diameter, or at the neck, extending from the lip
to the inflection point at the neck's base. They also have
characteristically small bases relative to their size. A
number of smaller shapes were found, with some of the same
features as the larger jars (Ruiz Estrada, 1973b, figs.
48-49). They vary in size from about 10 to 20 cm. in height.

Very few bowl fragments were analyzed for paste, but
those analyzed suggest a variety of different pastes. Most
are cream fired, but one fires to a medium orange, and
another consistently fires to a dull rose color. The cream
colored paste texture is a medium grained paste, tempered
with either sand, milky and smoky quartzite, or quartzite
with small black shiny particles. The medium orange and dull
rose colored pastes have a less granular appearance. Their
texture often resembles uncooked cookie dough, but in a few
cases, the texture is smooth as cement. The examples from

the Sillustani excavation appear to have no deliberate temper, but there are many sandstone, chalk and other particles in the paste.

The cream fired paste with milky and smoky quartzite temper is common among the analyzed jar fragments. The jar fragments analyzed were from surface collections at sites near Sillustani and represent both the thick rimmed and tall necked jars. Some jars from Sillustani have a medium orange surface color, suggesting the use of another kind of paste.

Of course, much remains to be known about the Sillustani style. The above description is certainly not thorough and was based on many fragments with no more than site provenience. As will be seen, many Sillustani style features can be observed in the Hatunqolla material. It is important to understand the context of these features in the Sillustani style before the impact of the Inca conquest made itself felt on the ceramic style in order to understand the process of style change.

PHASE ONE

Cuzco Related Bowls (Group I)

Bowls in this group are small and fairly shallow, like bowls in the Cuzco-Inca style. Only a few fragments belonging to this group were found in Phase 1 levels. No base fragments were recovered, but it is probable that these bowls had flat bases because of their other similarities to Cuzco-Inca bowls and because this group characteristically had flat bases in Phase 2 (see figs. 34, 37-39). Very characteristic

of these bowls is a fine surface finish on both inner and
outer surfaces. The inside is often slipped with one of
several pigments of red hue and finely polished to a shine.
The outside is less carefully finished, but always well
smoothed and polished over most of the surface. The outside
may be slipped. Other technological details differ and will
be discussed under the shape headings.

I:1. Bowl with flattened lip (fig. 1). The fragment
suggests a diameter of 15 cm. The lip is characteristically
flattened, so that if the bowl was turned over, it would rest
evenly on the lip surface. The flattened lip surface is not
wider than the thickness of the bowl wall below. The one
fragment with this shape is slipped with a dense purple pigment on the inside. This purple appears to be particularly
connected with Cuzco-Inca influence throughout the sequence.
The fragment was made of a paste closely connected with Cuzco
influence in the Hatunqolla sequence, referred to hereafter
as Paste C (Appendix).

I:2. Small shallow bowl with flattened lip (figs. 2-3
and one fragment not illustrated). No diameter could be
reconstructed from any of these fragments. The width of the
flattened lip surface is about the same or slightly smaller
than the width of the bowl wall below. These fragments
suggest a shallower bowl with straighter walls than the bowl
described above. One fragment is colored by a very thin slip
with a light red color (fig. 2). The slip darkens considerably when it is polished, but it was not polished in this
case. The fragment also exhibits black line decoration. The

lines blur around the edges, indicating that the black pigment is similar to the Sillustani style pigment already described (see note 3). Another fragment in this group was not
painted, but had a solution black stripe at the rim (fig. 3).
A third fragment in this group (not illustrated) was slipped
with a medium red color on the inside, with rows of upturned
crescents painted in solution black. All three fragments
have good interior and exterior surface finish, except the
fragment of fig. 2 which has no inside polish. One of the
fragments was executed in Paste C (fig. 3), and one in another majority paste, Paste D (Appendix). The remaining
fragment resembles Paste D in texture, but it seems to have a
fine sand temper in small quantity.

I:3.   Bowl with profile thinned toward the lip (fig. 4
and one fragment not illustrated). The one measurable fragment suggests a diameter of 15 cm. (fig. 4). Both fragments
have a rim profile similar to the "hooked" profile of the
Cuzco-Inca style (Bingham, 1930, p. 119, pl. 71, fig. 11a-g;
Eaton, 1916, pl. XIII, figs. 3, 6-7). The hooked shape
results from a concave interior profile. In the case of the
Hatunqolla fragments, the interior profile is only slightly
concave. The exterior profile is markedly convex just below
the lip and then tends to parallel the interior. Both fragments have an interior slip, but may also have some kind of
red slip on the exterior. Despite what looks like an
exterior slip, one of the fragments is less carefully polished than is usual for Cuzco related bowls (fig. 4). This
fragment has a design which can be related to the Cuzco-Inca

style, and it is almost convincing enough to suggest that it
was imitated from a Cuzco specimen. A pendent triangle band
hung from the lip line with two black stripes below it is
characteristically Cuzco-Inca.[5] The cross-hatched band below
is similar to one used on Cuzco-Inca vessels, but here it is
seen in circumferential position, unlike the Cuzco-Inca
standard arrangement where it crosses the interior in transverse position. The design is painted in purple and black
on a cream slipped surface. The black is not blurred about
the edges and may be a different pigment from the solution
black. The other fragment (not illustrated) has a similar
cross-hatched design, though the lines are not as narrow.
The black is faint, but does not seem to blur. In this case,
the design is painted on a medium red slipped surface.
Instead of purple dots, there are white dots painted in the
interstices. The white is chalky and not well preserved.
Both fragments were executed in Paste C.

Sillustani Related Bowls (Group II)

More variation in both shape and size is found among
bowls in this group. No base fragments of any size were
recovered, but by analogy with both pre-Inca and Phase 2
Sillustani related bowls, it is probable that most of these
shapes had a small, rounded base. Most of the Phase 1 bowls
are fairly deep and all but one have straight walls with
little or no convexity in the profile. There is a larger
size range in this group than in the Cuzco related group, and
some quite large bowls are represented. All fragments

exhibit a characteristic surface finish similar to the
finish of pre-Inca Sillustani style bowls. The Sillustani
style bowls from the test excavation at Sillustani were not
carefully smoothed and seldom polished. The Phase 1 bowls
from Hatunqolla were better smoothed. Sometimes the exterior
surface, especially the first few centimeters below the lip,
was wiped while wet, as horizontal wipe marks are often
visible. Some attention was usually given to polishing, but
the polish marks are widely separated and do not cover the
exterior surface very well.

   II:1. Bowl with inward bevel from the lip and outer
angle (figs. 5-12). Only a few fragments serve to reconstruct diameters for this class of bowls. They suggest a
diameter of 15-17 cm. Several fragments with thicker walls
may have had very large diameters, but they do not possess
enough of a rim to make a reliable measurement. Three sizes
seem to be in evidence. The shape itself is very common in
Phase 1. The beveled surface is characteristically wider
than the bowl wall below. The inner profile below the bevel
angle ranges from straight to very slightly concave. The lip
itself is slightly rounded. The exterior profile frequently
reflects the interior profile, but the width of a cross-
section through the lip is usually thinner than the width of
the bowl wall. The exterior angle is often not as sharp as
the bevel angle, and sometimes is represented only as a
slight depression in the outer profile, between .4 and 1 cm.
below the lip line. Below the bevel angle and corresponding

depression on the exterior, the plate wall maintains an even
thickness or thins slightly toward the lower edge.

II:1a. Black and white decoration on purple slipped
interior (figs. 5-6). This kind of decoration is directly
related to Sillustani style decoration. All decoration is
painted over a purple slipped surface. Both examples are
painted with Sillustani style band designs. The Phase 1
bands are wider than their pre-Inca equivalents, however.
Moreover, Sillustani style bands occurring on a purple
slipped surface consisted chiefly of two parallel black
lines with a row of white dots or an undulating white line.
These bands have a black zig-zag or scallop painted between
the parallel lines, as well as white dots or undulating white
lines. This kind of decoration was present in the Sillustani
style of pre-Inca date, but there it was associated with
bowls slipped with light red. Moreover, these Phase 1 fragments have bunches of vertical black stripes on the beveled
surface, something not found in the earlier Sillustani style.
A feature not usually seen in Sillustani style material is
the use of two or more adjacent narrow band designs. This
idea may have come from the Cuzco-Inca style, as adjacent
circumferential bands also occur in the Cuzco related bowl
group. The colors used for the bands were a matte white and
a solution black. One of the fragments has a purple exterior
slip and a better exterior surface finish (fig. 6). The
three fragments have different pastes. The one with the
exterior purple slip (fig. 6) is made of the cream fired

variant of Paste C (Appendix). The second fragment is
Paste D with the addition of a good quantity of fine mica
(fig. 5).

   II:1b. Black or black and white decoration on light red
slipped surface (figs. 7-10). There is considerable variety
in the decoration of this group. All fragments, though, have
a form of Sillustani style narrow band decoration with black
line zig-zag or scallop between two parallel black lines.
This kind of band, though narrower, was documented in association with a light red slip in pre-Inca contexts at
Sillustani. Like the last decorative group, some of these
fragments also have vertical black stripes on the bevel surface, sometimes with adjacent white stripes. Where enough of
the design is preserved, these plates have an adjacent upper
or lower black stripe. The one example with black and white
stripes on the bevel surface also has traces of white line
decoration on the zig-zag band (fig. 10). Another fragment
has a white wash painted over the zig-zag portion of the
zig-zag band (fig. 9). Three fragments were Paste D (figs.
7, 8 and 10), and another appears to be Paste D in other
respects but has little visible temper (fig. 9).

   II:1c. Black decoration on light red slipped surface
(fig. 11). The fragment suggests a 12 cm. diameter. The
shape and design details are similar to those described for
Group II:1b, except that this bowl is smaller in size. The
fragment was made of Paste D with very fine mica.

   II:1d. Black and red decoration on a white slipped surface (fig. 12). The motif on the interior surface of this

bowl is probably a standing human figure, holding a staff
and wearing a feather-like ornament on its back and head.
There are probable pre-Inca antecedents for this motif, and
it is certainly present in Phases 2 and 3 (Ruiz Estrada,
1973b, pl. 17a-b, figs. 47-51). This fragment has red paint
on the beveled surface. On the interior of the bowl below
the bevel angle there is first a black stripe, though little
black paint remains to suggest its existence, then a red
stripe. The alternating black and red stripe is very characteristic of Sillustani style bowls with a white slipped
interior, and this link demonstrates a continuity in style
(Tschopik, Marion, 1946, fig. 10g; Ruiz Estrada, 1973b, pls.
16b, d, 17d, h-j, 18b, j, 19a, c, d; fragments from
Sillustani surface). The colors used to execute the design
are similar to the colors employed in the related pre-Inca
bowls with some small differences. The white is the dense
matte white of the Sillustani style, but tinged with pink.
The red is a clear red, and not as dense or matte as the
Sillustani red, because the polishing was done after the red
was applied. The black is a solution black. This fragment
was made in the variety of Paste D with a large quantity of
fine mica.

II:2. Small bowl with inward bevel from the lip and
outer angle (fig. 13 and one fragment not illustrated). One
fragment suggests a diameter of 12 cm. The inside of this
fragment is slipped with an unusual color, partially obscured
by a grayed firing. Since there is an orange-red in this
phase, it can probably be identified as that color. A

second rim fragment was recovered (not illustrated), but it
was too small to give a diameter measurement. It has a good
outer surface finish, unlike other bowls in Group II. At the
same time, other details of paint and paste are closely
linked to the Sillustani style. The pigments are identical
to earlier Sillustani style pigments. The white is dense and
matte, the black, though faint, is a dense brown-black, and
the red is a dull, dark red. Though it is hard to see the
black, there were apparently vertical black stripes on the
bevel surface. At the bevel angle was another black stripe,
below it a red stripe and below that a pair of black diagonal
lines. Another Sillustani style feature is the narrower
width of these stripes. The fragment resembles several
others found in Phase 2 levels (figs. 64-66). The paste is
a very clear cream color with the temper characteristics of
Paste C. The other fragment (fig. 13) was fabricated in the
variant of Paste D with a large amount of fine mica.

II:3. Bowl with rounded inner lip or slight inward
bevel from the lip, and outer angle (figs. 14-17). This
group includes a number of bowls differing only slightly in
shape details. These minor differences may also be important,
and they will be discussed under the subheadings below. Only
a few fragments provide enough of the circumference to permit
a reconstruction of the diameter, suggesting a 12-19 cm.
diameter. The fragments have a very similar thickness, so
there may be less variation in diameter than the measurement
indicates.

II:3a. Black and red or orange-red on cream slipped or
unpigmented surface (figs. 14-15 and one not illustrated).
Two fragments have a very slight angular change in the inner
profile and an equally slight depression on the exterior
(fig. 14 and one not illustrated). Both have a red stripe
below the lip bordered by a black stripe which marks the
point of angular change with its lower border. A second
black stripe occurs below the point of angular change. The
orange-red color is clear on one fragment and dark on the
other (fig. 14). The clear orange-red was applied after polishing while the darker color was polished with the other
pigments. The black in both cases fades where it is painted
over the cream slip.[6] In one case (fig. 14), the design is
similar to a design found in the Sillustani style executed
on a white slip (tassel motif), except that the fine stripes
proceed from a single diagonal stripe on the left, rather
than stem from a single point (Tschopik, Marion, 1946,
fig. 10g; Ruiz Estrada, 1973b, pls. 20a, 21a). The third
fragment in this group is decorated with a motif borrowed
from the Cuzco-Inca style (fig 15). It has a rounded inner
lip and a pronounced outer angle. The execution of the
motif does not suggest deliberate imitation of the Cuzco-Inca
style, however. The band of vertical bars alternating with
parallel crossed lines (bar-and-x) is borrowed from the
Cuzco-Inca style as well.[7] The vertical stripes in alternating colors on the inner lip and the undulating black
line between two orange-red stripes were not. All three
fragments were made of Paste D with a large quantity of fine

mica on the surface. Other than the mica, there was very
little of the quartzite usually used as temper. Instead,
there were a number of inclusions including white quartzite
and sandstone grains of different colors.

II:3b. Black and red decoration on white slipped
surface (not illustrated). The two analyzed fragments are
quite different. One has a rounded inner lip and a pronounced
outer angle 4 cm. below the lip. The other has a rounded
inner lip and a very straight outer profile, tapering slightly
at the lip. The decoration also differs. The fragment with
the outer angle resembles a fragment described above (fig.
12) in the colors used and details of decoration. The black
used, however, fades to a very light gray over the white
slip. Again, high firing temperature or wear is indicated
(see note 6). There also appears to be only one black stripe
between the upper red stripe and the lower one. The interior
surface was polished over all pigments before the lower red
stripe was applied, and it was left unpolished. The other
fragment has very different pigments, though the surface is
too worn to permit detailed comparison. The white is
denser and creamier, the black is dark but washy and the red
is darker. The first fragment was made in Paste D with a
large quantity of additional fine mica. The other has the
visual aspects of Paste D, but only a small amount of fine
sand and no obvious temper. Its paste also contains a very
large quantity of additional mica.

II:3c. Black and white decoration on light red surface
(fig. 16 and one fragment not illustrated). Both fragments

have very slight angular change in the interior profile, but
this change occurs much further below the lip in one case
than in the other (fig. 16). The decoration is nearly identical. It consists of a band placed just below the interior
angle with grouped vertical black lines between two parallel
stripes. The area between the parallel stripes has a washy
white painted over it. The black is very dark and blurs only
slightly in some areas. The white is nearly worn away. This
use of the white pigment was documented on another fragment
(fig. 9). The width of bands with a washy white overlay and
the band designs chosen are reminiscent of earlier
Sillustani style bands.[8] The fragments were fabricated in a
paste resembling Paste D in visual aspects, but which fires
to a dark orange color. It contains a small amount of sand,
possibly a deliberate addition.

II:3d. Black and white decoration on purple slipped
surface (not illustrated). This fragment has a rounded inner
lip, the curve of which is repeated in the exterior profile.
In colors and some design details, this fragment closely
resembles those of Group II:1a. The placement of a
Sillustani style narrow band just below the lip is a conservative style feature, as is the width of the band. The
narrow band with closely spaced parallel black stripes and
white dots can be documented for the Sillustani style in
pre-Inca times. There may have been a washy white painted
over the surface of this band, despite the presence of white
dots. The paste has the textural aspects of Paste D, but it
has a moderate quantity of sand and is more of a cream color.

II:3e. Black and white decoration on a red-purple
surface (fig. 17). The rim is direct and the lip is very
rounded. The outer profile has a definite angle below the
lip. It also has an unusual thickening, thinning only
toward the base. The fragment was decorated with a zig-zag
band design bordered by a lower stripe. The upper stripe is
usually not as wide as in this example. Over the zig-zag
band there are traces of at least two white stripes. The
firing is grayed, and the colors are dull, but the interior
slip seems to have been red-purple. The exterior surface
was smoothed, but polished only near the lower edge. Toward
the lip, there are horizontal wipe marks. The fragment was
manufactured of a paste with the textural qualities of Paste
D, but with fine sand as the only temper.

II:3f. Black line decoration on unslipped surface (not
illustrated). The interior surface finish of this fragment
is different from the finish of others in this group. Horizontal striations indicate the surface was wiped while wet
rather than polished. The interior was slipped with a thin
medium brown color which may have been red at some time. A
black tassel motif is suspended from the lip. This kind of
decoration occurs in the Sillustani style (Tschopik, Marion,
1946, fig. 10g; fragments from sites near Sillustani). The
black pigment used is a solution black. The paste is cream
fired and very fine grained. A small amount of find sand may
have been used as temper. This fragment was from the lowest
levels of the excavation and may be stylistically earlier
than other Phase 1 material.

II:4. Bowl with evenly thinned rim (figs. 18-19).
Neither of the two fragments in this group can be used to
reconstruct a diameter or to reliably estimate the orientation of the profile. The fragments have relatively thin
walls, and no notable angular change in either the inside or
outside profile. They are both slipped with light red. One
has a wide band with a black line scallop between two black
stripes (fig. 18). The other has a narrower band with a
double zig-zag between two black stripes (fig. 19). Both
fragments apparently had washy white over the zig-zag, but
the white is very poorly preserved. The black is probably
solution black, as it is similar to the black used in II:3c
above, but it does not blur at the edges. The paste has the
textural aspects of Paste D, but is a clear orange color and
has fine sand as possible temper.

II:5. Bowl with straight inner profile thickening from
the lip (fig. 20 and fragments not illustrated). None of the
fragments will allow the reconstruction of a diameter, but
they represent a fairly deep bowl shape. The smoothing done
on the exterior surface of these fragments is less careful
than the finish of other fragments with ties to the
Sillustani style. All fragments have some kind of narrow
band design relatable to earlier Sillustani style antecedents.
The two bands used are the band with an undulating line
between two stripes and a band with bunched horizontal lines
also bordered by two stripes (fig. 20)(Ruiz Estrada, 1973b,
pls. 16c, 17c, f, 19b, 20b, c, 23a; Tschopik, Marion, 1946,
fig. 11a-c; fragments from Sillustani surface).

II:5a. Red and black decoration on a white slipped
surface (not illustrated). Both fragments have a similar
design; a narrow band with bunched horizontal lines is
placed immediately below the lip. The bunched lines alternate between black and red. Below this band is another with
a black undulating line between two red stripes. The paste
of these two fragments has the textural aspects of Paste D,
with a few sandstone inclusions and white quartzite particles,
but no obviously added temper grains, and a larger quantity
of fine mica.

II:5b. Black and white decoration on light red slipped
surface (not illustrated). A narrow band design consisting
of bunched horizontal lines is placed immediately below the
lip. A washy white covers the area between the two border
stripes. The paste is identical to the paste of II:5a.

II:5c. Black and white decoration on crimson slip (not
illustrated). A crimson slip occurs on Sillustani style
bowls with no features linking them to the Inca occupation of
the area. Two adjacent narrow bands, one wider than the
other, are placed below the lip. The black does not blur but
has other visual aspects of solution black. Solution black
tends not to blur over a very dense pigment. The white is
extremely faint. The paste has visual aspects of Paste D,
but it is a clear cream color and has fine milky quartzite
grains.

II:6. Deep bowl shape (fig. 21). The fragment suggests
a diameter of between 17 and 21 cm. The rim comes to a point
at the lip and thins toward the bottom edge. The interior

is decorated with a wide zig-zag band painted in solution
black over a polished light red surface. Traces of a lower
bordering stripe are preserved at the lower edge. The
exterior is not well smoothed and has horizontal wipe marks
except for the band below the lip. In addition, there are a
few narrow polishing marks. The fragment was made of Paste
D.

II:7. Small bowl shape (fig. 22). The fragment suggests
a bowl of 8 cm. diameter. The decoration consists of an
interior white slip with two parallel dark red lines below
the lip and some kind of decoration in red on the surface
below. The pigments are extremely like those used in Group
II:5a above.

II:8. Small bowl with vertical walls (fig. 23). The
bowl had a diameter of 9 cm. The rim is rounded, and the
profile thickens toward the base. The inside was smoothed
and very irregularly polished. The outside was very incom-
pletely smoothed. It shows a few wipe marks. Black line
decoration was the only decorative treatment used. The
paint used for decoration was solution black. The paste has
the visual aspects of Paste D, but contained few inclusions.

II:9. Miscellaneous bowl fragments. A number of bowl
fragments were found which give some indication of the lower
wall decoration of some of these deep bowl shapes. Four
fragments have a narrow band design with no adjacent decoration. Two of them are painted on a light red polished surface and appear to have a white stripe or band between two
black border stripes. The other two are painted on a

polished medium red surface. One fragment has thick walls.
It was painted with a white undulating line between two
parallel black stripes. All of these designs and this
design placement have conservative Sillustani style antecedents. Three have a paste with the textural aspects of
Paste D, a clear orange color and very little temper. The
fourth was made of Paste D, and has a fine exterior surface
finish with a red slip. One miscellaneous fragment has a
white slipped interior with alternating red and black tassel
motifs in series. Both the inside and outside were polished
over all pigments, and the outside was slipped with a medium
red. The fragment was made of the variety of Paste D with
fine mica. The final fragment has a black line design, possibly related to some of the non-geometric Sillustani style
designs painted on an unslipped surface. This fragment was
not slipped either, but was polished on both the inside and
outside surfaces. It was made of an orange fired paste of a
rather coarse texture, and tempered with fine angular gray
and white grits. The three fragments described with both
inside and outside polish come from the very lowest level of
the excavation and may be stylistically separable from the
other levels in Phase 1. The surface finish of these fragments, both interior and exterior, is better than for almost
any Sillustani tradition bowls among the Hatunqolla materials.

Utilitarian Shapes (Group III)

The only vessel forms to consistently show use in the fire were fabricated in Paste A (Appendix). Because this paste is also quite distinctive, vessels manufactured in it have been grouped together.

III:1. Jar with vertical strap handles (not illustrated). These jars apparently served as the principal cooking vessel during the occupation of Hatunqolla. The shape was very popular in Phase 2, and since the fragments in the lower levels are not noticeably different, its description is found under the same heading (III:1) in the Phase 2 section.

III:2. Shallow dish with vertical walls (fig. 24). No diameter can be reconstructed. The rim appears to have an outward bevel from the lip, though it is very irregular. The thickness of the fragment near the base angle also varies from being thinner than the wall above to being much thicker. The exterior surface has some kind of light red pigment on it that seems to be unaffected by the blackening of the surface beneath it. If the blackening was caused by use over the fire or reduction, then the red pigment should also show a strong gray factor. It does not, so the explanation must lie elsewhere. The inside surface is smooth and shows horizontal wipe marks. The outside is not as well smoothed, and there are some marks in several directions on the surface of the red pigment. The paste is Paste A of the low fired variety (Appendix). The blackened surface suggests reduction or smoking, but the problem with the light red pigment mentioned above indicates another possible reason for the blackening.

Other Shapes (Group IV)

IV:1. Jar with flaring rim (figs. 25-26). The
measurable fragment gives a diameter of 20 cm. (fig. 25).
The other jar probably had a smaller diameter. The larger
jar (fig. 25) has a pronounced flare at the rim, possibly a
result of Cuzco-Inca influence. The exterior profile is
very concave, constricting from the rim diameter to a diameter of 11 cm. at the lower edge. The other rim (fig. 26)
appears to be less concave and more like jars of possible
pre-Inca date with wider mouths and more nearly vertical
neck contours. Surface finish details confirm these relationships. The more concave neck has a slipped and polished
exterior and a broad band on the inner lip which is also
slipped and polished. The presence of this interior slipped
band is probably a Cuzco-Inca feature. The area immediately
below the lip on the exterior has horizontal polish marks,
applied when the slip was still quite wet. From the point of
inflection on the exterior the polish runs vertically. This
differential polish seems to be a local feature. The other
fragment probably was not slipped on the outside, though
there is some splotchy grayed red paint in one area. The
inside appears to have a black pigment over which the
red paint was applied. The black looks like scorched black,
or the result of fire clouding, but it may have been a
pigment of some kind. The inside surface is smoothed, and
there are some horizontal wipe marks near the lower edge.
The outer lip and the area just below it also have horizontal
wipe marks. The texture is otherwise fairly rough, due to

some kind of handling while the surface was still wet. The
more concave neck was made of the cream fired variety of
Paste C (fig. 25); the other fragment was fabricated in Paste
D (fig. 26) with a good quantity of fairly large grains of
clear quartzite and some large mica particles.

IV:2. Small bottle (not illustrated). A closed
container is indicated by the rough finish of the interior.
The base itself is flat and round, with a diameter of approximately 6.5 cm.   Not far from the base angle is a basal
gambrel, a shape feature of Cuzco-Inca bottles, jars and
dishes (Bingham, 1930, pl. 70, figs. 1a-d, 2a, 4b-c, pl. 71,
figs. 6a, c; Tschopik, Marion, 1946, figs. 19n, 22a, 23a,
25a). The base diameter of most Cuzco-Inca forms is usually
smaller in proportion to the diameter of the body at the
basal gambrel than this vessel was. The exterior was slipped
and polished to a shine. This slip spalls off over large
pieces of mica on the original surface. The interior of the
base was not smoothed after modelling. The walls were
smoothed, however, and show some wipe marks. The outside was
slipped a cream color and decorated in black and orange-red
line design. Very little design is preserved. The bottle
was made of Paste D with the inclusion of large pieces of
mica.

IV:3. Bowl with vertical walls (fig. 27). This bowl
probably had a diameter of more than 14 cm. The rim is very
unusual. The lip itself is thick and was probably built up
with an appliqué of clay to the lip's interior. The lower
edge of the appliqué was carefully smoothed, but the upper

edge was not, leaving a depression where the two clay
surfaces were joined. The interior surface was smoothed and
wiped while still wet, leaving horizontal wipe marks. The
exterior was imperfectly smoothed. Both surfaces were
slipped with a thin pigment. The outside and the surface of
the lip are a creamy white, while the inside below the bevel
angle is a dull brown. The paste is identical to the paste
of one of the fragments in Group IV:1 above (fig. 25).

    IV:4. Tumbler (not illustrated). No diameter can be
reconstructed. The fragment is very small, but some shape
and decoration details are reminiscent of Tiahuanaco style
tumblers. The outside was slipped a dull red-brown and polished. The inside was probably smoothed well, slipped and
left unpolished. The exterior was decorated with a creamy
white and a matte black. The black does not blur about the
edges, but it has other visual aspects of the solution black.
Only the surfaces appear to have been oxidized; the cross-
section reveals incomplete oxidation of carbonaceous material
in the paste. The paste is fine grained and well mixed and
probably was fired to a medium orange when completely oxidized. It contains a lot of fine angular white grains,
surely intended to serve as temper.

    IV:5. Modelled foot (fig. 28). The foot is not quite
flat; it is arched in the area of the ball. The toes are
destroyed but a reasonable calculation from the traces of
modelling that remain would be five toes. Some sharp instru-
ment was probably used to model them. The surface finish is
very careful, and no polishing traces remain. There are

traces of a possible light red slip. The foot was modelled
in Paste C, and the paste contained a good quality of
temper.

Imitation Inca Shapes (Group V)

Three shapes appear to have been borrowed from the
Cuzco-Inca repertory. These shapes are decorated in imitation of Cuzco-Inca vessels, but the use of local pigments
and paste and the misinterpretation of some style features
or their combinations allows fragments to be identified as
imitations. Most of the closed vessels have a slipped exterior with a very good finish, imitating Cuzco-Inca and not
local finish. Few fragments provide enough details for
shape reconstruction, so that the analysis mainly concerns
decoration and technology.

V:1. Cuzco bottle (figs. 177-180)(Rowe, 1944, fig. 8a).
A few Cuzco-Inca design compositions predominate. A very
common composition is the one John Rowe termed Mode A in his
early report on the Cuzco-Inca style (Rowe, 1944, p. 47).
This design composition consists of both narrow band and
panel designs in a distinctive arrangement covering one-half
the vessel's body, plus a number of decorative details for
the treatment of the neck, inner lip and back shoulder. The
local rendering of this design composition is fairly
faithful to the original, but there are some readily observable differences. Since there is a considerable amount of
variation, these differences will be discussed under the

subheadings that follow. First, fragments with Mode A decoration will be dicussed, then other kinds of body decoration
and decoration associated with different parts of the Cuzco
bottle will be considered.

V:1a. Mode A body decoration (figs. 177b, 178c, 179c, d,
e, 180c, d, g, h, i). Besides solid purple narrow bands, the
two bands of Mode A decoration represented among the Phase 1
fragments are the fern panel (Fernández Baca, 1973, figs.
100, 146, 161) and the bar-and-x band (Fernández Baca, 1973,
figs. 37, 149, 151-157). Fern panels commonly occur in
adjacent pairs in the Cuzco-Inca style, with the base of each
fern element uniting with an opposing fern element in a
common line or line design (Rowe, 1944, figs. 1, 3; Bingham,
1930, pls. 81b, d, 83-85). With one exception this pairing
of the panels does not occur. The exception is a three
strand, short stemmed fern executed in a brown-black on a
chalky white slipped background (not illustrated). The
colors are unusual, and the three strand fern is unique
among the ten fragments with fern panels in the Phase 1
levels. Other local features are evidenced by this fragment,
including the use of Paste D with large pieces of mica.
Other fern panels occur with band designs adjacent to the
stem side of the panel. They occur over a creamy white slip,
a chalky white slip, or an unslipped medium orange colored
surface. They uniformly have two and not three strands. In
most cases the only other color used is a purple. The fragments are made of Paste C, with two exceptions. One is a
bottle with fern stems sloping diagonally toward the base

(fig. 177b), and another is a bottle painted with obviously
local pigments, like a solution black which blurs around the
edges (fig. 180h).   The first bottle has a clear red color
below the basal gambrel which is associated with the variant
of Paste C with large mica grains.   The other bottle was made
of Paste D.

V:1b.   Purple slip (fig. 180b, j).   Purple slip decoration was fairly common.   The fragments with this decoration
were made of Paste C.

V:1c.   Areal decoration with a black grid on a red-purple
background (figs. 178b, 180a).   A peculiar areal design,
possibly related to the panel designs used in Mode B decoration, is a black line grid on a dark red-purple background,
combined with narrow bands of solid red-purple and white.
The fragments do not permit the reconstruction of the design
layout, except that the design does not appear to be a panel
on an unslipped field, but rather part of a larger areal
decoration.

V:1d.   Neck decoration (figs. 177a, 178a, 179a, 180e, 180f.)
Three kinds of neck decoration were found.   The one most frequently associated with Mode A decoration in the Cuzco-Inca
style is also quite common in Phase 1 (fig. 180e).   Among the
examples, some have a wider creamy white stripe on a shiny
dense black pigment more like the pigment used in the Cuzco-
Inca style, and others have a chalky white irregular stripe
painted over a matte black background.   The latter combination of pigments has a more local appearance.   Necks are also
painted a solid purple (figs. 179a, 180f).   The purple neck

can be associated with a wide white band at the neck's base.
The third kind of neck decoration was an allover chalky white
slip. The one example of a small size Cuzco bottle was a
neck fragment with this decoration (fig. 178a). An unusual
neck treatment consists of rows of diamonds painted in red-
purple on a white background (fig. 177a).

V:2. Cuzco jar (not illustrated)(Rowe, 1944, fig. 8e).
A small fragment from a Cuzco jar neck, slipped white, was
found, but not drawn.

V:3. Plates. Two small plate or bowl fragments, one a
base, were found. Both were similarly decorated. One was
painted with a red-purple like the local Sillustani tradition
red-purple, a creamy white and a thin, matte black. The red
and white were used in a cross-hatched narrow band design
borrowed from the Cuzco-Inca style (Fernández Baca, 1973,
figs. 284-285, 475). Cross-hatching in the same colors is a
feature of the Sillustani style as well, though not as part
of a band design.[9] The black hatching next to the other
band was probably also part of a narrow band design, probably also borrowed. These bands ran transversely
on the interior of plates, as in the Cuzco-Inca style
(Fernández Baca, 1973, lám. I, upper, and lám. II, upper).
The interior is polished without any traces. The exterior
has a good polish, but some narrow polishing marks are observable. The plate was made of Paste C. The second fragment
is from the base of a plate, perhaps imported from Cuzco.
The surface finish is very Cuzco-Inca, as are the colors
used in the decoration. The paste is obviously not local.

It fires to a medium orange and contains a small amount of
mica as well as fine grains of milky gray quartzite.   All
are characteristics which have been observed of a paste
common in the Cuzco area.   Decoration with bar-and-x bands
separated by purple bands and placed in transverse position
on the interior of a plate is very characteristic of the
Cuzco-Inca style.   This band arrangement is uncommon among
the excavated materials from Hatunqolla, and fragments with
this design composition may be imports.

Other Cuzco Related Shapes (Group VI)

VI:1.   Small bowl with hooked profile (fig. 29).   The
bowl has a diameter reconstructed at 13 cm.   The rim profile
is "hooked" like some bowls in the Cuzco-Inca style, and
similar to a Phase 1 bowl fragment in the Cuzco related
group (fig. 4).   The bowl is an example of blackware.
Blackware was not a part of the Sillustani tradition, though
earlier ceramic styles in the same area included blackware.
Some Tiahuanaco vessel shapes, executed in blackware, have
been found in the Puno area.   The blackened surface of this
fragment was a result of firing the vessel in a smudging
and reducing atmosphere (Shepard, 1965, pp. 88-90).   It is
very likely that this fragment indicates contact with the
coast.   A number of Inca influenced ceramic styles there
included blackware.   This fragment is deep black in cross-
section and has a very good finish, with only a few unpolished
streaks in evidence.   Because of these features, it is most similar to the blackware found in the Ica or Trujillo areas (Menzel,

1976, pp. 85, 122). The paste has the textural qualities of
Paste D, and contains very fine grains of clear quartzite and
some pink sandstone inclusions.

SUMMARY OF PHASE I MATERIALS

Influence from the Cuzco-Inca style can be clearly seen
in Phase 1. Cuzco-Inca shapes and decoration are imitated in
local clays, and innovations in the local ceramic tradition
are easy to recognize. Others are far more subtle and do not
reflect imitation of Cuzco-Inca features as much as using the
Cuzco-Inca style as a source of new ideas.

Bowls showing Cuzco-Inca influence are either outright
imitations or exhibit so many borrowed Cuzco-Inca features
that they more strongly resemble Cuzco-Inca bowls or plates
than Sillustani style bowls. The outright imitations will
be discussed in the section on imitation Inca vessels. Three
shapes fall into the first, or Cuzco related, group (figs.
1-4). These bowls are smaller than the Sillustani style
bowls, and fairly shallow. They have either a flattened or
thinned lip. Neither rim has antecedents in either the
Sillustani or Cuzco-Inca styles. Some of these bowls are
convex sided, probably a feature imitated from the Cuzco-Inca
style. There is no evidence to reconstruct their bases, but
Phase 2 bowls in this group characteristically have a flat
base with a diameter greater than half the rim diameter.
There is some variety in the shape of these bowls, but it
will be more convenient to discuss it when decoration and
paste are considered.

The most important feature borrowed from the Cuzco-Inca
style is exterior surface finish. The Cuzco related bowls
have well smoothed and fairly well polished exteriors including the surface of the base, unlike Sillustani style bowls.
This feature more than any other sets these bowls apart.

The Cuzco related bowls were fabricated in two local
pastes, each associated with different decorative treatments.
One paste has the color and consistency of the paste used in
the fabrication of Cuzco-Inca vessels (Paste C). It has a
granular aspect and fires to a light or medium orange (see
Appendix). The more faithful imitation Inca vessels were
manufactured in this paste, and bowls in the Cuzco related
group tend to have more borrowed features. Paste C bowls in
the Cuzco related group can be decorated with a solid color
slip, either a medium red or a dense purple (fig. 1). The
dense purple does not have local antecedents. The dense
purple pigment is consistently associated with both Cuzco
influence and Paste C throughout the sequence. One bowl is
decorated with two band designs borrowed from the Cuzco-Inca
style (fig. 4).[10] A small bowl with an unpigmented interior
is decorated with a black stripe on the flattened lip. A
single black stripe at the lip is probably a Cuzco-Inca feature (fig. 3). The other bowls were made in a more local
paste (Paste D; see Appendix). These plates have more
obviously local decoration. Black line decoration has
Sillustani style antecedents (fig. 2). Other motifs used
have no ties to the Cuzco-Inca style.

The Sillustani related bowls are strongly tied to the
pre-Inca Sillustani style, though some features suggest that
a certain amount of style change has occurred to separate
Phase 1 from the style unit represented by Testpit 12 at
Sillustani. These bowls cover a larger size range than the
Cuzco related bowls. Most of the specimens are moderately
shallow when compared with Sillustani style bowls, but some
very deep bowls are also represented. The bowls characteristically have very straight walls, like pre-Inca Sillustani
style bowls. The only curvature ever exhibited is in the
exterior profile. Though no bases were identified, it is
probable that bases were either very small and flat or small
and rounded. The number of fragments is small, so the
description of these bases relies on analogy to earlier and
later Sillustani tradition bases. Most of the bowls in this
group exhibit some kind of angle in the profile near the lip.
Some have a steep inward bevel from the lip mirrored by an
angular change in the outer profile. Others have a less pronounced bevel from the lip. A third class of rims resembles
the direct rim of the pre-Inca Sillustani style, except that
these rims are not as thin in profile relative to the bowl's
diameter. Their thickness is compensated for entirely by
curvature of the outer profile near the lip.

The Sillustani related bowls are decorated with a number
of band designs and motifs on differently slipped surfaces.
Again, the color of the surface affects the choice of decorative elements. The fragments recovered are mainly from red
or purple slipped bowls, many with zig-zag band designs

(figs. 5-11, 17-19, 21). Even the white slipped bowls tend to
have band designs and not other motifs, though a human figure
motif and a tassel motif are also in evidence (figs. 12 and
14). The zig-zag band in use is wider than the known pre-
Inca Sillustani style examples. It occurs on unpigmented,
medium red, light red, and purple surfaces, unlike the earlier Sillustani style examples which are known only to occur
on unpigmented surfaces. It is nearly always accompanied by
an immediately adjacent band or stripe of some kind. The
stripe may be placed either above or below the band. Pre-
Inca Sillustani style bands usually occur singly and without
border stripes.[11] As in the pre-Inca Sillustani style, white
lines and dots are used to complement the zig-zag. In the
earlier style, white lines and dots are associated with a
purple or crimson slip, but in Phase 1 white lines can occur
over any shade of red. Some zig-zag bands have a thin white
wash painted over the entire band except for the border
stripes, a feature which may not have a Sillustani style
origin (figs. 9 and 19). Other Sillustani style bands, like
a narrow band with bunched parallel lines, also have this
additional feature (figs. 16 and 20). Bowls with a steep
inward bevel at the lip have an added feature in association
with the zig-zag band. They frequently have bunches of
parallel lines on the beveled surface (figs. 5-8, 10-11).
The lines may be black or alternate between black and white.
This feature probably does not go back to the pre-Inca
Sillustani style, and it seems to be associated with
inwardly beveled rims.

White slipped bowls are in the minority. A very small
bowl with convex sides may be a new addition to the shape
inventory (fig. 22). An unpigmented surface or a cream
slip with very strong brown tones is associated with the
kind of decoration usually seen only on white slipped bowls
(fig. 14). An orange-red pigment is also associated with
bowls painted in this manner. One fragment painted with this
orange-red pigment is also decorated with a Cuzco-Inca style
band design, the bar-and-x band (fig. 15). Other non-Cuzco
features are part of the design composition, and the combination of features exhibited by this fragment is very
unusual. Some fragments with a white or unpigmented surface
have stripes in alternating color arrangement on the beveled
surface and below the bevel angle, relating them to the
pre-Inca Sillustani style (fig. 12).

The paste most frequently used in the fabrication of
these bowls is Paste D. Very often only a small amount of
clear quartzite was present, in smaller quantity than was
usual in the later phases.

Fewer generalizations can be made about other shapes
because few diagnostic fragments were found. Many fragments
from a single jar shape were included in Phase 1 levels,
most of which give evidence for use in the fire. The shape
of these jars is similar to the shape of some large jars
Ruiz Estrada found at Sillustani, but none of the Sillustani
jars showed evidence of use over the fire and all were much
larger than the Hatunqolla jars. Moreover, the Hatunqolla
jars were manufactured in a distinctive paste (Paste A; see

Appendix). This paste is unlike the pastes of pre-Inca

Sillustani style material studied so far. It may have had

a non-local origin; though the cooking jar was well repre-

sented throughout the sequence at Hatunqolla, the vessel

shape was also common at other sites in the Lake Titicaca

region during the time the area was under Inca control

(Cordero Miranda, 1971, fig. 13; Rydén, 1947, p. 206 and

fig. 85V, pp. 216-217 and fig. 88T, p. 254 and figs. 108a,

c, p. 264 and fig. 113m, and p. 268 and figs. 117N, O).

The cooking jar was well represented in Phase 1. Its absence

in Testpit 12 at Sillustani indicates a stylistic lapse

between the Sillustani style unit and Phase 1.

A couple of fragments possibly related to the tall necked

Sillustani jars were also found (figs. 25-26). One was made

in Paste D, and the other, in a cream fired variant of

Paste C (Appendix). The cream fired variant of Paste C

was used in the manufacture of all tall necked jars found at

sites in the area with pre-Inca Sillustani material on the

surface.

Several Cuzco-Inca shapes and the decoration appropriate

to them were imitated. Deciding what is an imitation and

what is an import is complicated, and only vessels made in

an identifiable local paste can be argued to be local imita-

tions. Fortunately, most of the fragments fall into this

category. Very few fragments were drawn, primarily because

a photograph provides almost as much information as a draw-

ing. The majority of imitation Inca fragments came from the

Cuzco bottle shape, and many of them were decorated with

Mode A decoration borrowed from the Cuzco-Inca style (Rowe,
1944, p. 47). Small details, none of which detract much from
the Cuzco-like appearance of these bottles, show that these
bottles were locally made, as does the use of Paste C. A
non-Cuzco decorative feature is the use of a narrow band
between fern panels or the use of single fern panels,
instead of the standard Cuzco arrangment of paired fern
panels with fern stems articulating in a line or line design
(figs. 177b, 180c, h, i). Only two other body designs were
represented among the fragments: a solid purple decoration,
common in the Cuzco-Inca style (fig. 180b, j), and an
unusual black grid design painted over a red-purple background (figs. 178b, 180a). Cuzco bottles have a number of
decorative details associated with them, but only in the case
of neck decoration did the Phase 1 fragments offer any information. The Hatunqolla fragments imitated standard Cuzco-
Inca neck decoration. A wide purple band, in good Cuzco-Inca
style, even occurred on the inner lip.

Cuzco jars are represented by a single fragment (see
V:3{2}), and of the two plate fragments in the collection,
one is probably an import.[12]

In summary, Cuzco-Inca decorative motifs or compositions
made their way into the local style. A number of panel and
band designs were being imitated as early as Phase 1, and
these were incorporated into the decoration of non-Cuzco
shapes (figs. 4 and 15). Whole design compositions were probably not used on these shapes. Obviously the Cuzco-Inca
style had its greatest effect on local bowl shapes.

Non-cooking jars were also replaced to some extent by Cuzco-
Inca bottles. No other shapes were replaced to any degree at
all. Considering what we know of the vessel classes of the
Sillustani style, ceramic containers probably served similar
needs in this first phase as in the pre-Inca Sillustani
style.

A small blackware plate was also part of the assemblage
(fig. 29). Its presence indicates contact with the coast,
probably brought about through policies of the empire.

PHASE TWO

Cuzco Related Bowls (Group I)

The small shallow bowls of Phase 1 are still in evidence
in Phase 2, but a greater variety of rim profiles and decorative compositions were present. Some of these bowls are
even shallower than Phase 1 examples, and the base fragments
which can be associated with them show a thickening of the
base in comparison with the thickness of the bowl's walls. A
large bowl appears to be new in Phase 2 in this group. This
bowl is also fairly shallow and has a flat base. Again,
bowls in the Cuzco related group have characteristically
fine surface finish. Many fragments exhibit even finer
exterior surface finish than their Phase 1 counterparts.

I:1. Bowl with flattened lip (figs. 30-32). The three
fragments suggest a diameter of 13-17 cm. Shape and surface
finish details seem analogous to the Phase 1 shape with a
flattened lip (Group I:1{1}). In Phase 2, however, the
flattened lip, depth and less careful exterior surface finish

are conservative style features. The decoration of these
bowls is not apparently related to either the Sillustani or
the Cuzco-Inca style. The pigments were applied over a possibly unpigmented surface. The black is definitely a solution, but blurs around the edges in only one case (fig. 30).
The white is chalky and used only for small details. One
fragment was made of Paste C, fired to a strong orange color
(fig. 30). Another fragment was made of an orange fired
paste of very fine consistency, with little visible temper
(fig. 31). The third fragment was made in Paste D (fig. 32).

   I:2. Shallow bowl with inward bevel from the lip (figs.
33-40). A diameter from 13 to 17 cm. for the lip and 4.5
to 7 cm. for the base can be reconstructed from the available fragments. The outer profile is convex with a very even
curvature throughout its length. This curvature is probably
a result of the comparative shallowness of this bowl (compare with Group I:1). The rim has a slight inward bevel from
the lip. The width of this beveled surface tends to be the
same as the width of the bowl wall below, or slighly narrower.
The interior profile maintains an even, if somewhat sharper
curvature, probably to accommodate a base somewhat thicker
than the walls. Because of this feature, the wall tends to
thin below the lip. One fragment (fig. 33) is decorated with
a dense purple pigment, a pigment associated with Cuzco
influence throughout the sequence. Most of the fragments
were decorated with a new decorative composition, one without
any obvious Sillustani or Cuzco-Inca style antecedents (figs.
34-38). The bowl interior is divided into an upper wide band

and a central medallion space. The arrangement may possibly
be related to the placement of a lower narrow band design on
Sillustani style bowls, and the similar division of space
this placement creates. The most complete example of this
new treatment of the design space has a wide band slipped a
medium red with a large beaked bird painted in a faint black
on its surface (fig. 34). The medallion space is slipped a
chalky white. On its surface, a stylized lake catfish
(suche) is painted in medium red and black. This suche
motif was probably symmetrically opposed to another suche
motif, each suche's head facing the other's tail. Superimposed on the suche motifs is an unidentifiable figure
painted in black. Quite a number of nearly complete specimens of this kind of bowl were found at Sillustani. One
of these bowls provides an explanation for the black figure
painted at the center of the medallion; it is a bird. It
grasps one of the suches in its beak (bowl in the Sillustani
Museum). Between the medallion space and the wide band is
a black stripe. A third kind of decoration associated with
these bowls is a wide zig-zag band painted in solution black
on a light purple slipped surface (fig. 39). The zig-zag
band is bordered on the lower edge by an additional black
stripe. A fourth kind of decoration is black, red-purple
and white line decoration, painted over an unpigmented surface (fig. 40). All of these bowls were fabricated in Paste
D, with the exception of the bowl slipped with dense purple
pigment (fig. 33).

I:3. Bowl with inward bevel from the lip and Cuzco-Inca protuberance (fig. 41). The bowl fragment suggests a diameter of 18 cm. The only shape detail at variance with Group I:2 above is the addition of a Cuzco-Inca style protuberance at the lip. The protuberance does not have a depression at its center, as frequently occurs in the Cuzco-Inca style. Cuzco-Inca protuberances occur in closely spaced pairs. If another protuberance was attached to the lip of the Hatunqolla fragment, it could not have been as closely spaced as was usual in the Cuzco-Inca style. The plate has an unslipped, but finely finished surface and was made in Paste D.

I:4. Small bowl with inward bevel from the lip (figs. 42 and 43). One rim fragment allows a reconstruction of 17 cm. for the diameter. The shape is similar to Phase 1 fragments from Groups I:1 and I:2, but none of the fragments in those groups had Cuzco-Inca protuberances. In these Phase 2 examples, the upper surface of the protuberance bevels downward, more like known Cuzco-Inca examples. Both examples have solution black line design on a medium red slipped surface, and some exterior polish. Both fragments were executed in the variant of Paste D with the addition of a lot of fine mica.

I:5. Shallow bowl with flattened lip (fig. 44). This fragment is also similar to the Phase 1 bowls of Group I:2. Judging from the thickness of the walls, the diameter should have been about 11 cm.

I:6. Small bowl (fig. 45). The bowl had a diameter of
11 cm. Four pigments were used in its decoration. The
beveled lip was painted with a purple pigment. The interior
below the bevel angle was slipped with a white pigment that
has a pinkish cast. Immediately below the bevel angle are
two black stripes. The black is lightened where painted over
the white slip (see note 6). Another black stripe is barely
visible at the lower edge. On the field of white are irregular red circles with central dots. Both a purple and a red
were used, to make a total of four distinct pigments. The
bowl was fabricated in Paste C.

I:7. Bowl with inward bevel from the lip (fig. 46). The
fragment suggests a diameter of 16 cm. The outer profile is
usually convex at the lip, straightening out after the first
centimeter. The inner profile has an inward bevel from the
lip, like some Group II bowls in Phase 1. Also similar to
Group II bowls of Phase 1 is the width of the beveled surface, in this case .9 cm. Below the bevel angle, the inner
profile parallels the outer, narrowing slightly toward the
base. The fragment was decorated with medallion decoration.
The upper wide band was painted with a dense purple pigment.
The beveled surface was not specially handled, but the lip
was painted with a black stripe. The medallion space may
have been slipped with a slip the same color as the paste.
The black pigment is lightened when it occurs over the
unpigmented surface (see note 6). A black stripe was painted
between the two major color areas. This bowl was fabricated
in Paste C, the paste associated with the dense purple pigment.

I:8. Large bowl with inward bevel from the lip (figs.
47-51). The fragments suggest a diameter of 22-29 cm. This
bowl is a larger version of the bowl just described (I:7),
except that it is shallower in proportion to the diameter.
One base fragment shows a flat base, but no marked base angle
(fig. 47). The base is thinner in cross-section than the
walls. The design spaces of this shape are the beveled surface below the lip and the bowl interior below the bevel
angle. The beveled surface has a vertical stripe design
which is not continuous around the rim. This feature was
observed on some Group II bowls in Phase 1. In the case of
the bowls considered here, placement of these bunches of vertical stripes does not appear to relate to the spacing of
design motifs on the interior. The striping is painted in
black on a purple surface. Below the bevel angle the bowl
interior is slipped a creamy white which sometimes appears to
be slightly pink. Immediately below the bevel angle are two
black stripes. The interior motif repeats itself, perhaps
four to six times, in radial fashion around the center. The
largest fragment offers the most details for the reconstruction of this motif (fig. 48). The motif is a human figure
holding a staff in the left hand. The staff has a projection
on top, like the Phase 1 example of this motif, painted red.
The staff is thickened where the hand grasps it, and there
are white dots on the thickened part and on the staff itself.

The figure can be further reconstructed by comparing it
with one other Phase 2 example (fig. 47) and several surface
sherds, though the details vary somewhat. The figure often

has a bucket shaped head, a rectangular shirt, feet pointed
in the direction of the staff, the lower trunk painted in
purple and a strange black leafy projection which probably
covers the right hand, but extends to the ground and is
covered with white dots.[13] A feathery red ornament is
attached to the head. The white dots are not always in evidence, perhaps due to wear, but most of the other features
are common to all Hatunqolla examples. The Phase 1 bowl
with a motif of this kind (fig. 12) and two surface fragments
which are very similar to it show the figure facing right
instead of left. The surface fragments have other conservative features linking them to Phase 1. A human figure motif
similar to this one has been recorded in other Inca related
contexts, on other shapes as well as bowls (Cordero Miranda,
1971, fig. 12; Lumbreras, 1974, fig. 231). There is also a
pre-Inca precedent for these figures at Sillustani (Ruiz
Estrada, 1973b, pl. 17a-b).

These bowls comprise the most elaborately painted vessel
category at Hatunqolla. The fanciest bowl was decorated with
four different pigments (fig. 48). The beveled surface is a
very deep purple color. The circumferential stripes, staff,
head and torso of the figure are black. The black is fairly
dense but shows signs of being part solution. The background
white is pinkish and fairly dense, though not thick, and has
a slight shine. The red in the feathery ornament is not the
same as the purple. The white dots are a true white. They
are poorly preserved but probably were quite dense and
matte. The red and probably the white were applied after

the surface was polished. Other fragments do not have both
red and purple. Instead, only red is used. A creamy white
can be substituted for the matte white. All fragments have
excellent surface finish, both inside and out. They were
made in Paste C and fired to a medium orange color. Some
slight irridescence often appears on the exterior. The fragment with the fanciest decoration (fig. 48) also exhibits the
highest temperature firing, as evidenced by some slight
cracking in the paint.

I:9. Shallow bowl with rounded lip and bevel angle
(figs. 52-53). The two fragments suggest a diameter of
16-21 cm. Compared with other bowls in this group, these
bowls are unusually shallow relative to their diameter. The
rim has an inward bevel from the lip, with a rounded bevel
angle and lip edge. Both bowls have excellent interior and
exterior surface finish. They were decorated with a faint
black pigment, probably lightened during firing (see note 6).
It does not blur around the edges. The pigment may have gone
over an interior slip the same color as the paste, as a slip
of this kind has been observed on Phase 2 fragments. The
paste looks like Paste C, but it has a very fine sand temper
without any shiny black grains.

I:10. Bowl with thickened profile near the lip (fig. 54).
The rim suggests a diameter of 16 cm. The walls thin toward
the lower edge of the fragment like the bowls of Group I:8
above. Both the interior and exterior are well smoothed and
well polished, though unpolished areas are visible on both
surfaces. The bowl was coated with a medium red slip and

painted with a black line design related to Sillustani
tradition zig-zag band design. The black does not blur but
has other visual aspects of solution black. The lines are
painted unevenly. The fragment was manufactured in Paste C.

I:11. Shallow bowl with rounded lip and extreme curve
in the profile (fig. 55). A diameter of 17 cm. is suggested
by the fragment. The fragment was smoothed, slipped on both
surfaces, and polished. The exterior was slipped purple,
and the interior was decorated with black lines on a cream
slip. The paste used in the fabrication of this bowl was
cream fired and has a fine sand temper.

I:12. Bowl with rounded lip (fig. 56). The fragment
suggests a diameter of 15 cm. Both the inside and outside
have a good finish. The black line motif was painted with a
solution black on an unslipped surface. The exterior has a
firing ghost with traces of the same design as painted on the
interior. Below the lip on the exterior are two crossed
lines, scratched into the surface after the vessel was fired.
The paste has textural and visual aspects of Paste D, but
very little temper. There is a fine scatter of mica particles on the exterior, suggesting the variant of Paste D
with a large quantity of fine mica.

I:13. Shallow bowl with rounded lip (fig. 57). The
fragment suggests a 14 cm. diameter. Both interior and
exterior surface finish are good, but the interior was
treated with a little more care. The design was executed
with a faint solution black, possibly lightened by a high

temperature firing (see note 6). The paste has the visual
aspects of Paste D, but only a small quantity of quartzite
temper.

I:14. Shallow bowl with inward bevel from the lip and
thick walls (fig. 58). The fragment suggests a diameter of
13 cm. Both the interior and exterior have a good finish.
The interior and beveled lip surface are decorated with a
faint solution black, again suggesting a high temperature
firing (see note 6). The paste has a light orange color and
a large amount of what appears to be sand temper.

Sillustani Related Bowls (Group II)

The Sillustani related bowls still show more variation
in size than the Cuzco related bowls. The small and regular
sizes continue, and two large bowl shapes are added to the
inventory. A few base fragments from Phase 2 levels could
be assigned to the Sillustani related group on the basis of
surface finish and paste. These fragments either have no
angular change at the base, having instead a small roughened
area, or they have a flat base, very small in diameter and
roughened on its surface. Group II bowls have a finer
exterior surface finish. The smoothing of the exterior of
Group II bowls prior to polishing is still not as good as
the smoothing of Group I bowls, even Group I bowls of Phase
1. The exterior is often covered more completely with polishing marks than was common in Phase 1. Still, when there
is a depression in the exterior profile below the lip, this
area remains characteristically unpolished. Wiping of the

exterior, exhibited by several Phase 1 fragments in this
group, is not in evidence among fragments with similar
features of shape, decoration and paste.

II:1. Bowl with inward bevel from the lip and thinning
toward the base (figs. 59-60). One fragment suggests a
diameter of 15-16 cm. (fig. 59). This shape is similar in
some shape details to shape I:8 (figs. 47-51). One fragment
has the new design composition with an upper wide band and
central medallion space, except that the medallion space is
somewhat larger in this example than it is in the Cuzco related group (fig. 59). The upper wide band is painted light
red. Below it the medallion space is painted with a slightly
pinkish white. Irregular elliptical shapes are painted on
the surface in both the light red and solution black pigments. The medallion space is bordered by two stripes in
solution black, painted over the white slip. The other bowl
has a medium red slipped interior (fig. 60). Both bowls
were fabricated in Paste D.

II:2. Deep bowl with inward bevel from the lip and
outer angle (figs. 61-62). The fragments suggest a bowl of
20-21 cm. in diameter. Though the rim profile of these
bowls is similar to Phase 1 fragments of Group II:1, these
bowls are much deeper and thinner walled than bowls of a
corresponding size in that group. Both fragments are
slipped a medium red and have black line decoration, but
without accompanying vertical stripes on the beveled surface.
One fragment has what appears to be a variant of the wide
zig-zag band (fig. 62). The upper point crosses the bevel

angle and covers the beveled surface. Both fragments were
fabricated of Paste D, one in the variant with a large
amount of fine mica (fig. 62).

II:3. Small bowl with straight walls (fig. 63). The
diameter cannot be reconstructed, but it is probably between
13 and 17 cm. The bowl was probably slipped with a matte
white and decorated with red-purple stripes. The firing is
grayed. It was made of Paste D.

II:4. Small bowl with inward bevel from the lip and
outer angle (figs. 64-66). The fragments suggest a diameter
of between 13 and 17 cm., but the rims are very small. All
three bowls have very steep walls, and steeply beveled lips.
The exterior is well smoothed, and polished over most of the
surface, excluding the angle near the lip. The interior is
slipped a dense matte white. One fragment has both black
and dark red line decoration (fig. 65). The others only
indicate the use of dark red. The fragment with both pigments has vertical striping on the beveled lip and two
narrow stripes on the interior below the bevel angle (fig.
65). The other two have some kind of horizontal stripe on
the rim and two narrow stripes on the interior below the
bevel angle. All three fragments are made of a cream fired
paste that is well mixed but not fine grained, and is tempered with milky quartzite grains and some fine sand. The
shiny black particles characteristic of Paste C are not in
evidence, but otherwise this paste has the visual aspects
of the cream fired variant of Paste C.

II:5. Large bowl or plate with inward bevel from the
lip and outer angle (fig. 67). The diameter can be reconstructed at 34-38 cm., making this bowl the largest bowl in
the excavated sample. The outside is finished like most
other bowls in this group, with imperfect smoothing and polishing marks which do not cover the entire surface. There
are very faint traces of a thin red pigment on the interior.
The paste is cream fired and was tempered with milky quartzite and some black particles.   The black inclusions are
larger and rounder than the shiny black particles characteristically found in Paste C.

II:6. Bowl with straight inner profile (figs. 68-70).
The diameter of these bowls is between 13 and 18 cm.
Details of the profile are similar to a Phase 1 bowl in
Group II:6 (fig. 21). The exterior surface of these fragments is not smooth, and little attention was given to polishing it. The interior was slipped a very light red and
painted with black line design in solution black. One
example has a zig-zag band with an additional black stripe
above and below it (fig. 70). Another example appears to be
identical (fig. 68). The width of the black lines in all
three cases is irregular. All the fragments were made in
Paste D.

II:7. Small bowl with vertical walls (figs. 71-72). The
two fragments suggest a diameter of 10-11 cm. The shapes
represented have walls which thin toward the lip. The lip
bevels inward. One fragment is fairly complete, and allows
the shape to be totally reconstructed (fig. 71). It has a

raised bump at the center of the base. Otherwise the base is
thinner than the walls. The base is flat and 4.5 cm. in
diameter. Its surface is very rough, and small particles of
pink sandstone are imbedded in it. In some details the bowl
is similar to a Phase 1 bowl of Group II:8 (fig. 23). Both
have similar decoration, though one bowl is slipped with a
washy red-purple slip, and the other is slipped in the same
color as the paste. The latter bowl has an exterior white
slip in keeping with a fairly careful surface finish for
bowls of Group II. The design of the red-purple slipped
bowl is painted in solution black and matte white. The
other bowl is painted with a faint white and a black which
was probably lightened by high temperature firing (fig. 72).
Both bowls are decorated with a black line motif with white
line or dot details. This motif is probably a new development in the Sillustani tradition, as it has no known antecedents in the Sillustani style. The paste of both fragments
is cream fired, almost temperless and very fine grained.

   II:8. Deep bowl with inward bevel from the lip (figs.
73-74). The diameter suggested by the fragments is 19-22 cm.
In one case the beveled surface is wide (fig. 73). In the
other case, it is narrow (fig. 74), and the lip exterior is
correspondingly convex. The fragments also differ in exterior surface finish. The finish of one (fig. 74) is careful,
while the exterior of the other (fig. 73) is neither well
smoothed nor well polished. The carefully finished fragment
is slipped with a medium red and painted with a faint black.
The other fragment is slipped with light red and painted with

a line design in the same faint black. Both fragments have
the same design motif, a very wide zig-zag band similar to
the one observed on a bowl in Group II:2 (fig. 62). The
light red fragment was made of the cream fired variant of
Paste C. The other fragment was made of a cream or light
orange fired paste with large grains of sand. The paste
also contains a large quantity of fine mica.

II:9. Bowl with rounded lip and convex profile (fig.
75). The diameter of this bowl was between 16-17 cm. The
interior is well smoothed and polished. The exterior is not
as well smoothed and was polished over only about half of its
surface. The design was executed in black on a medium red
slip. The black does not blur, but bears a visual resemblance to the solution black. The bowl was made of a cream
fired paste with a very small quantity of sand. In some
areas, there is a thin band of orange coloration below the
surface.

II:10. Large bowl with flattened rim and thick walls
(fig. 76). The fragment has a measurable diameter of 23 cm.
Both interior and exterior were smoothed and polished, but
the interior has a more careful finish. The decoration was
painted with a black design on a medium red slipped ground.
The black does not blur, but may still be the solution black
because of other visual similarities. The fragment was made
of Paste D.

II:11. Miscellaneous (fig. 77). The orientation of
this fragment is approximate. The surface finish is like the
finish of Group II bowls in Phase 1. The bowl was slipped

with a purple slip and decorated with a Sillustani style
narrow band design (Ruiz Estrada, 1973b, pl. 22d-e; fragments
from Sillustani surface; fragments from Level 5, Testpit 12,
Sillustani). Both features are more characteristic of Phase
1 and are not in evidence in Phase 2 except for this fragment. Nothing suggests the fragment is not an antique. The
fragment was made of Paste D with the addition of a large
quantity of fine mica.

Utilitarian Shapes (Group III)

The one vessel to show signs of use in the fire was a
jar shape made of Paste A. A number of other shapes are
made in this paste in Phase 2. Some, like the cooking jar,
were not completely oxidized in the initial firing. Others
were oxidized to a medium orange, often showing irridescent
pink in some areas. All of these shapes will be included
under the utilitarian heading on the basis of sharing a
common paste with the cooking jar.

III:1. Jar with vertical strap handles (figs. 78-84).
A group of 20 measurable rim fragments have diameters from
15 to 27 cm. One measurable base fragment has a 4 cm. diameter (fig. 82).   A nearly complete example of this jar was
recovered as part of the grave furnishings of a single individual buried in Barrio Azoguini in the town of Puno (fig.
84). On the basis of the ceramic contents, this grave can
probably be cross-dated to Phase 3 of the Hatunqolla
sequence, or possibly to late Phase 2. The Azoguini jar
has a 16 cm. rim diameter, a 6.2 cm. base diameter and a

height of 25.6 cm. Applying these proportions to a jar with
a 27 cm. rim diameter, a height of 42 cm. would be in proportion. Some of the Phase 2 jars and the Azoguini jar have
pronounced constrictions in the neck. The degree of constriction varies a lot, and some necks are no more than
slightly convex in profile. The edges of the handle characteristically flare upward, though the handle width remains
constant. Because of this distinctive flare, the handle
appears to have a central trough, beginning just below the
lip. This trough is seen on similar jar fragments from as
far away as sites near Pucarani on the Bolivian side of Lake
Titicaca (Cordero Miranda, 1971, fig. 13).

Below the lower attachment of the handle, the vessel
walls thin a great deal. Also useful as an identifying
characteristic is the blue-red slip applied to the inside of
the neck from the lip to the inflection point at the base of
the handle. This slip exhibits horizontal wet-polishing
marks unless the surface is too worn for identification.
Both the interior below the slip and the exterior were wiped.
In some examples, including the Azoguini jar, the exterior
has a special polish. Parallel groups of polishing marks,
obviously applied when the surface was quite wet, radiate
diagonally from the circular base. On the Azoguini jar,
there are four groups at the base. At the point of maximum
width, the direction of these marks is nearly horizontal.
The inside of the neck has horizontal wipe marks and the
handle has vertical ones. The polish does not continue
above the point of maximum width on the body. As noted

before, these jars frequently have thick post-fire carbon deposits on the exterior. The carbon penetrates the walls, and the vessel below the neck is usually thoroughly smoked. Some of the jar fragments appear not to have been used in the fire, and the paste description relies on these fragments for some details. The jars are consistently made in Paste A of the low fired variety.

III:2. Jar with thick handle extending above the lip (figs. 86-87). The rim fragment illustrated has a 14 cm. diameter. The lip flares slightly. As it flares, it thickens before ending in a rounded lip. The rim flare and thickened lip are more pronounced in this shape than in III:1 above, but other shape details are very similar, such as the neck constriction, the placement of the handle base, the thinning of the wall below the handle base and the contours of the shoulder profile. The handle itself, though, is much thicker in cross-section and extends upward above the lip following the flare. The inside and outside surfaces are smoothed, and the inside is wiped below the attachment of the handle. The inside of the neck and the outside surface are wet polished. The other fragment exhibits an exterior angle, probably near the base (fig. 87).

The surface coloration of these fragments is not easy to explain. The black appears to be fire clouding, as it only appears in some areas and does not seem to be a deliberate application. However, there is a light red painted on the surface near these black areas, and the red pigment is dragged by the polishing over the surface of the black,

creating a distinctive mottled appearance. If the black
areas were fire clouds, the deliberate mottling could not be
planned; moreover, the light red would be equally blackened,
which it is not. One explanation for this kind of surface
coloration is that the black was painted on the surface and
only bears a resemblance to fire clouding. Quite a number of
these fragments were found in Phase 2 levels, but the surface treatment exhibited by these fragments may have been a
feature of Phase 1 (III:2{1}). Both fragments were fabricated in Paste A of the high fired variety.

III:3. Colander (fig. 88). When drawn the fragment was
thought to be from the neck of a jar. Another interpretation
of the shape features would be as the rim of an open bowl or
dish shape. A diameter of about 25 cm. is indicated. The
rim flares outward and appears to have been cut at the lip
instead of modelled. The arrow indicates the cut edge.
The lip surface is very irregular and may have been cut to
the shape of an undulating curve or scallop. The surface
finish is very like the wiped finish of the Group III:1
jars. The holes were pierced from the face of the sherd, as
drawn, through to the other side. Both the greater diameter
of the holes on the face side and the presence of excess
clay around the opening on the reverse help determine the
orientation. The paste used to make the fragment was the
low fired variety of Paste A. The fragment shows no signs
of use in the fire.

Other Shapes (Group IV)

IV:1.   Large jar with flaring rim (fig. 85). The jar
has a diameter of 28-29 cm. In many details it is similar
to the jars of Groups III:1 and III:2 above. The rim is
more strongly flared and thickened toward the lip, however.
If the resemblances to Group III:1 jars allow the reconstruction of the jar's height, it would have been about 45 cm.
tall. A fragment of the base was found. It is flat and has
a diameter of 9 cm. A small flat base is in keeping with the
evidence given above for utilitarian jars. The surface
finish is also very similar to the finish of Group III:2,
except that many more polishing marks are visible. Also,
like the Phase 1 jar in Group IV:1, the direction of polish
is a decorative feature (fig. 25). Polishing marks are horizontal from the lip to the point of inflection at the base of
the flare. Below this point, and over the entire surface of
the neck down to the jar's shoulder, the polishing marks are
all vertical. The jar is painted in the same fashion as the
jars of Group III:2, except that there is only one blackened
area right below the flare at the neck. Nonetheless, the
light red pigment is still deliberately polished over this
spot. The light red does not cover the entire neck's surface. There are areas where the surface of the cream
colored paste shows through. The red pigment is also dragged
over some of this surface. The body of the vessel is more
completely covered with light red. The jar was made of the
cream colored variant of Paste C.

IV:2. Small jar with flaring rim (fig. 89). A
diameter of 14-16 cm. can be reconstructed. The jar has a
pronounced flare toward the lip. Both the inside and outside surfaces are smoothed, but not polished. The exterior
is less well finished than the interior. The paste has the
visual and textural aspects of Paste A, but it is tempered
with red sandstone, white quartzite, yellow and gray particles (probably sandstone) and white chalk, in good
quantity.

IV:3. Miscellaneous jar fragments (fig. 90 and a fragment not illustrated). A neck base and a body fragment were
decorated in an unusual manner. The neck fragment (fig. 90)
suggests a diameter of 24 cm. for the base of the neck,
which compares very favorably with the diameter of the neck
base of the jar described in Group IV:1 above. The only
decoration is an appliqué strip applied to the base of the
neck with small dots excised from its surface. The inside
and outside surfaces were well smoothed, but not apparently
polished or wiped. The surface of the appliqué strip cracks
near the excised dots, perhaps due to a drying problem. The
fragment was manufactured in Paste D and has a large quantity of temper. The body fragment recovered (not illustrated) was painted with a medium red and had some kind of
areal decoration in solution black on it. The fragment was
smoothed on both surfaces, but not polished. It was made of
Paste D.

IV:4. Deep bowl with hooked profile (figs. 91-92). The
two fragments suggest a diameter of 20-22 cm. Though one

fragment has a flattened lip with an inward bevel (fig. 91)
and the other a rounded lip (fig. 92), both are characteristically hooked inward.   Both fragments are decorated on the
outside and inside, but in different ways.   One fragment has
a washy red interior slip which shows brush strokes.   The
surface it was applied on was very smooth (fig. 91).   The
exterior was polished when wet.   The polishing strokes are
short and horizontal.   The light red pigment has been applied
over some of the surface.   The other bowl has a polished
light red on both surfaces and a black line at the rim (fig.
92).   The first fragment was made of the cream fired variant
of Paste C.   The second was made of cream fired paste with
a fine sand temper.

IV:5.   Bowl with straight interior profile and convex
outer lip (fig. 93).   The bowl has a 15 cm. diameter.   This
fragment was finished and painted like one of the bowls in
Group IV:4 above (fig. 92), except that it had no black
stripe at the lip.   There may be a fire cloud on the exterior
near the lower edge.   The paste has a strong orange color and
a lot of sandstone and chalk inclusions.   It has a very
unusual cement-like texture which appears again only in
Phase 4.

IV:6.   Bowl with inward bevel from the lip (fig. 94).
The bowl has a diameter of 15 cm.   In the shape of the rim,
this fragment bears some resemblance to another fragment
(fig. 74).   It is a smaller and probably shallower bowl.
The inside surface is well smoothed and coated with a red
slip from the lip.   The outside is not well smoothed, but a

few polishing marks are evident. The profile reveals a
sandwich effect in the firing color of the paste. The surfaces fired to a cream color and the center to an orange. A
small amount of fine sand and mica was included in the paste.
The exterior has a small fire cloud near the lower edge.

IV:7. Bowl with rounded lip (fig. 95). The bowl has a
diameter of 15 cm. Some attention was given to smoothing,
but no polish is evident. The surface is blackened on both
outside and inside and the area not blackened is coated with
a red slip like other Phase 2 fragments already described.
The firing is grayed. The paste is coarse grained and has a
very coarse sand temper. Besides what appears to be sand,
there are some particles of basalt included in the paste.

IV:8. Shallow bowl with rounded lip (fig. 96). The
paste has the same color and texture as Paste A, but with
some sand, yellow sandstone and white chalk particles.

IV:9. Unfired clay basin (fig. 97). This basin is 10.2
cm. long, 4.5 cm. wide and 2.5 cm. tall, at its maximum
extent. The shape is extremely irregular, as seen in the
drawing. The color is a very medium gray with a brownish
cast. Some white material was deposited on the inside of
the container, as were remains of ashes. The container was
found in an ash lens. It was obviously finger modelled, and
no surface finish was effected. The clay was not fine
grained, and it does not seem to be of the quality usually
chosen for ceramics.

IV:10. Spindle whorl (fig. 98). A complete spindle
whorl was found, with a diameter of 3 cm. The whorl appears

not to be decorated. Because of the quantity of fine mica
visible on the surface, the object was probably fabricated
in Paste D.

Imitation Inca Shapes (Group V)

Many more shapes were borrowed from the Cuzco-Inca
inventory. The borrowed shapes continue to be decorated
with imitation Cuzco-Inca decoration.

V:1. Cuzco bottle (figs. 99-101, 181-184). Only one
specimen provides enough data to suggest the height of these
bottles. A bottle was restored on the basis of seven diagnostic fragments with a rim diameter of 23 cm., a diameter of
the neck base of 15 cm., a maximum diameter of 43-44 cm. and
a height of 71 cm. (fig. 99). Though these measurements are
hypothetical, they are probably fairly close to the original
measurements of this bottle. The other two fragments from
which diameters were taken probably represent smaller bottles.
Comparing their neck dimensions with the neck of the reconstructable bottle, they had heights of 45 cm. (fig. 101) and
50 cm. (fig. 100).[14] The exterior surface finish of these
bottles is usually very good though some examples have a
less careful smoothing than their Cuzco-Inca prototypes.

V:1a. Mode A body decoration (figs. 99, 181a, b, d, e,
g, h). In addition to the fern panel, the bar-and-x band
and the purple band, a version of the Huatanay band
(Fernández Baca, 1973, figs. 418, 420-422) and a hatched band
similar but not identical to bands in the Cuzco-Inca style
(Fernández Baca, 1973, figs. 196-198).[15] Both two and three

strand fern panels are represented, always painted on medium
orange surfaces. Only two of the fern panels provide evidence for the design bordering the stem end. In both cases,
the stems border on a narrow purple band. Both the variety
and number of fragments in Mode A decoration have diminished,
yet it is still the dominant decorative mode. All examples
except the reconstructable bottle have pigments related to
Cuzco-Inca pigments and were made in Paste C. The reconstructable bottle (fig. 99) has a purple, a solution black
and a chalky white more characteristic of the area. It was
also made in the local utilitarian paste, Paste A. Other
details of this one specimen are worthy of note. A large
number of fragments from this bottle were found. Missing
were the base, handles and protuberance at the base of the
neck. The design, though it includes many features of
Cuzco-Inca design, usually has a number of narrow band designs
on the center front without any space between them. This
example has two bands similar to the Huatanay bands of the
Cuzco-Inca style flanking a central purple band, but leaving
a considerable amount of open space on either side of it.
The Huatanay related band also occurs at the base of the neck,
a feature not regularly seen on Cuzco-Inca style bottles.
Also, there was no wide purple band on the inside lip, as is
the case with most Cuzco-Inca examples. In conclusion, the
artist followed most of the canons of the Cuzco-Inca style,
but chose the local utilitarian paste and made some non-Cuzco
modifications in the design.

V:1b. White slip (fig. 183e).

V:1c. Purple slip (fig. 183b).

V:1d. Areal decoration with a black grid on a red-purple background (fig. 184a-d).

V:1e. Panel decoration (figs. 181f, 183a, c, and possibly 181c, 184c). Two kinds of panels, one with a pin-wheel design (fig. 181f) and the other with a meander com-posed of black and white stripes, are present. Both kinds of panels are found in the Cuzco-Inca style (Bingham, 1930, pls. 73, 81, 82a, 117c; Valcárcel, 1934a, fig. 55; Valcárcel, 1935, pl. IV, fig. 1/269, pl. VIII, fig. 1/130). They usually occur on the front body of Cuzco bottles, placed at the level of the handles, and several fragments from these levels suggest this placement. The Phase 2 panels have certain features which distinguish them from Cuzco-Inca panels, particularly in the choice of pigment and in their execution. The pigments chosen are local ones, including solution black. Less attention was given to rendering straight, even lines and perpendiculars than is usually the case in the Cuzco-Inca style. Though there is very little evidence, the scale of the bands seems to be larger than in Cuzco-Inca examples, taking the size of the vessel into account.

V:1f. Neck decoration (figs. 100-101, 182). Several neck designs found in Phase 1 levels were also found in Phase 2. Most common again was the black neck with horizon-tal narrow white stripes, associated with Mode A in the Cuzco-Inca style (figs. 101, 182d-f). The same range of

variation is observable. Both white (figs. 100, 182a) and
purple slipped necks were found (fig. 182b). Unfortunately,
neck bases were not available to confirm the association of
white neck bands with the purple slipped neck. In addition
to the purple neck, there was a red slipped neck similar to
the red of the Mode A fragment in the lowest of the Phase 1
levels (fig. 182c). An unusual neck fragment has a Huatanay
related band painted in the local pigments on an unslipped
surface (not illustrated). The band appears to occur somewhere near the middle of the neck. All fragments of Group
V:1 were made of Paste C, except for the neck fragment just
described, a white slipped neck and the reconstructable
bottle. The red neck fragment was made in the Paste C variant with large pieces of mica. The reconstructable bottle
and the white neck fragment were made in Paste A.

V:2. Small Cuzco bottle (fig. 105). A rim fragment
and several neck fragments from a smaller bottle shape were
found (fig. 105 and other fragments not illustrated). The
neck fragments are probably from small Cuzco bottles with
pointed bases, like Group V:1 just described, because of the
pronounced flare toward the lip and the concavity of the
outer profile associated with it. The flared rim occurs
only rarely with a flat base. The rim has a diameter of
11 cm. All the fragments recovered have a white exterior
finish. The rim fragment has a wide purple band on the
exterior just below the lip, and a similar band just below
the lip on the interior. All fragments were made of
Paste C.

V:3.   Cuzco jar (figs. 102-103).   One jar fragment
suggests a 33 cm. diameter (fig. 102), the other a 42 cm.
diameter (fig. 103).[16]   Both have relatively taller necks
than do vessels of a comparable size in the Cuzco-Inca style.
The decoration of the two jars is very similar.   Both have
white slipped exteriors, a black band at the outer lip, and
a wide purple band on the inner lip.   The smaller jar (fig.
102) probably had an interior white slip.   The larger jar
(fig. 103) has a black stripe at the point of inflection
marking the neck's base, below which is a purple area.   The
outer surface is covered with a deposit suggesting use in
the fire.   Jars of this shape may have been used in beer
(chicha) preparation, and cooking the ingredients prior to
fermentation in a jar with a similar shape has been recorded
in the Cochabamba region (Cárdenas, 1969, pp. 240-262).   Both
vessels were made in Paste C.

V:4.   Flat bottomed Cuzco bottle (fig. 106)(Rowe, 1944,
fig. 8h).   The one example of this shape has a diameter of
about 10 cm. at the basal gambrel.   The design is like one
seen on a Cuzco-Inca vessel from Sacsahuaman (Valcárcel,
1934a, fig. 68).   The pigments are very dense and exhibit no
blurring.   Purple and black were used over a creamy white
slip.   Below the basal gambrel, the body was slipped purple.
The paste used was Paste C.

V:5.   Tall necked bottle (fig. 107)(Rowe, 1944, fig. 8d).
The fragment suggests a very narrow neck, perhaps 3 cm. in
diameter.   Attributing this fragment to the Cuzco-Inca tall
necked bottle shape was done on the basis of rim and shoulder

fragments from Phase 3 levels with the same paste and decoration as this fragment, but with more shape information. The
Hatunqolla fragment is decorated with cat spot motifs
painted with a solution black pigment over a white slip with
a slight pinkish cast (Fernández Baca, 1973, figs. 59-60).
The motif itself has been observed on white paste ceramics
from the area (Tschopik, Marion, 1946, fig. 18a-c) and
on Spanish colonial era ceramics from Cuzco (Fernández Baca,
1973, fig. 67; John Rowe, personal communication). The
paste has the visual and textural aspects of Paste C, but
it has no temper except for a moderate amount of fine yellow
chalk.

V:6. Deep dish (not illustrated)(Rowe, 1944, fig. 8f).
No rim fragments were found, only a body fragment almost
certainly from this shape. It was decorated with a Huatanay
band and painted in local pigments, including solution black.
Neither the interior, nor the exterior surfaces were slipped.
The surface finish was similar to the finish of Cuzco
bottles. The fragment was made in Paste C.

V:7. Shallow dish (fig. 108)(Valcárcel, 1934a, figs. 56,
78-80). The fragment has a diameter of 26 cm. Because of
the size of this dish, it may be a mistake to relate it to
the Cuzco-Inca shallow dish, a uniformly smaller vessel.
However, some of the shape features are very reminiscent of
the Cuzco-Inca dish, including the slipping of both interior
and exterior surfaces, the horizontal strap handle and the
basal gambrel. The Cuzco-Inca dishes have a different rim
profile, more like that of the tumbler described below

(Group V:9). This vessel was slipped inside and outside
with light red slip and then polished while wet. The paste
used in its manufacture was Paste A.

V:8. Pedestal dish (fig. 109)(Rowe, 1944, fig. 8j). The
fragment suggests a diameter of 15 cm. This fragment is probably from a pedestal dish, although no fragments of the
pedestal were found. Both rim fragments and a pedestal
fragment were found in Phase 3 levels where the number of
fragments of this shape was higher. The pedestal dish was
used as a cooking pot in the Cuzco area. Such vessels in
museum collections are usually manufactured in the same kind
of paste used for deep dishes and have walls of about the
same thickness. Surface fragments from pedestal pots with
thin walls are found at Inca sites in the Cuzco area, and
they may be similar to the Hatunqolla examples. The one
fragment in Phase 2 levels does not show use in the fire. It
has no decoration other than a red slip on the inner lip.
It was executed in the high fire variety of Paste A, and has a
surface finish similar to the finish of utilitarian jars of
Group III:1.

V:9. Tumbler (figs. 110-111)(Rowe, 1944, fig. 8i). One
tumbler has a 14-15 cm. diameter (fig. 110), and the other a
12 cm. diameter (fig. 111). The larger tumbler may have
been an import. It has the everted lip characteristic of
Cuzco-Inca style ceramic tumblers (Bingham, 1930, pl. 121a;
Valcárcel, 1935, pl. VII, figs. 14/828, 1/573). The tumbler
was painted with a creamy white and had a purple band on the
inner lip. The paste is a medium orange color and has small

grits of what appear to be lava temper. The other tumbler
has a very different rim profile, with an inward bevel from
the lip. The reason for the different shape may be to
approximate the contours of wooden cups, suggested also by
the imitation wooden cup design painted on the exterior
(Schmidt, 1929, p. 434; Llanos, 1936, pl. VII, figs. 5/740,
5/741, 5/742, 5/743). The decoration was painted in solution
black and a faint cream color on a slightly irridescent
red-purple surface. The slip extends to the inside of the
vessel, just beyond the inner bevel angle. The cup was
executed in Paste C.

   V:10. Bowl with hooked profile (figs. 112-114). The
fragments allow the reconstruction of a 13-16 cm. lip diameter and a 6 cm. base diameter. These bowls are very shallow.
They have a distinctive profile like the "hooked" profile of
some Cuzco-Inca bowls with an exterior angle .7 to 1 cm.
below the lip. A hooked rim with an exterior angle is frequently associated with a figurehead handle in the Cuzco-Inca
style (Bingham, 1930, p. 119, pl. 71, fig. 11a-g; Eaton,
1916, pl. XIII, figs. 3, 6-7). One of the bowls has a pair
of protuberances borrowed from the Cuzco-Inca style (fig.
112). Such protuberances almost always occur opposite
figurehead handles when they occur on bowl shapes, so a
figurehead handle is also suggested by this feature. Both
bowls have a stripe at the lip line, also a common feature
in the Cuzco-Inca style. One of the two is slipped with a
dense purple slip and has a black stripe at the lip edge
(fig. 113). The other may be coated with a slip the same

color as the paste or be left unslipped. It has a very dark
purple stripe at the lip, extending over the edge to the
exterior angle (fig. 112). The protuberance may be painted
with a lighter purple. A third bowl had a figurehead handle,
a feature borrowed from the Cuzco-Inca style (fig. 114). It
was the only example of this kind of handle excavated at
Hatunqolla, and only a few fragments with handles were collected on the surface. The bowl represented by this fragment was not slipped on the outside or inside. The handle
was slipped a purple color and a black stripe, possibly a
rim stripe, was painted at the base. The paste of this
fragment is a very strong orange color. All three bowls were
fabricated in Paste C.

V:11. Plate with concave sides (figs. 115-117)(Rowe,
1944, fig. 8g). The one fragment useful for estimating a
diameter suggests one of 20 cm. (fig. 115). All three of
these plate fragments seem to have been imported from somewhere with stronger ties to the Cuzco-Inca style, probably
from the Cuzco area itself.[17] The two rim fragments have a
distinctive concave shape characteristic of Cuzco-Inca
plates with pairs of protuberance handles opposite each
other on the rim. Both plates had these handles. One has
a pair (fig. 115); the other only has traces of a protuberance, apparently broken off (fig. 116). The surface of the
protuberance bevels downward. The protuberance does not have
indentations in its upper surface as many Cuzco-Inca examples
of this shape do.[18] The protuberances are closely spaced,
following the customary spacing of Cuzco-Inca style plates

with band decoration. The largest of the three plates considered here has both circumferential and transverse banding
in a very typical Cuzco-Inca design arrangement (fig. 115)
(Bingham, 1930, pls. 89e, 90, 91, 100a, 123d). The two band
designs that appear on this plate are often used in such a
design arrangement, but this fragment exhibits almost the
only occurrence of the combination in the Hatunqolla sample.
The pigments used are also common in the Cuzco-Inca style.
The black is matte but does not blur, the purple is a
specular hematite purple and the white is dense and slightly
creamy. The unslipped surface was finished before any pigments were applied. The specular hematite purple was the
only decorative pigment to be polished. The other rim fragment probably represents a plate with similar design arrangement, but with the substitution of a Huatanay band in the
circumferential band position (fig. 116). This plate had
an exterior black slip and an interior purple slip, both
unusual for this kind of plate. The pigments bear some
resemblance to local ones but still could have been used in
Cuzco. The third fragment was a base with black llama figures on a creamy white slip (fig. 117). Because of its
shallowness, the fragment has been included with this group.
This llama motif is unknown in the Cuzco-Inca style. The
llama looks backward over its shoulder and was drawn like
a similar motif from the Copacabana area (Bandelier, 1910,
pl. LI, fig. 3). The paste of this base fragment is a dark
cream color with small grits of what appears to be lava
temper. The other two fragments are a bright orange color

with a sand temper consisting mainly of white quartzite
grains.   A very small quanitity of mica is visible on the
surface.

V:12.   Lid (fig. 118)(Llanos, 1936, lám. II, 5/690, lám.
III, 5/306, 5/307, lám. VI, 5/94).   It was completely flat
on one side, like some Cuzco-Inca style lids.   The flat
side is painted with a dense purple pigment with a lot of
wear on its surface.   The surface also appears to be blackened in the area where the wear is heaviest.   The fragment
was executed in Paste D, tending to an orange color.   A
large quantity of fine mica was included.   This fragment is
unique in the Hatunqolla sample; it has been interpreted as
a lid because it resembles this Cuzco-Inca shape, but the
identification is tentative.

Other Cuzco Related Shapes (Group VI)

VI:1.   Large tumbler (figs. 104 and 119).   One tumbler
could be completely reconstructed (fig. 104).   It has a 22
cm. rim diameter, a 16 cm. base diameter and a height of
23 cm.   The shape was restored on the basis of three fragments, although many more fragments from this vessel were
found.   The other vessel included in this category was
probably a large tumbler as well.   At the point indicated
in the drawing, the vessel has a 15 cm. diameter (fig. 119).
A pair of large tumblers are known from the Sacsahuaman
collection at the Cuzco University Museum, but they have an
everted rim characteristic of the Cuzco-Inca style.   The
reconstructed tumbler has a number of distinctive shape features

including indentations about 2 cm. above the base and the
same distance below the rim, as well as a modelled band about
two-thirds of the distance from the base to the rim. The
modelled band is rectangular in cross-section, but its form
is changing toward one of the broken ends. This tumbler also
shows some stylistic similarities to Arica style tumblers,
especially the modelled band and possible modelled figure
attached to this band (Latcham, 1938, p. 184, fig. 51). A
tumbler found in an Inca related burial in La Paz is somewhat similar (Portugal, 1957, p. 388, fig. 147). The
Hatunqolla tumbler was slipped black on the exterior, the
exterior of the base and the flattened lip. An orange slip,
the same color as the paste, was painted over the black in
the two indentations. The black slip was polished, but still
remains quite matte. The other fragment also has modelled
decoration (fig. 119). The modelling consists of a raised
band, which is changing its shape near one broken end, a
modelled hand and a modelled mouth. The raised band probably represents the waist of the figure. Right behind the
mouth is a groove, a feature which often occurs on the
inside of Cuzco-Inca tumblers (vessels in the Cuzco
University Museum). The groove may occur near the lip or
somewhere on the inside of the upper part of the body. The
outer surface was finely finished but left unpigmented.
Both vessels were manufactured in Paste C.

VI:2. Small bowl with rounded inner lip (fig. 120).
The bowl had a diameter of approximately 14 cm. The lip
bevels inward slightly. The surface of the bevel is convex,

and the bevel angle is rounded. The bowl is an example of
blackware and resembles the fragment described in Phase 1
(Group VI:1). This fragment exhibits a glossy finish, an
even blackness and numerous polishing marks. Like the
Phase 1 bowls its stylistic links are probably closest to the
Late Horizon blackware of the Ica valley or to roughly
contemporary blackware from the Trujillo area (Menzel, 1976,
pp. 85, 122). The paste has the textural aspects of Paste
D and a very fine clear quartzite temper.

VI:3. Bowl (fig. 121). The bowl had a 19 cm. diameter.
The rim has a steep inward bevel from the lip. The bowl
walls are very convex. The base is thinner than the walls
and shows a concave profile. The peculiar shape of the
base and the unusual decoration combine to give the impression that a pyro-engraved gourd bowl was being imitated in
ceramics. The interior was painted a creamy white which
is badly worn. The creamy white also covers the beveled
surface. The exterior design was painted with solution
black on an unpigmented surface. The design motif itself
seems to repeat, but does not have identical elements in
each of the repetitions. Some kind of insect or other
creature is probably being represented. A similar gourd
bowl with a similar design was found in Huacho (Schmidt,
1929, p. 438). The bowl was executed in Paste C.

VI:4. Small bowl (fig. 122). The orientation is approximate. The inside and outside are very smooth, and have no
traces of polishing marks. No decoration is evident. The
bowl was fabricated in a kaolin paste which fires to a clear

white. A few quartzite particles can be observed in the
breaks, but there are no temper grains apparent. Because of
the wall width of this bowl, it can best be compared with a
number of small white paste bowls with very fine decoration
found on the surface at Hatunqolla. These bowls characteristically have a pendent triangle band around the rim, and
may also have a design using the color orange or the cat
spot motif (Schmidt, 1929, p. 300). A large expanse of
undecorated surface is also characteristic. The paste of
these bowls is very white. The tiny fragment from the
Phase 2 levels also compares well to the Hatunqolla surface
fragments in paste and surface finish.

SUMMARY OF PHASE II MATERIALS

The distinction between Cuzco related and Sillustani
related material remains clear in Phase 2. Again, the stylistic emphasis seems to be on bowl shapes. The number of
Cuzco related bowl shapes proliferates, and most of the decorative innovation occurs in this group. In addition to the
division of the material into two groups on the basis of surface finish and shape, another division becomes meaningful.
Paste adds another dimension to the analysis. As in Phase 1,
both Paste C and Paste D are used in the fabrication of
bowls in the Cuzco related group. Among imitation Inca
vessels and other vessels strongly tied to Cuzco influence,
Paste C predominates. In the Sillustani related group, Paste
D predominates to the complete exclusion of Paste C. Paste C
resembles Cuzco-Inca pastes, and it is perhaps for this

reason that it was chosen for use in these contexts. For
the purposes of highlighting the differences between Pastes
C and D, the two pastes are segregated in the following
discussion of bowls.

Cuzco related bowls of Paste C occur in many more shapes
and have a larger size range than the same group in Phase 1.
At least one of the Phase 1 bowl shapes continues unchanged
into Phase 2 (figs. 30-32). The flattened lip profile is
a conservative shape feature in Phase 2, though, and most
rims exhibit an inward bevel from the lip. Among the shapes
with this inward bevel is a large bowl, represented by a
number of fragments (figs. 48-51). These bowls are especially
elaborate and may have served as some sort of prestige ware.
The beveled surface is particularly wide, resembling Phase 1
Sillustani related bowls of Group II:1. As a class, these
bowls are larger (22-29 cm. in diameter) than any other Cuzco
related bowls of Phases 1 or 2. A small bowl was also made
of Paste C (fig. 45)(11 cm. diameter). This size range of
Paste C Cuzco related bowls is quite a bit larger than the
size of these bowls in Phase 1 (15 cm. diameter), though
there were fragments from some possibly smaller bowls.

The majority of Cuzco related bowls made in Paste C
were slipped white and decorated with motifs related to
earlier white slipped Sillustani style bowls. A Phase 1
antecedent to the most popular composition, a human figure
motif repeated several times on the interior, was made in
Paste D and classified as part of the Sillustani related
group (fig. 12)(Cordero Miranda, 1971, fig. 12; Lumbreras,

1974, fig. 231). A number of details are significantly
different, including the treatment of the beveled surface
and the area just beneath it. The use of bunched parallel
stripes on the rim, a Sillustani related feature associated
with a red slip in Phase I, is now associated with a white
slipped bowl shape executed in a Cuzco related paste. Also
notable is the use of a creamy white background slip
instead of a flat white, and the use of four different pigments on a single specimen. In all, four different pigments
can be observed on these plates, including red, purple,
white and black. These four colors can be documented in the
Cuzco-Inca style, but the use of so many pigments on a single
vessel is rare. A bowl slipped a dense purple like the
purple used in some of the Hatunqolla bowls with a human
figure motif was also found (fig. 33). This pigment was
also used in the decoration of a bowl with a new kind of
design composition called medallion decoration because
of the division of the design space into a central medallion
and an upper wide band (fig. 46). In this example, the
wide upper band is painted with the dense purple pigment
associated with Paste C. This pigment is consistently
associated with Paste C throughout the sequence and appears
to also have particular ties to the imitation Inca and other
strongly Inca influenced vessel categories.

Cuzco related bowls of Paste D also occur in a variety
of shapes (figs. 41, 42, 43, 56 and 57), including medium
and small sized bowls like those of Group I:2 of Phase 1.
New shapes are shallower, more convex in profile and have a

slight inward bevel from the lip. The width of the bevel is
usually not greater than the width of the bowl's walls, and
it is often smaller. Base fragments from these shapes are
thick in proportion to the width of the walls and conform to
Cuzco-Inca proportions of base diameter to rim diameter.
Cuzco-Inca style protuberances can occur at the lip (figs.
41, 42 and 43).

Several kinds of decoration are associated with these
bowls. Medallion division is among them (figs. 34-38).
When medallion design is used in association with Paste D,
the medium red and not the dense purple is used for the wide
band. Small bowls with the Paste D variant including fine
mica are decorated with black line design on a red slip
(figs. 42-44). One of these bowls exhibits a Cuzco-Inca
protuberance at the rim (fig. 42). An unslipped bowl with a
Cuzco-Inca protuberance and another medium sized bowl with
a Sillustani style zig-zag band were also found (figs. 39
and 41) as well as a design without known antecedents (fig.
40).

A number of shapes do not readily fit into either of the
two groups above, though they exhibit the appropriate surface finish for the Cuzco related group. Some of these fragments were decorated with black line design on an unpigmented
surface (figs. 52 and 53). The paste chosen for these bowls
was Paste C or some other cream or orange fired paste, so
that the surface is characteristically light. Some of the
designs are similar to material recovered in the southern

Lake Titicaca basin, as is the use of black line design on
an unpigmented surface.[19]

Only a few of the Sillustani tradition shapes of Phase 1
continue into Phase 2, and some modifications are evident
in these shapes. A few fragments of bowls with a beveled
inner lip and outer angle were found (figs. 61-62 and 64-67).
One of these bowls (fig. 62) is deeper and more convex than
similar Phase 1 bowls (figs. 6-10). The bowl with a straight
inner profile and thickened cross-section also continues
(figs. 68-70). Its shape is more convex and shallower than
the Phase 1 example (fig. 21). The small bowl with vertical
walls also continues (fig. 23). The two Phase 2 fragments
exhibit a thinned lip with a slight inward bevel from the
lip (figs. 71-72). Another small bowl with inward bevel and
outer angle also continues (figs. 64-66). A large shallow
bowl shape (fig. 67) and a large deep bowl (figs. 73-74) may
be new in Phase 2 (but see fig. 10). The deep bowl shape
exhibits some kind of inward bevel from the lip. A medium
sized bowl shape is also new. It, too, has an inward bevel
from the lip (figs. 59-60). Like the Cuzco related shape
of Groups I:7 and I:8, this bowl has a wide beveled surface
extending inward from the lip, and its walls tend to thin
toward the base.

The new bowl just mentioned and the small bowl with
vertical walls are decorated with motifs not seen in Phase 1.
The small bowl fragments have motifs peculiar to them. One
of the bowls with a steep inward bevel from the lip is decorated with medallion decoration (fig. 59). A light red is

used for the wide band. The central motifs may be related
to Sillustani style motifs. The use of color alternation
underlines this possibility.

All of the other Sillustani related shapes are decorated
with line and band designs with conservative Sillustani style
roots. The white slipped bowls were painted with conservative Sillustani style pigments and made of a cream fired
paste typical of conservative Sillustani style fragments from
the surface of sites with pre-Inca occupations (figs. 64-66).
Features like exterior surface finish, rim profile with
inward bevel from the lip and bunches of parallel stripes on
the beveled surface are conservative features. Other bowl
shapes were slipped either with a medium or a light red slip,
depending on the shape chosen. Only one bowl fragment exhibited a purple slip (fig. 77); it was decorated with a band
design typically associated with a purple or crimson slip in
the Sillustani style. Two band designs are used on the red
slipped bowls, either a zig-zag band of about the same width
as similar bands in Phase 1 (figs. 68 and 70), or a wide
zig-zag band (figs. 62, 73 and 74). Either band may be
painted with an angular zig-zag or a line which has the
appearance of a scallop suspended either from the stripe
below the bevel angle or from the lip edge. In the wide
zig-zag band, the upper ends of the scallop commonly meet on
the beveled surface. No white line or dot details were associated with any of the zig-zag bands. White dots appear only
in association with the purple slip in a conservative
Sillustani style band (fig. 77).

Fragments from the utilitarian category, defined on the
basis of paste, were very numerous in Phase 2, and several
shapes were represented. Principal among them was a cooking
jar (figs. 78-83). Fragments from these jars were found in
other parts of the Lake Titicaca region, at sites with
Inca influenced ceramics (Cordero Miranda, 1971, fig. 13;
Rydén, 1947, figs. 88T, 128G; McBain, 1961, pl. XIV, fig. f).
A cooking jar from a burial in Barrio Azoguini in the city
of Puno was analyzed and found to be stylistically indis-
tinguishable from the Hatunqolla jars (fig. 84). A colander
of some kind was also made in this paste (fig. 88), as was
another jar shape (fig. 89). The utilitarian jar shapes
have a very unusual surface treatment, involving the use of
a light red and possibly a black pigment.

The quantity of fragments from other jar and unclassi-
fiable shapes is not large, and again, few generalizations
can be made. One large jar shape may be related to
Sillustani tradition wide necked jars with a thickened lip,
but the lip profile is much thinner (fig. 85). A jar fragment with a decorative appliqué fillet has obvious ties to
the Sillustani style (fig. 90). Among the other miscellaneous shapes, a deep bowl with a hooked profile stands out
(figs. 91-92). The wide necked jar fragment and one of the
deep bowl shapes can be linked together on the basis of
surface treatment, paint and paste (figs. 85 and 91). Both
were made of the cream fired variant of Paste C, painted
with a light red pigment and wet polished. The light red
pigment was used on other bowls in this group.

Quite a few additional Cuzco-Inca shapes were borrowed
in Phase 2. Though a smaller quantity of materials was used
to define Phase 1 than Phase 2, there were as many imitation
Inca fragments in the Phase 1 levels as there were in Phase 2
levels. Therefore, the jump in number of shapes may be meaningful. Only a few shapes in the Cuzco-Inca repertory were
not represented in Phase 2. Several Cuzco-Inca shapes were
even copied in Paste A, the local utilitarian paste, including fragments from Cuzco bottles, pedestal dishes and
shallow dishes (figs. 99, 108 and 109). Pedestal dishes
were used as cooking vessels in the Cuzco area, so that it
is not surprising that this shape was copied in the paste
associated with cooking vessels at Hatunqolla (Bingham, 1930,
p. 148). The comparison of imitation Inca material from
Hatunqolla with Cuzco-Inca style material is involved, and
exact details can be found in the preceding description
section. In general, some very faithful copies of Cuzco-Inca
vessels were made, though size canons were not observed.
Only a few design compositions from the Cuzco-Inca
style found their way into the Phase 2 material from
Hatunqolla, however, and most of these compositions were
already around in Phase 1. A couple of fragments seem to
represent local embellishments on the Cuzco-Inca style, such
as the use of the cat spot motif on tall necked bottles (fig.
107), but the precise origins of the decorative features
involved cannot be pinpointed.

For the first time, Cuzco-Inca concave sided plates
appear among the ceramic materials (figs. 115-117).[20] None

of the fragments was made in an obviously local paste, and
all could have been imports. Two base fragments with the
kind of transverse and circumferential banding frequently
associated with concave sided plates in the Cuzco-Inca style
were found in Phase 1 levels. These fragments may also have
been from concave sided plates, so that the shape may not
have been new in Phase 2.

A new category of unique shapes executed in Paste C has
been added. Because of a lack of antecedents for these
vessels, their uniqueness and their association with Cuzco
related surface finish and paste, this group may be a prestige ware category. Drinking vessels, in particular, were
prestige markers during the time of the Inca empire. The
small tumbler appears to be a ceramic copy of a wooden
tumbler (fig. 111). Dorothy Menzel has argued that tumblers
were an indication of the rank of civil servants in Ica, and
that ceramic tumblers probably had lower prestige than
wooden ones (Menzel, 1976, pp. 230-231, 236, 240). This cup
is a mixture of the ceramic and wooden tumbler styles, so
its reference to a particular status appears to be somewhat
ambiguous. Another bowl was probably the imitation of a
gourd container in ceramics (fig. 121). The design is similar to the design of a pyro-engraved gourd bowl from Huacho
on the central coast (Schmidt, 1929, p. 438). Gourds were
produced for export in Chincha during the time of the Inca
empire, and the ceramic bowl may be a copy of a gourd imported
into the highlands (Lizárraga, 1909, cap. LIX, p. 519). A
blackware bowl also indicates contact with the coast (fig. 120).

PHASE III

Cuzco Related Bowls (Group I)

Small shallow bowls continue in Phase 3. However,
larger bowls are also common. A deep bowl shape is new.
Bowls in the Cuzco related group show more variety in exterior surface finish than before. Some fragments exhibit an
exterior surface finish as fine as that of the finer Phase 2
examples, but very few fragments are in this category. The
remainder are well smoothed, with evident polishing traces.

I:1. Bowl with flattened lip (fig. 123). The diameter
suggested by this fragment is 20 cm. The profile compares
very neatly with the profiles of Group I:1 of Phases 1 and 2.
The bowl was probably decorated with the human figure motif
of the earlier phases. The decorative details at the rim
associated with this figure are certainly present. The pigments, however, are grayed, and the surface has no shine,
despite polishing. Though the pigments may have been different, the fragment was overfired as evidenced by surface sintering. A base fragment with a human figure motif may also
belong to this group (fig. 124). It exhibits the same
altered pigments, but there is less of a gray factor in the
white slip. The paste of the first fragment is probably
Paste D (fig. 123). The second fragment was made of Paste
C (fig. 124).

I:2. Shallow bowl with inward bevel from the lip (figs.
125-127). One fragment suggests a 16 cm. diameter at the
lip (fig. 125), and another, a base diameter of 7 cm. (fig.
126). In depth, size and rim profile, these bowls are

similar to bowls in Groups I:2 and I:3 in Phase 2.   Two of
the fragments have Cuzco-Inca style protuberances (figs. 125
and 127), with fingernail impressions in their upper surfaces.   One fragment has a protuberance which bevels downward; the other example has no bevel.   The three fragments
are decorated with conservative Sillustani style narrow
bands, last seen in Phase 1 (fig. 6).   The narrow band is
combined with a wide zig-zag band; the latter band is too
wide by Phase 1 standards.   These elements are associated
with Cuzco related shape features and Cuzco-Inca style protuberances, resulting in a mixture of the two substyles.   The
pigments used are a creamy white, a solution black and a
dark red-purple.   All these fragments were executed in
Paste C.

I:3.   Small bowl (figs. 128-130).   The fragments suggest
a diameter of 12-15 cm.   All three fragments have a nearly
flat lip.   The bowl walls are nearly parallel, showing no
thinning toward the base.   The lip is rounded in one case
(fig. 128), but fairly angular in the other two cases.   One
of the bowls (fig. 129) is decorated like a Phase 2 bowl of
Group I:6 (fig. 45).   The irregular circles are elongated
and pointed, and there is a "swallowing bird" motif adjacent
to the row of circles.   The other two fragments are decorated with narrow bands like those used on bowls of Group I:2.
Again, the narrow band is placed immediately below the bevel
angle.   Below the narrow band is probably a zig-zag band of
some kind, possibly related to Phase 1 bands with Cuzco-Inca
influence (compare figs. 128 and 130 to figs. 4, 15 and 19).

One fragment has solution black and faint white line decoration on a red-purple slipped surface (fig. 128). The other has solution black and red-purple line decoration on a slip the same color as the paste (fig. 130). The solution black is lightened where it occurs over the light orange surface (see note 6). All three fragments may have been manufactured in Paste C, but one is nearly temperless (fig. 129).

I:4. Bowl with thickened lip (fig. 131). The fragment suggests a 16 cm. diameter, but the contour of the lip is irregular and may have given a misleading measurement. The rim profile is unusual and unlike anything discussed so far in the degree of thickening toward the lip. The interior surface was slipped with a dense purple and has a solution black stripe of even width painted on the lip. The fragment was made of Paste C.

I:5. Large deep bowl with inward bevel from the lip (figs. 132, 133 and 134). One measurable fragment allows a tentative reconstruction of 25 cm. for the diameter (fig. 132). This shape is similar in some details to a number of Group I shapes including I:2, I:7 and I:8 in Phase 2, though it bears a closer resemblance to Group II:1 in the same phase. This kind of deep bowl shape seems to break the rules for a Group I shape. However, one of these bowls was made of Paste C, which is never associated with Group II, and all three bowls have Cuzco related exterior surface finish. One bowl is decorated with the lake catfish design first seen in Phase 2 (fig. 132). Like the Phase 2 bowl in the Cuzco related paste, the wide upper band is painted with a dense purple pigment. Also similar is the use of a slip

the same color as the paste instead of white in the medallion

space. The suche is also drawn differently from the suches

drawn on a white medallion. .The black used was the solution

black. It was .lightened, probably because of a high tempera-

ture firing (see note 6). Wear is a less likely possibility

because the fragment looks new. A second bowl (fig. 133)

has a medium red slip on the interior and beveled lip. The

third bowl has a medium red slip on the interior and a purple

stripe on the beveled lip (fig. 134). The first bowl was

made of Paste C, and the other two were manufactured in

Paste D, one with the addition of a good quantity of fine

mica (fig. 133).

I:6. Miscellaneous bowls (fig. 135 and other fragments

not illustrated). One base fragment and a number of other

fragments too small to draw are included in this group. The

base has a 9 cm. diameter (fig. 135). Both the inside and

outside have an excellent finish, very like the finish

seen on a plate possibly imported from Cuzco (fig. 115).

This bowl or plate may be slipped with a very light red.

There is a hint of reddish coloration on the surface. At

the same time, the black is lightened, suggesting a high

firing temperature (see note 6). The decoration is unusual

among the Hatunqolla materials. The bowl was fabricated in

Paste C. Another fragment (not illustrated) is related to

Group I:8 of Phase 2. It has a dense purple pigment on the

beveled surface with bunched vertical black stripes, but no

decoration below the bevel angle. Two rim fragments of

bowls like those of Group I:2 of Phase 2 were found. Both
had medium red slip, and one fragment is large enough to
show a lower black stripe, indicating the medallion mode of
decoration. Several body fragments of these bowls were also
found. Another bowl fragment has a bird depicted on the
upper wide band outlined with narrow white lines. A bowl
shape similar to bowls of Group I:1 in Phase 2 has already
been documented, also labelled Group I:1 in Phase 3. Some
of the undrawn fragments have similarities in decoration,
including decoration of the beveled surface with stylized
llamas and cross-hatching.

Sillustani Related Bowls (Group II)

A number of Phase 2 shapes continue relatively unchanged
into Phase 3. At the same time, a shallow bowl with a
thinned base appears to have no Phase 2 antecedents. Most
of the fragments exhibit the same kind of surface finish as
their Phase 2 counterparts.

II:1. Bowl with inward bevel from the lip (fig. 136).
This bowl had a 15 cm. rim diameter and a 5 cm. base diameter. In many ways it resembles the bowls of Group I:2.
Because of the exterior surface finish, this fragment has
been considered as a relative of Group II:1 bowls of Phase 2.
It should be noted that one of the fragments in Group I:5
has a similar shape and was also fabricated in the Paste D
variant with a lot of fine mica (fig. 133), so that this
identification, and the other one, are somewhat ambiguous.
The bowl has a medallion design layout. The upper band was

painted with a light red. The medallion has a thin white
slip with pinkish tones. The black pigment applied over it
blurs at the edges. Like the bowls in Group II:1 of Phase
2, the wide band is proportionally less wide than the wide
bands of bowls with similar design layouts in Group I:2 of
Phase 2. There are a number of other similarities, including
similar pigments, pastes and the use of two black stripes to
border the medallion space. The motif used is a swallowing
bird seen in part in the decoration of another bowl in Group
I:3. Seven or more of these birds appear to have been
arranged on the medallion space. As mentioned before, the
bowl was made of Paste D with the addition of a large amount
of fine mica.

II:2. Bowl with inward bevel from the lip and outer
angle (fig. 137). The fragment has a measurable diameter of
15 cm. The shape represented by this fragment is similar in
some respects to a bowl of Group II:2 in Phase 2 (fig. 62).
Like this bowl, the Phase 3 bowl has a lip that is thin in
cross-section. The shape is still quite deep, but it is not
as deep as the Phase 2 bowl, and the walls are correspondingly convex. The fragment was decorated with a wide zig-zag
band. This band is bordered at the lower edge by an additional black stripe. Like the Phase 2 example, the zig-zag
line is hung like a scallop from the upper border stripe.
The bowl was slipped with a light red and painted with solution black. The black tends to blur around the edges. The
fragment was made of Paste D.

<u>II:3</u>.   Large deep bowl with an inward bevel from the
lip and outer angle (figs. 138 and 139).   The one measurable
fragment suggests a diameter of 23 cm. (fig. 138).   The
other fragment is probably a bowl of similar size (fig. 139).
Like the Phase 3 bowl just described, and unlike similar
Phase 2 bowls, this bowl shape was somewhat shallower and had
more convex walls.   Both fragments were decorated like the
fragment described in Group II:2 above.   They were painted
with solution black over a medium red slip.   One fragment
(fig. 138) was made of Paste D, and the other (fig. 139)
was made of a cream fired paste with sand temper.

<u>II:4</u>.   Deep bowl with straight walls (fig. 140).   This
fragment does not have a measurable diameter, but must represent a fairly large bowl.   Both the thicker lip and the
straight walls are features more characteristic of Phase 1
than Phase 2.   The fragment was decorated with vertical rim
stripes and an irregularly painted zig-zag band which may
not have been as wide as similar bands on other deep bowl
shapes in Phases 2 and 3.   The bowl's interior was slipped
with a medium red and painted with solution black.   The
fragment was made in Paste D.

<u>II:5</u>.   Large deep bowl with inward bevel from the lip,
outer angle and handle (fig. 141).   The fragment suggests a
diameter of 16 cm.   It has a vertical strap handle that
extended from the lip to a place fairly high on the body.
The thickness of the lip with relation to the walls might
have suggested the possibility of a handle, even if it was
not present.   Both the outside and inside have a washy

purple slip and fairly good surface finish. The inside is
decorated with a wide zig-zag band painted with solution
black, and the beveled surface has bunches of vertical
stripes in the same pigment. The stripes occur at the point
where the handle attaches. Other deep bowl fragments from
Phase 3 levels have bunches of vertical stripes (fig. 140).
Such stripes are associated with large semi-circular protuberances in some cases. The protuberances are unlike the
paired protuberances of the Cuzco-Inca style. The rim striping of these bowls is associated with zig-zag band decoration, as in Phase 1. The handled bowl is slipped purple on
both the interior and exterior. The paste used was a cream
fired paste with a small quantity of milky and clear
quartzite.

II:6. Bowl with rounded lip (fig. 142). A 13-14 cm.
diameter was obtained from this fragment. Both the orientation and the diameter are suspect because of the size of
the fragment. The lip profile is similar to that of one of the
Group II:6 fragments of Phase 2 (fig. 68). In the use of
the light red slip and solution black line decoration, as
well as the quality of surface finish, the fragment also
resembles Group II:6 fragments of Phase 2. The band is
painted with lines of a more even thickness than the Phase
2 fragments, though, and the execution of the band resembles
that of another Phase 3 band (fig. 137). The bowl was made
in Paste D.

II:7. Bowl with steep inward bevel from the lip (fig.
143). The bowl had a diameter of 11 cm. Its profile is

unusual and resembles some of the Group I rim profiles.
The exterior surface finish, though, is definitely like the
usual Group II finish. The first centimeter below the lip
has wipe marks. Below it, the surface is not well smoothed
and the polishing does not hide cracks. The bowl has an
unpolished light red surface and a solution black stripe
painted just below the bevel angle. The bowl was made of
Paste D.

II:8. Deep bowl with rounded inner lip and outer angle
(fig. 144). The fragment suggests a diameter of 15 cm.
Both the shape and decoration of this fragment revive Phase
1 features with strong links to the Sillustani style (figs.
12, 15 and 17)(Tschopik, Marion, 1946, fig. 10g). The exterior is well smoothed and polished over most of its surface,
except for the depression created by the angle. The pigments
are closer to Sillustani style pigments, like the bowls of
Group II:4 of Phase 2. The white is more dense and chalky,
the red is a dull red-purple and the black is dense and
matte. The black blurs where it is painted over the red-
purple pigment, indicating a solution. The bowl was made of
Paste D with the addition of a small quantity of fine mica.

II:9. Deep bowl with direct rim (fig. 145). The fragment suggests a 17 cm. diameter. Compared with similar
Phase 1 and 2 shapes, this bowl has considerably thinner
walls. The interior surface was decorated with a narrow
band design similar to one used on bowls of Groups I:2 and
I:3 (figs. 125-128 and 130). These narrow bands are
reminiscent of conservative Sillustani style bands. The

bowl was slipped with a dense matte white with a pinkish
cast and was painted with a dull red-purple and washy
green-black. It was manufactured in Paste D.

II:10. Deep bowl with direct rim and thick profile
(fig. 146). The fragment suggests an approximate diameter
of 16-19 cm. Very little of the rim remains. This kind of
rim profile is characteristic of bowls of Group II, but the
exterior surface finish is much better than usual for Group
II. The bowl was slipped with a slip the same color as the
paste. The stripe decoration was painted in black and
red-purple. The black is lightened, probably due to high
temperature firing (see note 6). The color order is hard to
determine, but the slip was painted first, the black stripes
second and the red-purple stripe last. The plate was made
in Paste D.

II:11. Small bowl (figs. 147, 148 and 149). The bowls
have measurable diameters of 9 and 9.5 cm. They are probably related to the small bowl with vertical walls of Phases
1 and 2 (II:8{1} and II:7{2}), except that they are all considerably shallower. All three bowls also have a fairly
rounded lip. They were each decorated in a different manner.
One bowl has a black line design on an unslipped surface
(fig. 147). Heavy abrasion obscures the design. Another
bowl has a slipped and polished interior (fig. 148). The
slip is a medium red, and a solution black and faint white
pigments were used for the line decoration. Apparently, the
decoration chosen was the Sillustani style narrow band
design associated with other Phase 3 bowl shapes. The

design layout, a composition of transversely crossed bands, is not something linked to the earlier Sillustani style. The third bowl was not slipped and only partly polished (fig. 149). Its design has no known antecedents in the Sillustani style. It was painted with solution black. Two of the bowls were made of Paste D with the addition of fine mica (figs. 147 and 148). The third fragment was made of Paste D (fig. 149).

II:12. Shallow bowl with rounded lip (fig. 150). The bowl had a diameter of 14 cm. This shape is apparently new in Phase 3. It is far shallower for its diameter than any shape discussed so far. The interior was well smoothed and wiped. The outside was not so well smoothed, but was still wiped. The base diameter is about 2.5 cm., much smaller than the base of a Cuzco-Inca style bowl or plate. Its surface is very rough. The bowl was decorated with a very faint black pigment which has a brownish cast. The firing is slightly grayed, so that color is hard to determine. The bowl was fabricated in a paste with sparse grains of milky quartzite and other small particles, probably a sand.

II:13. Small, deep bowl (fig. 151). The bowl had a diameter of 11 cm. Its shape and the colors used in its decoration are very reminiscent of another Phase 3 bowl. It is identical in every respect to a bowl found in a grave lot in Barrio Azoguini in the city of Puno, except that the Azoguini bowl has a black stripe at the rim (fig. 152). The exterior of these bowls was not well smoothed. It was polished very carelessly except for the last .5-1 cm. where

the surface was wiped horizontally. The pigments are a
white slip with a pinkish cast, a dull red-purple and a solution black. The white slip was brushed on the Azoguini bowl.
Brush marks can be seen. Apparently the surface was polished before the red and black line decoration was added.
The Azoguini bowl has a firing ghost on the exterior which
appears to be from a bowl with similar decoration. Both
bowls were made of a nearly temperless Paste D with the addition of a moderate to a very large quantity of fine mica.
The Azoguini bowl has a base diameter of 3.5 cm. Its surface is rough, and like one small bowl of Group II:7 in
Phase 2 (fig. 71), it appears to have been set in fine red
sandstone while still wet enough to pick up particles of
sandstone.

   II:14. Miscellaneous bowl shapes (fig. 153). The bowl
had a base diameter of about 5 cm. Though some of the Phase
2 bases are thinner than the body of the same bowl, none are
this thin. The exterior surface is poorly smoothed and not
polished. The base itself is not even and has some rough
spots and lumps. It is also not very round. The bowl was
slipped red-purple on the interior and decorated with a
solution black and a faint white. The decoration is similar
to the decoration of small bowls of Group II:7 in Phase 2.
The bowl was made of a very fine grained cream colored paste
with a minute quantity of fine sand.

Utilitarian Shapes (Group IV)

III:1. Jar with vertical strap handles. This jar was described under utilitarian shapes in Phase II (Group III:1). The shape continues, as described, in Phase 3.

III:2. Jar with thick handle extending above the lip (fig. 154). A rim fragment from this shape was found in Phase 3 levels, similar to the one described for Group III:2 in Phase 2 (fig. 86). A body sherd from a vessel with similar surface treatment can probably be included with this group (fig. 154). It exhibits an angle in the lower body profile (fig. 154).

III:3. Colander. These fragments can be oriented vertically as neck fragments like the Group III:3 fragment of Phase 2, but an open bowl shape with an everted rim may be the shape represented (see fig. 88). In all details of manufacture, these Phase 3 fragments are like the Phase 2 one. The largest fragment in the Phase 3 group is not punctured over the entire surface, but has some unpunctured space.

III:4. Small plate with thinned base (fig. 155). The plate had a 13 cm. rim diameter and a 4.5 cm. base diameter. The lip is very rounded. Like the bowl of Group II:14 above, this vessel has an extremely thin base. Both inside and outside were smoothed and wiped. Neither surface was decorated. The bowl was made of Paste A of the high fire variety.

Other Shapes (Group IV)

IV:1. Jar with flaring rim (fig. 156 and one fragment
not illustrated). One fragment (not illustrated) is very
similar in shape and decoration to a Phase 1 fragment (fig.
25). The Phase 3 fragment is somewhat grayed in cross-
section, but it was evidently slipped with a red-purple
color and painted with a black stripe at the lip edge. The
second example of this shape has a 20-21 cm. diameter (fig.
156). This jar was slipped with a purple slip on both the
exterior and interior. Both inside and outside were smoothed
and polished over the slip, though many unpolished areas are
evident. The second fragment was made of the Paste C
variant which fires to a cream color (fig. 156).

Imitation Inca Shapes (Group V)

No new shapes were borrowed from the Cuzco-Inca repertory, but there is some evidence for style change in the
imitation Inca group between Phases 2 and 3. Moreover, some
of the bowls in this group exhibit non-Cuzco shape features.
They have been included in this group because they are decorated in a fairly standard Cuzco-Inca manner.

V:1. Cuzco bottle (figs. 185-188). No fragments were
drawn. Fewer diagnostic fragments with standard Cuzco-Inca
decoration were found.

V:1a. Mode A body decoration (figs. 185a, c, d, e, f,
g, h and other fragments not illustrated). Mode A decoration
is in evidence, executed on both white slipped and medium
orange surfaces. The few fragments with fern panel

decoration have three strand ferns, not two strand ferns.
The pigments are purple, tending to irridescence in some
spots, a creamy white and a black which is obviously solution
black in some cases and may be in others. Both Paste C and
Paste A were used.

    V:1b. Mode B body decoration (figs. 185b, j and other
fragments not illustrated)(Rowe, 1944, p. 47). This kind of
decoration is also present for the first time. The elements
of Mode B are very careful imitations of Cuzco-Inca Mode B
elements, and their arrangement is also faithful to the
Cuzco-Inca style (Rowe, 1944, fig, 18, nos. 21-22, pl. V,
figs. 4-6; Bingham, 1930, pl. 74, 80c, 81a, 82d-3; Llanos,
1936, pl. I, fig. 5/825). The designs are painted with the
same colors used in Mode A decoration described above,
except that the white is not creamy and has a streaked
appearance. The careful execution and the Cuzco look of
these fragments would be enough to suggest they were imported,
were it not for the fact that they were manufactured in Paste
C. Several very fancy bottles with variations of Mode B
decoration were also found at Sillustani.

    V:1c. Panel decoration (fig. 186c, d and other fragments
not illustrated). Panel decoration is also evident. Pinwheel panels, like those seen in Phase 2, were common. The
pinwheel was rendered in alternating black and purple
triangles on a white background. One of the fragments has a
panel with a wide purple stripe outlining it. The panel was
painted on an unpigmented surface. The other panel has a
simple black stripe outline, but it was painted on a slipped

surface. The purple in this case is very dark and, like the

black, contrasts strongly with the white. This effect prob-

ably results from the special firing conditions discussed

earlier (see note 6).

V:1d. Spiral tipped triangle decoration (fig. 187)(cf.

Fernández Baca, 1973, figs. 307-310, 353). The triangle has

a point from which two opposing spirals stem. The design

is painted in black on a white surface. It is very possible

that all the fragments with this design are from the same

vessel. This vessel is similar to the reconstructable

bottle found in Phase 2 levels (fig. 99). A number of fea-

tures, including the spacing of lines, pigments, surface

finish and fabrication in Paste A, are shared with the Phase

2 bottle.

V:1e. Miscellaneous body decoration (fig. 186e-f and

other fragments not illustrated). Other kinds of body deco-

ration are also represented, but cannot be reconstructed

from the fragments available. They have no local antecedents

or obvious links to the Cuzco-Inca style, but occur in the

paste related to Cuzco-Inca influence and probably come from

Cuzco bottle shapes. The designs include triangles in black

and red, sometimes outlined in white, and border stripes. The

design is painted on an unpigmented surface. Two nubbins

like those usually found on the front shoulder of Cuzco bottles

(fig. 186e-f)(Bingham, 1930, pls. 73, 74, 76, 78, 79, 82-85,

86, 88) were also found. One has an incised face on its

upper surface, a design seen frequently in analogous position

on Cuzco-Inca bottles. The other has an incised grid.

V:1f. Neck decoration (fig. 188 and others not illustrated). The neck decorations described for Phase 2 were found in Phase 3 levels as well. In addition, unslipped necks were found, some of which had black line decoration (not illustrated). The entire design cannot be reconstructed, but the fragments suggest it was a floral design like one found in the southern Lake Titicaca basin (Rydén, 1947, fig. 117P).

V:2. Cuzco jar (not illustrated). One fragment from a small Cuzco jar was found. It had traces of a faint white slip.

V:3. Tall necked bottle (fig. 157 and others not illustrated). Several fragments from bottles with decoration like the bottle of V:5 in Phase 2 were found, including one shoulder fragment and other rim fragments. The shoulder fragment was made in the same paste as the Phase 2 fragments. Apparently the opening of the body cavity was deliberately impressed, perhaps with the fingernail, to promote the adherence of the neck tube when it was attached.

V:4. Deep dish (figs. 158 and 159). The fragments suggest a diameter of 10 to 18 cm. Like the Cuzco-Inca deep dish, these fragments were made in an orange fired paste and decorated with Cuzco-Inca band designs. The larger dish has a good Cuzco-Inca profile, and a number of other details which closely follow the Cuzco-Inca style (fig. 158). The colors look very much like Cuzco-Inca pigments, and the treatment of the rim is also very Cuzco-Inca. The only feature which suggests some non-Cuzco affiliation is the use of

unoutlined white lines as both an undulating white line and
a crossed line design. The dish is made of Paste C. The
other deep dish is a miniature and may possibly be an import
(fig. 159). The painting is not as careful as the painting
of the first deep dish and wear obscures details of the band
design. The paste is not Paste C, but has a very similar
look. It was tempered with milky quartzite particles and
grains of fine sand.

V:5. Shallow dish (fig. 160). The rim diameter is 9.5
cm., and the base diameter is 7 cm. The dish is much
smaller than its Phase 2 counterpart (fig. 108). Both
vessels were slipped inside and outside, polished while
still wet, and were made in Paste A. The base does not
indicate a basal gambrel, but rather a flat base almost as
large as the rim in diameter.

V:6. Pedestal dish (figs. 161-163). The rim fragments
suggest a diameter of 12-14 cm. The diameter of the pedestal
was 10 cm. These fragments are very similar to a fragment
described in Phase 2 (fig. 109). All of the rim fragments
have a red slip at the lip and on the interior to the bevel
angle, polished while still wet. Some fragments are
blackened from use over the fire. All fragments were made in
Paste A.

V:7. Tumbler (fig. 164). The fragment suggests a
diameter of 19 cm. The profile of this tumbler is very like
Cuzco-Inca tumbler profiles. It is like the unusual black
tumbler of Phase 2 in its size, a size matched by two
tumblers in the Cuzco University Museum, but otherwise rare

in collections. This fragment also has Cuzco-Inca finishing
details, such as a black stripe at the lip and a red band
from the lip edge to the inner angle. The pigments are also
very like Cuzco-Inca pigments, except that the white is not
at all creamy. The fragment was made in Paste C.

   V:8. Bowl with hooked profile (figs. 165-167). The
fragments suggest a rim diameter of 12-14 cm. and a base
diameter of 4-5 cm. Two fragments have a flat base (figs.
165 and 167), but the base of another is slightly rounded
(fig. 166). The fragment with a flat base probably had a
figurehead handle (fig. 165). This kind of handle seems to
be associated with a hooked rim in the Cuzco-Inca style, but
at Hatunqolla, actual evidence for these handles is very
rare. The little that remains of this kind of handle
suggests that this example was painted black and had white
dots over some of its surface. Two bowls were decorated with
a series of birds, probably about four, painted in black
near the center of the bowl (figs. 165-166). The birds
appear to be circling the base in a clockwise direction.
The depiction of the birds differs between the two bowls,
suggesting that different kinds of birds may be represented.
The bowl with the suggested figurehead handle has a bird
with no wings and very long crooked feet (fig. 165). White
paint was painted over its beak. The other bowl shows a
bird with a white tipped wing, purple beak and feet and a
triangular tail (fig. 166). This bowl had a very unusual
double "v" design incised on the base prior to firing. Both

bowls were made of a medium to bright orange fired paste
with particles of lava temper, like a bowl described in
Group V:11 of Phase 2. The third bowl (fig. 167) was slipped
purple on the exterior and white on the interior (cf.
Tschopik, Marion, 1946, fig. 22g-h). The lip has a black
stripe on its edge. The interior is decorated with black and
purple pigments. The black is part solution. The particular
design arrangement is not common among well provenienced
Cuzco-Inca vessels, but it is a combination using a common
Cuzco-Inca band design. The bowl was made of Paste D with
the addition of a moderate amount of large grains of mica.

V:9. Bowl with thinned base (fig. 168). The fragment
has a diameter of 16 cm. The rounded lip is slightly thicker
than the bowl's walls, like some of the Inca related material
from Chucuito (Tschopik, Marion, 1946, figs. 14a, g, 15f). The
shape may not be closely similar to shapes borrowed from Cuzco.
The walls do not thin until just above the base angle, then
the profile thins markedly. The bowl is decorated with band
decoration arranged both circumferentially and transversely on
the interior in good Cuzco-Inca style. Its interior is badly
worn and was affected by sintering due to high heat and other
factors (see note 6). The bowl was made of a paste very
similar to the one used for the tall necked bottle in both
Phases 2 and 3 (see V:5{2}).

V:10. Bowl with outer curve (fig. 169). A diameter of 18
cm. could be reconstructed. Like the bowl discussed above,
it is not identical with a Cuzco-Inca shape. The outer
angle may be an imitation of the hooked profile of the

Cuzco-Inca style bowls. The bowl was decorated with black
and purple decoration on an unpigmented surface, possibly
slipped the same color as the paste. All elements of the
design and their combination were imitated from the Cuzco-
Inca examples (Bingham, 1930, pl. 89c; Valcárcel, 1935,
lám. III, fig. 1/559). The black fades except where it comes
into contact with the purple pigment, due to high temperature
firing (see note 6). The bowl was made of Paste C.

V:11. Bowl with rounded lip (fig. 170). A diameter of
19 cm. can be reconstructed. The rounded lip of this fragment is a feature it shares with the bowl described under
V:9, but this bowl did not have a thinned base. The rounded
lip may be related to the Chucuito material illustrated by
Tschopik (Marion, 1946, figs. 14a, b, g, 15d, 17f, g). It
was decorated with the same pigments used to decorate a
Sillustani tradition bowl (fig. 145), but the band design
was imitated from the Cuzco-Inca style. The outside may
have been slipped, as it is several shades darker than the
paste. The exterior finish is good, but this surface finish
usually does not darken the surface color very much. The
fragment was manufactured in Paste C.

Other Cuzco Related Shapes (Group VI)

VI:1. Bowl with rounded and thickened outer lip (fig.
171). A diameter of 17 cm. could be reconstructed. The
bowl has a thickened lip, similar to contemporary materials
from Chucuito (Tschopik, Marion, 1946, figs. 15h, 22g). The
band design used on this bowl is similar to Cuzco-Inca

"hourglass" bands (Fernández Baca, 1973, figs. 178-180, 279),

except that filled triangles are substituted for the

hourglass motifs. A number of vessels with this design,

said to come from the Sillustani area, are found in the Puno

Municipal Museum. A nearly identical fragment was found in

the southern Lake Titicaca basin (Rydén, 1947, fig. 89B).

This band may be a particular feature of provincial variants

of the Cuzco-Inca style in the Lake Titicaca region (cf.

Fernández Baca, 1973, figs. 131-142). The Phase 3 fragment

at Hatunqolla was made in a kaolin paste, but the nearly

identical fragment found further south was not. Both

fragments have a wide stripe painted with an orange pigment,

however. The occurrence of an orange pigment is unique among

the excavated materials from Hatunqolla. The color of the

paste is a slightly grayed white. Apparently some kind of

iron mineral occurred as an inclusion in the paste, and

there are small red spots in the cross-section. Other

particles, probably sand, can also be identified.

SUMMARY OF PHASE III MATERIALS

Sorting the Hatunqolla material into two groups,

depending on resemblance either to the Cuzco-Inca style or

to the Sillustani style, is a bit more arbitrary for Phase 3

than for the earlier phases, and some of the features that

were used to separate the two groups in Phase 2 no longer

work as well. Some shape features are shared. For example,

a flat, fairly wide base now occurs in both groups. The

deep bowl shape formerly reserved for Group II now occurs in

Group I. A very shallow bowl is part of the Group II
inventory, when this feature was exclusively associated with
Group I in Phase 2. The revival of a Sillustani style narrow
band design also complicates matters, because it is more
frequently seen on Cuzco related material than on Sillustani
related material. While some decorative overlap occurred in
earlier phases, more overlap occurs in Phase 3. Surface
finish and stylistic links to Phase 2 help to maintain the
distinction between the two bowl groups. Some conservative
Sillustani style shape features are revived in the Sillustani
related group, also aiding in the differentiation of two
stylistic subgroups. In the non-bowl groups, a great deal of
continuity from Phase 2 is obvious. Some interesting devel-
opments take place in the imitation Inca material, better
discussed in a later paragraph. In all, many Phase 2 shapes
and decorative compositions continue into Phase 3, giving the
impression that the pace of innovation has slowed. The
innovations which occur, however, are consistent, and it is
clear that Phase 3 is a separate stylistic unit.

Cuzco related bowls made of Paste C occur in several
shapes, including some new ones. Continuing shapes are a
bowl shape with a flattened lip (fig. 123)(I:1{2}) and a
shallow bowl with an inward bevel from the lip (figs. 125-
127)(I:2{2}). A large deep bowl (figs. 132, 133 and 134) may
be related to the bowl with a wide inward bevel from the lip
(I:7{2} and I:8{2}). They also bear a resemblance to the
Sillustani related bowl with an inward bevel and a profile
that thins toward the base (II:1{2}). Both shapes have a

very similar rim profile and tend to thin slightly toward
the base. Deep bowls in Phase 2 had Sillustani related
features, while the Phase 3 example has an extremely fine
exterior finish and other decorative details heretofore
associated only with Cuzco related bowls. Some smaller
bowls were found (figs. 128-130), some of which seem to be
smaller versions of Group I:2{3}. The small bowls with
straight sides resemble a Phase 2 bowl group (I:6{2}). Two
other shapes without Phase 2 precedent are a bowl shape with
a thickened lip and a shallow bowl with fairly thin walls
and base for its size (fig. 131 and 135).

The decoration of Cuzco related bowls can usually be
related to decorative compositions used on bowls of the same
category in Phase 2. Medallion decoration was used, utilizing four and possibly five pigments. A bowl (fig. 132)
executed in Paste C with medallion decoration has a wide
band painted in the dense purple pigment associated with
Paste C and an unslipped medallion space just like a similar
Phase 2 example (see fig. 46). Decoration on a white slipped
surface with motifs related to the Sillustani style is also
found (compare figs. 123-124 with figs. 47-51 and fig. 129
with fig. 45). A new motif, the swallowing bird, was also
used (see fig. 129). Another new decorative composition is
the use of a more conservative Sillustani style narrow band
in conjunction with a wide zig-zag band (figs. 125-127).
Unlike Phase 1 bowls with similar decoration (fig. 6), Phase
3 examples characteristically have Cuzco-Inca protuberances
at the lip. These plates do not have bunched parallel

stripes on the beveled surface near the lip, and the zig-zag
band is wider than Phase 1 bands. The bands, including
undulating white lines detailing the zig-zag band, are
painted on a purple slip, like their Phase 1 antecedents.
Two of the bowls with a flattened lip (figs. 128 and 130)
also have the revived narrow band design, used with some kind
of motif involving paired diagonal lines, also seen in Phase
1 (figs. 4, 15 and 19).   One of the new shapes was decorated
with a bird motif, a spiral design and another line motif
(fig. 135). The spiral design consists of two spirals
united in a common stem. The Hatunqolla example may be
related to similar designs in use on unslipped bowls in the
southern Lake Titicaca basin in Inca related contexts
(Rydén, 1947, figs. 74Q, 79Q, 92B, 102G, 106Q, 106R, 113D).
Birds are another motif commonly painted on an unslipped surface in the same area (Rydén, 1947, figs. 87Q, 87S, 101f,
101g, 101h, 105X, 108T, 126C).

Only two fragments in the Cuzco related group were made
in Paste D (figs. 133 and 134). They are very similar to
bowls of Group II:1{2}, except for a Cuzco related exterior
surface finish. These two fragments have solid color
decoration.

Many Sillustani related shapes from Phase 2 survive into
Phase 3, including bowls with an inward bevel from the lip
and an outer angle (figs. 137-138)(II:2{2}), a shallow bowl
with a rounded lip (fig. 142)(II:7{2}) and a small bowl
(figs. 147, 148 and 149)(II:11{2}). The first bowl in the
list just mentioned has a more convex profile than the

Phase 2 examples. The two Phase 3 fragments have a thin lip
profile and a narrow beveled surface like one of the Phase 2
fragments (fig. 62). A related shape with a wide beveled
surface, a thick lip profile and a vertical handle attached
to the lip is without antecedents in the Hatunqolla materials (fig. 141). Some shapes in this group recall Phase 1
Sillustani related bowls in such features as a slightly
rounded inner lip profile (fig. 146, compare to figs. 20 and
21) and an inward bevel from the lip and straight walls (fig.
140, compare to figs. 6 and 10). One shape is more conservative yet and resembles pre-Inca Sillustani style bowls (figs.
145 and 151, compare to figs. 18 and 19). At the same time,
a very shallow plate shape was associated with these conservative fragments (fig. 150). The direct rim and small base
are non-Cuzco features, but the shallowness of the bowl
follows a trend related to Cuzco-Inca influence. Another
new shape feature is a thinned base (figs. 153 and 155; cf.
fig. 168). One Phase 3 bowl (fig. 136) combines some
shape features like those of Group I:2{3}, with surface
finish, paste and decorative details like a Sillustani
related bowl in Phase 2 (fig. 59).

A number of conservative decoration features are evident
in the Sillustani related material. Some bowls with shape
antecedents in Phase 2 are also decorated in the same manner
as Phase 2 bowls (fig. 142). Again, a zig-zag band of moderate width was used on the shallow bowl shape, and a very
wide zig-zag band was used on the deeper bowl shape. A
certain preference for the suspended scallop version of this

band is exhibited. Phase 3 rim fragments with this design
show the scallop suspended from the upper border stripe and
not the lip edge. The band was also painted with wider,
more even lines. Some special shape and decoration features
are associated with some of the deeper bowl shapes, particularly when these bowls are also decorated with the angular
version of the zig-zag band. Protuberances, handles and
bunches of parallel stripes appear on some deep bowls (figs.
140 and 141). Bunches of parallel stripes on the bevel
surface are a decorative feature of Phase 1 not seen in
Phase 2. Protuberances and handles are first found in Phase
3. Bowls with even more conservative shape features also
have conservative decoration features. A striking example
is the fragment with a rounded inner lip (fig. 144). It is
decorated with Sillustani style tassel motifs suspended from
stripe decoration on the inner lip. Another kind of tassel
motif, also suspended from the lip but in the reverse direction, appears in Phase 3 (fig. 151); these tassels are
associated with white background slips, but they are drawn
as line figures without the filling characteristic of
Sillustani style tassel motifs. They are probably still
related to the conservative tassel motif, and they exhibit
color alternation. Another fragment has the revived narrow
band design used on Cuzco related bowls in Phase 3 (fig. 145,
compare to figs. 6 and 15).

New designs are associated with the new shallow bowls.
A design composition consisting of narrow bands, or just
paired stripes, crossing at right angles on the interior of

the bowl is common (figs. 148 and 150). This design composition can be seen on the interior of bowls from the southern
Lake Titicaca basin (Rydén, 1947, figs. 74M, 108A). These
designs are painted on unpigmented, and sometimes unpolished,
surfaces. Another new design is a narrow band with a red-
purple stripe painted between two black outline stripes (fig.
146). A final example of a new design is the swallowing
bird motif painted on the medallion space of a bowl (figs.
129 and 136). Medallion decoration, when executed on
Sillustani related bowls, is the same as it was in Phase 2.
The upper band is fairly narrow, painted in light red and
bordered with two black stripes (see fig. 59).

All three shapes made of Paste A continue in Phase 3,
without any new additions. Very few diagnostic fragments
from other shapes were found. Two purple slipped tall
necked jar fragments were found (fig. 156). One is quite
similar to a Phase 1 jar fragment (not illustrated). The
other has almost no flare, except right at the lip edge
and has a much finer surface finish than any other tall
necked jar (fig. 156).

Fewer Cuzco-Inca shapes are represented in the Phase 3
levels than in Phase 2 ones. Some of the missing shapes
were represented by few fragments in the Phase 2 levels, so
their absence in Phase 3 levels may not be meaningful.
Little can be said about minor shape details, except in the
case of bowls. Bowls seem to have a number of local features, including a thickening at the lip and a thinning of
the base (Rydén, 1947, fig. 117J; Tschopik, Marion, 1946,

figs. 14a, g, k, 15c, d, f, h, 17d, e, f, g, i, 22g). These
bowls have been included in the imitation Inca group because
they are decorated with standard Cuzco-Inca decoration,
though the new shape features do not appear to have come
from Cuzco.

Decorative details are less constant between Phases 2
and 3 than between Phases 1 and 2, especially where imitation
Cuzco bottles are concerned. Mode A decoration continues,
over both white slipped and unslipped surfaces, but the fern
motif is rendered with a three strand stem exclusively. One
example of this kind of stem occurred in Phase 1, and both
two strand and three strand stems were common in Phase 2.
Surface and excavated material from the southern Lake
Titicaca basin with strong stylistic links to Phase 3 material at Hatunqolla exhibit only three strand stems (Rydén,
1947, figs. 74Z, 103I, 106J, 113W). Mode B decoration, carefully imitated from Cuzco-Inca models, is represented for the
first time (fig. 185b, j)(Rydén, 1947, figs. 47R, 74Y, 74e,
88F, 88G, 103D, etc.). Another decorative motif well represented in Phase 3 levels is the pinwheel panel (fig. 186c,
d)(Rydén, 1947, figs. 74U, 79M, 85R, 88B, 98G, 102A, 108V,
113Z). At the same time, the areal design with a black grid
on a red-purple background is missing. This design was not
in good Cuzco-Inca style, if indeed it was imitated from that
style. In Phase 3 another design also lacks an exact Cuzco-
Inca model. It consists of geometric shapes, particularly
triangles, in red and black on an unslipped surface, often
with white outlines.[21] A neck design, not seen in earlier

phases, appears to be a floral motif, perhaps similar to
one in use in the southern Lake Titicaca basin (Rydén, 1947,
fig. 117P). The leafy stem and calyx of the flower are
represented by the fragments.

Three kinds of design are represented by the imitation
Inca bowl fragments. One is a standard band arrangement
with transverse and circumferential banding (figs. 168-169
and possibly 170). Shape details of these bowls are not
standard for Cuzco-Inca bowls. Both the pigments used and
the firing are closer to local pigments and firing. Another
bowl has adjacent circumferential bands, an arrangment in
use in Phase 1 (fig. 167). The third kind of design involves
the use of repeated bird motifs on the bowl's interior near
the base (figs. 165-166). These bowls may be imported from
somewhere with closer stylistic ties to Cuzco. There is a
bowl almost identical to them in the Cuzco University Museum.
The Hatunqolla bowls have grits of lava used as temper. The
surface finish is very like the finish of Cuzco-Inca bowls
and plates with no interior slip. This kind of surface
finish occurs on another Phase 3 bowl with decorative similarities to material from the southern Lake Titicaca region
(fig. 135), and the use of repeated bird motifs is also a
characteristic of that area (Rydén, 1947, figs. 87S, 101f,
101g, 101h, 108T, 126C).

Other imitation Inca shapes continue from Phase 2. Some
very elaborate deep dish fragments were found (figs. 158-159).
The Phase 2 fragments of this shape were few in number and
not as fancy. A fragment from a large white tumbler was

found (fig. 164). It has a standard Cuzco-Inca rim profile
and decorative treatment. Fragments from tall necked
bottles with a cat spot design are evidence for the
continuance of this shape (fig. 157).

Copying Cuzco-Inca shapes in the local utilitarian paste
also went on in Phase 3, and the same three shapes were
copied as in Phase 2. A pedestal fragment was found, confirming the likelihood that pedestal dishes and not deep
dishes were being copied in the utilitarian paste (fig. 161).
Another fragment from what appears to be a shallow dish was
found (fig. 160). Like the fragment attributed to this
shape in Phase 2, it is not a close copy of the Cuzco-Inca
shallow dish. A Cuzco bottle imitated in the utilitarian
paste was decorated with non-Cuzco motifs, including spiral
tipped triangles. The spiral tipped triangle motif is also
found on Cuzco bottles in the southern Lake Titicaca basin
(Rydén, 1947, figs. 74S, 85Q).

Other shapes related to the vessels identified as
prestige ware in Phase 2 were not found. A fragment from a
kaolin paste bowl was recovered (fig. 171). It has a
thickened lip like some Chucuito bowls (Tschopik, Marion,
1946, fig. 22g). The design of this fragment is like a standard Cuzco-Inca band design, but filled triangles are substituted for a filled hourglass motif (Tschopik, Marion,
1946, figs. 15h, 22g). This fragment is extremely similar to
one found in the southern Lake Titicaca region (Rydén, 1947,
fig. 89B), except that the second fragment was not made in
a kaolin paste. It was slipped white instead. The color

purple was used for the solid triangles in one of the band
designs in the Hatunqolla fragment, while only the color
black was used in the bands of the southern Lake Titicaca
basin fragment. Both fragments have orange bands separating
the Cuzco related band design. The color orange occurs in
very special contexts, in association with vessels manufactured in kaolin paste or vessels related to them, or in
association with an elaborate polychrome decoration referred
to as Urcusuyu Polychrome.[22] These Lake Titicaca region
features are found far from the Titicaca area in other
provincial Inca styles, indicating non-Cuzco input into
the Cuzco-Inca style at this time.

SUMMARY OF PHASE IV MATERIALS

Phase 4 does not follow immediately after Phase 3, as
evidenced both stratigraphically and stylistically. Since
this material was not analyzed in the same detail as the
material of Phases 1-3, only a brief sketch of its characteristics will be presented here. The fragments recovered
were smaller, so that less complete information can be
obtained for shape and decoration.

Convex sided shallow bowls of small size predominate in
the refuse, many with Cuzco related surface finish. The
majority of the fragments belong to the Cuzco related group,
and there are very few fragments of Sillustani related
bowls. The one shape clearly represented among the
Sillustani related bowls with Phase 3 antecedents is a deep
bowl shape with a wide zig-zag band painted on a red slipped

surface. Design compositions for Cuzco related bowls with Phase 3 antecedents are the human figure motifs in series and medallion decoration. Many bowl fragments are simply decorated with a pair of black stripes, a long standing Sillustani tradition feature, set below the bevel angle on the interior. A small number of imitation Inca fragments were recovered from Cuzco bottles with pinwheel panels or elements of Mode A decoration (fig. 189) and from bowls with transverse and circumferential band designs. The band designs used in these bowls are not easy to distinguish, in part because the surface sintering noted in Phase 3 is even more pronounced in Phase 4 (see note 6).

New shapes are an open bowl with probable European influence (figs. 172-173) and a jar with an everted lip (figs. 175-176). Two large fragments of the bowl were recovered, one with a medium red slip (fig. 172) and the other with two black stripes below the bevel angle on an unslipped surface (fig. 173). Another new motif is a suche painted in a cream color with black spots, sometimes with no outline (fig. 174). This motif occurs on a medium red slipped surface. The bowls just described have a very fine paste. It fires to a light cream or light orange color and has almost no temper, except in the case of fig. 172 which may have milky quartzite as temper. One of the jars has a very thick vertical strap handle and a diameter of 23 cm. (fig. 175). The other jar has only a 16 cm. mouth diameter and a probable height of about 24 cm. (fig. 176). It was obviously used in the fire and may have replaced the cooking

jar common in Phases 1 and 3 to some degree, as only a few
fragments from the earlier cooking jar were found. The
paste of the two jar fragments in Phase 4 is quite coarse.
It fires to a light orange color and has large grains of
white quartzite, yellow and white chalk, gray particles and
red sandstone as temper. Fragments from very large jars
obviously made on the wheel were also recovered. These fragments turned up on the surface of sites in the southern Lake
Titicaca basin, particularly at a site occupied into the
Spanish colonial era (Rydén, 1947, fig. 114, pp. 263,
312-313). The vessels represented by these fragments may be
connected with wine importation. Phase 4 levels also
contained a round Venetian glass bead, steel knife fragments,
nails, glass fragments and a piece of four strand braid with
yarns wrapped in silver tinsel. This association confirms
the ceramic evidence in suggesting that this phase dates to
the early Spanish colonial era. No glazed pottery was
recovered in the Phase 4 level, although it was recovered
stratigraphically above materials similar to the Phase 4
materials elsewhere at Hatunqolla (Testpit 7).

Notes to Chapter V

[1]Material from sites in the vicinity of Sillustani, and roughly contemporary with the material from Testpit 12 at that site, has been used occasionally in the analysis. This material comes from the sites of Ale, Esturi, Escalera and Maluchane, all located in the hilly region near Lake Umayo.

[2]The name Sillustani has been consistently used in two ways. By "Sillustani style" ceramic material from the Sillustani area dating to the time before the arrival of strong Cuzco-Inca influence is meant. By "Sillustani tradition" the reference is specifically to the local ceramic tradition during the time period covered in this study, that is, from the time just before to the time just after the period the area was under control from Cuzco.

[3]This black is the most common black pigment in use at Hatunqolla. It behaves differently on different surfaces, so that its identification is sometimes difficult. Blurring, for example, does not always occur. The black is particularly affected by high firing temperatures (see note 6).

[4]A great number of reds can be identified, some of which are not different pigments, but result from different surface

finishing, different firing, or a different paste used underneath. No attempt has been made to identify these pigments
chemically. Several have a bearing on the style analysis,
and these pigments have been called attention to in the
description sections. The drawings have also been keyed to
show differences in pigments apparent from visual examination.

[5]Bingham, 1930, pl. 89a, c, e, 99h, 100a, 109b, 123c, d,
127f; Eaton, 1916, pl. XI, figs. 5-6; Llanos, 1936, lám. II,
figs. 5/90, 5/325, 5/326, 5/327 and others; Valcárcel, 1934b,
lám. III, figs. 1/84, 1/85, lám. V, fig. 1/81, lám. VI, fig.
1/86.

[6]This effect was probably caused by high temperature
firing in most cases. The organic material in the solution
can be entirely burned out if the firing is hot enough.
Apparently, contact with certain pigments, especially the
red pigments, inhibits the lightening of the black for some
reason, so the same black stripe can be black when applied
over a red pigment and faint gray when in contact with an
unslipped or white surface. In some specimens, surface sintering further confirms a high firing temperature. This
effect is apparent in Phase 2, but it gets more serious in
Phases 3 and 4.

[7]Bingham, 1930, pl. 80b, 82c, 83, 84, 109c, 113 and
others; Llanos, 1936, lám. II, fig. 5/297. lám. VII, fig.
5/336; Valcárcel, 1934b, lám. II, fig. 1/406, lám. IV, fig.
1/407 and others; Valcárcel, 1935, lám. I, fig. 1/125, lám.
V, fig. 1/201 and others.

[8]The zig-zag band was documented on a fragment from Level 5, Testpit 12, Sillustani, and at other sites in the area. The other band has been illustrated elsewhere (Ruiz Estrada, 1973b, pl. 18b, cf. pls. 20b, 23a).

[9]Bingham, 1930, pl. 79; Rowe, 1944, figs. 18, 20-21, figs. 19, 9; Valcárcel, 1934a, fig. 65; Valcárcel, 1935, lám. VII, figs. 14/828, 1/573; Llanos, 1936, lám. I, fig. 5/825; Ruiz Estrada, 1973a, pls. 17d, h, 18a, f; Tschopik, Marion, 1946, fig. 10c, o; fragments from Sillustani surface and other nearby sites.

[10]Bingham, 1930, fig. 99k. Two plates in the Lowie Museum of Anthropology, University of California at Berkeley, with the lower band design were collected by Max Uhle in the Cuzco area (4-8004, 4-8005).

[11]Level 5, Testpit 12, Sillustani; fragments from Sillustani surface and nearby sites. Some of the fragments illustrated by Ruiz Estrada have multiple adjacent band designs, but the testpit at Sillustani did not contain fragments with this kind of decoration.

[12]A shorthand notation to identify shape numbers with particular phases has been adopted. It consists of the shape number, followed by the phase number in brackets, as for example, II:7{2}.

[13]Some dance costumes in the Puno area resemble this figure (see Bandelier, 1910, pl. XVI, and Paredes, 1966, pp. 156-168). Feather headdress is a very common element of the costume.

[14]All three bottles are outside the two size classes
observed for Cuzco bottles by George R. Miller using measurements taken from specimens in the Cuzco University Museum.
Cuzco bottles are either 8-37 cm. or 80-97 cm. tall. The
proportions of the Hatunqolla bottles are also somewhat
different. The Cuzco bottles usually were about as wide as
they were tall and had necks which were 1/3 the total height
of the vessel. For the reconstructable bottle from
Hatunqolla, the width is only 2/3 of the height, and the
neck is only 1/4 the height.

[15]Rowe, 1944, p. 49; Bingham, 1930, pls. 108a-d, f, 109c,
f, 119c; Valcárcel, 1934a, fig. 52; Valcárcel, 1935, lám.
V, fig. 1/271, lám. VI, figs. 1/642, 1/183, lám. VII, figs.
1/111, 1/197, 1/639 and others.

[16]When the height of these jars is calculated using
proportions from measured Cuzco-Inca specimens in the Cuzco
University Museum, the smaller jar has a height of 38-50 cm.,
and the larger jar, a height of 46-64 cm. Two sizes are
represented in the Cuzco-Inca material. Small jars are from
5 to 14.5 cm. in height, and large jars are from 60 to 97 cm.
in height. As can be seen, one jar is clearly outside the
usual range for Cuzco-Inca jars. Again, the measurements
were taken by George R. Miller.

[17]A comparative collection from sites in the Cuzco area
was used in the hopes that a Cuzco origin for some of the
material could be established. These three fragments are
within the range of variation of the Cuzco area pastes.

[18]Eaton, 1916, pl. XIII, figs. 3, 6, 7; Bingham, 1930,
pls. 89c, e, 91, 98f; Llanos, 1936, lám. II, figs. 5/731,
5/327, 5/329, 5/320 and others; Valcárcel, 1934a, figs. 69,
71, 75, 76; Valcárcel, 1935, lám. 1, figs. 1/125, 1/550,
1/83.

[19]The southern Lake Titicaca region bowls are mainly
decorated in this fashion. No emphasis on different
colored slips is apparent (Rydén, 1947, figs. 101W, 101X,
102C, 1050, 105U, 105W, 105T and others). Medallion decoration may be represented among the fragments from the same
area (Rydén, 1947, figs. 79R, 102A). This material bears
much stronger resemblances to Phase 3 at Hatunqolla and
is referred to often in the next section.

[20]Bingham, 1930, pl. 72, fig. 12a-c; Llanos, 1936, lám.
II, figs. 5/331, 5/335; Valcárcel, 1934a, figs. 76-77;
Valcárcel 1934b, lám. VI, fig. 1/165; Valcárcel, 1935, lám.
I, figs. 1/396, 1/256, 1/550, 1/561 and others.

[21]Rydén, 1947, figs. 79M, 790, 85U, 88B, 103J, 106E,
108V, 113Z, 120L. All but one of these fragments is probably from a pinwheel panel. None is painted on an unslipped
surface, but rather over a white pigment.

[22]Rowe, 1944, fig. 49, 5-7; Tschopik, Marion, 1946, figs.
18, 19, pl. 10f, g; Bingham, 1930, pl. 78; Menzel, 1976, p.
149, 150, pls. 61, 62.

6

FINAL DISCUSSION: OVERLAP IN HISTORICAL AND ARCHAEOLOGICAL RESEARCH

To this point, the historical and archaeological studies have proceeded separately. The research was designed neither to use archaeological evidence to check inferences from historical sources nor vice versa, for reasons outlined at the beginning of the text. The two methods followed independent courses. At the same time I hope it is clear that more has been learned about the occupation of Hatunqolla than might be learned using either the archaeological or the historical method alone. The problem addressed was the nature and degree of Inca control in the Lake Titicaca region, and most particularly in the Qolla province of 'Urqosuyu with its capital at Hatunqolla. The historical sources indicated that many aspects of Inca rule can be documented in the Lake Titicaca region. The archaeological materials reflected a strong Inca presence.

The area of overlap between the two methods is small in the present study, and it is the subject of this chapter. The discussion focuses on two major points. One is the use of historical information to provide some kind of time scale for the ceramic sequence defined for Inca Hatunqolla. The other is the interpretation of the impact of Inca influence

on local cultural materials in light of what we know about
the Qollas from other sources. It should become clear during
the discussion of the latter topic that what we would con-
clude from the historical evidence alone is that the Qollas
were fiercely independent, while our natural conclusions from
the archaeological evidence would be that the Qollas strongly
identified with the goals of the Inca empire. An alternative
explanation suggests itself when both kinds of evidence are
considered together.

CHRONOLOGY

So far no argument has been advanced about the length
of time Inca Hatunqolla was occupied. In a number of early
written accounts, Inca activities in the Lake Titicaca
region were reported as part of a general history of the
Inca conquest and events subsequent to it. Within this
general framework it is often possible to suggest a relative
date for a particular event by referring to a military campaign that had or had not yet occurred or by simply placing
the event within the rule of a particular emperor. One
writer ventured to suggest dates for the last three reigns.
These dates may not be reliable, but they are reasonable
estimates (Rowe, 1945, p. 277).

Determining the span of time Hatunqolla was occupied
relative to this chronology is not a simple task. The foundation of Hatunqolla was not mentioned by any writer. Archaeological exploration revealed that the site was occupied
from a time when the local material tradition was

beginning to come under strong influence from Cuzco. Though
influence is not equatable with control, the relative leap in
the amount of Inca influence seen at this time is a strong
indicator that Hatunqolla was founded after the Incas took
control. Moreover, Hatunqolla appears to have been planned
by the Incas, and no materials antedating the strong shift
in the local ceramic tradition were found at the site, either
on the surface or in test excavations in various parts. A
Hatunqolla may have existed before this time, but its site
was located in another place.

Determining the likely date for the foundation of
Hatunqolla on its present site is complicated by a lack of
agreement among the historical sources regarding the chronology of the Inca conquest of the Lake Titicaca region. Two
authors, Cieza de León and Juan de Santa Cruz Pachacuti (see
pp. 39-40), mentioned an independent Qolla dynasty in the
time of Wiraqocha 'Inka, the eighth Inka. According to
Cieza, Wiraqocha intended the conquest of the northern Lake
Titicaca region, but because Qari was able to defeat Zapana
before Wiraqocha's arrival, a peace pact between Wiraqocha
and Qari was the only result of his venture into the area
(1967, cap. XLIII, pp. 145-146). Not until Pachakuti's
reign, and following campaigns this Inka made into Soras,
Vilcas and Condesuyu, did the Lake Titicaca region become a
focus of Inca attention again. At that time, when the
Incas had an alliance with the Chancas, Pachakuti sent a
brother of his, Thupa Wasqo, with a Chanca captain off to
the Lake Titicaca region to conquer the area. Pachakuti

later joined their army at Chucuito, where the captains had
fought a number of successful battles (1967, cap. XLVIII,
pp. 160-161). Since, in Cieza's account, Qari had already
defeated Zapana and taken everything from him, the Incas
appear to have annexed the entire northern Lake Titicaca
region before the midpoint of Pachakuti's rule.

Given Cieza's chronology of events, the founding of
Hatunqolla occurred during the time of Pachakuti's rule, and
perhaps during the early part of it. As noted earlier,
Pachakuti was said to have been involved with planned resettlement, and particularly with moving people away from hilltops to the flat lands (Sarmiento de Gamboa, 1906, cap. 39,
p. 80; Cieza de León, 1924, cap. XCIII, p. 275, cap. C, p.
290, and 1967, cap. XXIV, p. 83). On a second trip to the
northern Lake Titicaca region, after a campaign in Jauja,
Pachakuti congregated people into nucleated settlements in
the Qolla province of 'Urqosuyu, and it was perhaps at this
time, if not before, that Hatunqolla was founded (1967,
cap. LII, p. 175).

Inca control of the area was interrupted by at least two
armed rebellions, and Inca activities following pacification
of the area may also have led to the founding of towns
(Sarmiento de Gamboa, 1906, cap. 41, p. 83, cap. 49, p. 96,
cap. 50, pp. 97-98, cap. 51, pp. 98-99, cap. 52, pp. 99-100).

Pinpointing the arrival of Europeans is equally difficult.
The Spanish first arrived in the Lake Titicaca region in
December, 1533, when Pizarro sent two Spanish scouts to make
a report on the area (Sancho de la Hoz, 1938, p. 175).

Several other contacts were probably made between that date
and the Spanish military occupation of the area in 1538
(Sitio del Cuzco, 1934, p. 121). Spanish influence on local
materials was therefore probably negligible until 1538 or
later. Hatunqolla was said to have been inhabited in 1543,
but was reportedly abandoned before 1549 (Vaca de Castro,
1908, p. 439; Araníbar, 1967, p. xxi). Hatunqolla may have
been resettled at some time between 1565 and 1585 when the
Spanish administration was recongregating dispersely settled
people into nucleated settlements. In 1573 the people of
the district were settled in three nucleated settlements,
none of which bore the name Hatunqolla (Toledo, 1975, p. 98).
By 1586, the population had been recongregated in Hatunqolla
(Miranda, 1906, p. 193). Some small population may have
remained on the site throughout this time period, but it is
unlikely that it was very large.

It is also unlikely that Hatunqolla was repopulated by its
former residents. The depopulation of Inca administrative
centers following the Spanish conquest has been documented in
other cases (Morris and Thompson, 1970, pp. 358-359). Many
of the people resident in these centers were there on government business, and when Inca provincial government ceased to
function, they had no reason to remain. Moreover, administrative centers were located along the imperial roads and
were particularly vulnerable during the time of civil dis-
ruption following the Spanish invasion. The Lake Titicaca
region was an area where the fighting connected with the
Spanish civil wars of 1544-1548 and 1555-1556 was heavy; it

was on the royal road to Arequipa and was probably severely
affected by Spanish demands for troops and supplies (Crespo,
1972).

The break in occupation found in Pit 1/1A may well
coincide with the abandonment of Hatunqolla sometime between
1543 and 1549. It was both complete and of some duration.
The break occurred before any European influence on the
materials was in evidence, and when the site of Pit 1/1A
was reoccupied, the ceramic materials reflected considerable
style change and were associated with some ceramics of
European manufacture and other materials such as steel
knives and nails, and bottle glass and beads. The refuse
used to define the last phase (Phase 4) of the ceramic sequence almost certainly dates to the time after 1573 when the
site was officially reoccupied.

The refuse used to define the first three phases,
therefore, was deposited before 1573 and probably before
1549. The ceramics of the earliest levels, as noted earlier,
suggest that these levels relate to a time when the local
tradition began to undergo heavy influence from the Cuzco-
Inca style of the Inca capital. The founding of an administrative center may have been part of what produced this
transformation in the local ceramic tradition. If so, the
ceramic sequence established at Hatunqolla may begin near
the time the site was founded. The deposition of refuse
continues unbroken until the site of Pit 1/1A was abandoned,
at some time before 1549. No European influence can be
detected in the materials it contains.

Plausible estimates in calendar years for the duration of several of the later emperors' reigns were given by Cabello Valboa (see Rowe, 1945, p. 277).   If Hatunqolla was founded during the reign of Pachakuti, the eighth Inka, then it falls within the span from 1438 to 1471 estimated for the duration of his reign.   The conquest of the northern Lake Titicaca region probably occurred early in Pachakuti's reign, during the time before his son Thupa 'Inka took control of the army, or between 1438 and 1463.   If Hatunqolla was founded soon after the Inca conquest of the area, or during Pachakuti's second trip into the region, then the foundation occurred at some time during those years. Absolute dates for the abandonment of Hatunqolla have already been suggested; the site appears to have been abandoned sometime between 1543 and 1549.   A range of 98 to 111 years is therefore an approximation of the length of time represented by the refuse used to define Phases 1 to 3.

The length of time represented by the levels used to define each phase cannot be estimated, but on an average, they span something like 32-37 years each.   The chronology for Hatunqolla, therefore, is based on a very fine division of archaeological materials.   Distinguishing style phases among units of material which represent a period of time as short as 100-110 years is not impossible, and others who work with ceramics expect this kind of precision from style analysis (Menzel, 1976, pp. 6-7).

INCAIZATION

Historical information can also be used to provide a context for the strong identification with Cuzco expressed by the material remains. The stylistic transformation of material remains, including ceramics and domestic and burial structures, associated with the occupation of Hatunqolla will be referred to as Incaization, for ease of reference.

The ceramic sequence is the most complete record of Cuzco material penetration we have, and the refuse obtained from Pit 1/1A can be made the basis of general observations about the penetration of the Cuzco-Inca style. It was obtained from a single refuse deposit, but that deposit was continuous and appears to have been associated with a house cluster. There is a fair possibility, then, of continuity in the social group associated with the refuse over the period during which it was deposited. Moreover, the materials recovered in Pit 1/1A indicate that pottery was not produced solely for use by the producers. The emphasis on particular pastes and their apparently non-functional association with different pigments and different surface finishing techniques suggests that pottery was being consumed from several local sources. Information about the organization of ceramic production during the Inca empire corroborates the existence of production beyond household requirements; it still leaves open the possibility of rigid government control. The Hatunqolla refuse indicates that no monopolization of ceramic production by any single entity occurred. Materials very similar to those found in Pit 1/1A were recovered on the

surface all over the site of Hatunqolla, so generalizations
about changes in the ceramic materials may be made based on
the contents of Pit 1/1A. The most significant limit to
generalization is that Pit 1/1A is a consumption pattern, or
a selection of materials from a larger range, and will
probably not be a complete selection of materials in use at
the time.

Even if the selection of materials is incomplete, it
is still clear from analyzed ceramics at Hatunqolla that
little Cuzco-Inca influence had affected the local ceramic
tradition before the founding of Hatunqolla. It is also
clear that ceramic materials were directly related to the
local tradition and that the Cuzco-Inca style was not borrowed whole. The sequence allows the impact of the Cuzco-
Inca style on the local ceramic tradition to be understood
as an ongoing process.

In Phase 1, imitation of Cuzco-Inca shapes and the
decoration associated with them occurred, an interest that
continued throughout the sequence. The Cuzco bottle was
the focus of this attention. This vessel appears to have
been the Cuzco-Inca shape most copied abroad, and if ceramics
were used to symbolize Inca rule, this shape was its most
important symbol. A Cuzco jar appears to have been imitated
at this time, and there is some small evidence for imitation
Cuzco-Inca plates or bowls. Besides these imitations, the
Cuzco-Inca style was used as a source of new ideas. Features
of vessel firing, paste color and surface finish had a tremendous impact on local ceramic production, most obviously

in Phase 1. Bowls, a major component of the local ceramic
shape inventory, also became considerably shallower under
Cuzco influence.

The Incaization of ceramics reached its greatest extent
in Phase 2. Many more Cuzco-Inca shapes were imitated, and
extremely fine imitations were produced. Moreover, some of
these imitations were made in the local utilitarian paste.
At the same time, it is clear that local imitations cover only
a certain range of the Cuzco-Inca style as represented by
provenienced collections in Cuzco. Although imitations of
individual Cuzco-Inca vessels could be excellent, there is no
evidence that the relationships between Cuzco-Inca vessel
shapes, evident from associated Cuzco-Inca materials, were
perceived by local imitators. Moreover, in the case of two
vessel shapes, the Cuzco bottle and the Cuzco jar, the reconstructed size of the Hatunqolla imitations fell outside the
size ranges of these vessels in the Cuzco-Inca style. The
rules which governed the Cuzco-Inca style, like the grammar
of a language, were not understood. At the same time, it is
apparent that the degree of Cuzco-Inca influence on local ceramics is greater in Hatunqolla than in many parts of the empire.

In Phase 3, almost the same group of Cuzco-Inca shapes
and their decoration were imitated, with the exception of
bowls. The bowls were decorated with standard Cuzco-Inca
band designs in a Cuzco-Inca design composition, but a few
shape features which appear to have originated locally
were incorporated. Changes in the other vessels appear to
be related to changes in the Cuzco-Inca style itself. For

example, Mode B decoration, a distinctive arrangement of
band and panel designs associated with the Cuzco bottle,
appears for the first time, and though pinwheel panels
appeared in Phase 2, they are more common in Phase 3.
Imitation Inca vessels continue to be made in the local
utilitarian paste. The same shapes are made in Phase 3 as
were made in Phase 2, but there is a marked increase in the
number of pedestal dish fragments in Phase 3. These vessels
were used for cooking in the Cuzco region, and their increased
importance in the Hatunqolla refuse may indicate an increased
penetration of aspects of Inca culture.

Throughout the sequence, style change occurred which was
unrelated to Cuzco-Inca influence. The innovation in Phase
2 is especially notable. A purely local development was the
adoption of a popular new design composition called medallion
decoration. A tremendous variety in shapes with local antecedents was also produced, particularly in the bowl categories.
It was during Phase 2 that the inventory of imitation Inca
shapes greatly expanded, and it appears that a wave of innovation affected the entire style. It is interesting to note
that this round of innovation did not occur at the beginning
of strong Cuzco influence, though strong Cuzco influence was
detectable in the first phase.

Another index of Incaization in the local material
tradition is the presence of clustered rectangular dwellings
in Phase 3 and perhaps earlier. Little is known about pre-
Inca house types or planning in the Lake Titicaca region,
but evidence from the Lupaca province, the Pacajes provinces

and from Sillustani itself, suggests that houses were round
and arranged in rows (Hyslop, 1977b, p. 221; Rydén, 1947,
pp. 185-186, 288-289, maps 33, 34, 38, figs. 119, 131, 132,
134; Tschopik, Marion, 1946, pl. IIa, d). If the remains of
a wall in Levels 7 and 8 of Pit 1/1A indicate a house construction, it was probably circular. This wall was much less
substantial than the excavated house of Pit 1/1A, like
circular houses excavated in the southern Lake Titicaca
basin. Stone was used only as a foundation, and the upper
portion of the structure appears to have been built of some
other material. The house uncovered in Pit 1/1A was rectangular and was part of a house cluster. This pattern
probably resulted from contact with Cuzco. The superposition
of this house on an earlier circular one is another likely
example of Incaization.

A third example is provided by the use of fancy Cuzco
stone masonry in the burial towers of Sillustani. As mentioned earlier, Sillustani was very likely the necropolis of
the Qolla dynasty resident at Hatunqolla. Burial in burial
towers or chullpas was a high status form of burial, commented
upon by several early writers (Cieza de León, 1924, cap. C,
pp. 291-292, cap. CI, p. 293). Sillustani is the location of
more chullpas in good Inca style masonry than any other site
known in the Lake Titicaca region (Hyslop, 1977a; Tapia Bueno,
1975, Ruiz Estrada, 1973a; Tschopik, Marion, 1946). The occurrence of elaborate Inca stonework in the provinces is rare
enough to make the amount of it present at Sillustani seem
remarkable. Fancy Cuzco masonry is usually associated only

with constructions undertaken by the Inca government. The
chullpas in the Lake Titicaca region were part of a very
elaborate burial ritual that was unlike Cuzco practice, and
the use of Cuzco stone masonry techniques was probably of
Qolla inspiration. Parallel to the ceramic evidence, the
chullpas are evidence for a vigorous local tradition
incorporating ideas from Cuzco.

The chullpas are silent evidence for the degree of Inca
penetration into Hatunqolla material culture, evidence the
refuse could not provide for its lack of specific association
with individuals. There were 26 burial towers which appear
to have been built mainly or entirely using Cuzco masonry
techniques. Many others had lower courses built of this
kind of masonry, with other material used in the construction
of the walls above. The number of burial towers which
incorporated Cuzco masonry indicate that quite a few individuals were buried in Cuzco influenced burial towers.
These numbers could be greatly increased if each chullpa
contained multiple burials. At the same time, the number of
burial towers indicate that not everyone from Hatunqolla
was buried in chullpas with Cuzco style masonry. Moreover,
Ruiz Estrada was able to associate materials contemporary
with the occupation of Hatunqolla with Sillustani chullpas
built with field stone masonry (vessels in the Sillustani
Museum).

The Incaization of Hatunqolla is apparent from the
material remains, but interpreting it is another matter.

The question is an open one, though historical information
adds an interesting dimension to its consideration.

The material remains appear to express some kind of
identity between Hatunqolla and Cuzco. Hatunqolla was like
Cuzco in many respects. The town was founded during the time
of the Inca empire and was presumably laid out by Inca
planners (Julien, 1979). The layout of shrines was also
patterned after the layout of shrines in Cuzco, although
this similarity may not have been physically evident to the
observer. Hatunqolla was also the location of numerous
Inca buildings, including a temple of the state religion
and a multitude of storehouses. A convent of women chosen by
the Inca government was located there; these women and other
individuals served the official state religion. A great number of foreigners were also resettled in the area. Finally,
Hatunqolla was one of four highland storage centers
designated for the deposit of coastal tribute.

Like Cuzco, Hatunqolla was the center of administrative
activities. The centralization probably afforded the local
people a number of opportunities in exchange for their participation in the Inca government. Local elites staffed a
recruitment organization, but a number of other individuals
of more common descent participated in the government as
officers in charge of permanently assigned tributaries, a
number of whom were craft specialists who produced for the
Inca government. These officers very likely gained some
prestige through their association with the Inca government.

It is apparent from a study of ceramic and architectural styles that these relationships with the empire were given material expression. The analogy between the roles of Cuzco and Hatunqolla was a strong one, and it was obviously perceived by the local residents.

At the same time, the people of the Lake Titicaca region, who shared a Qolla identity (Chp. II), had a reputation for being rebels. At least two major rebellions were staged, one of which was urgent enough to require Thupa 'Inka, the tenth Inka, to leave a military campaign in progress and hasten to reconquer the Lake Titicaca region, a feat which took an estimated three years. One of the intriguing aspects of Qolla rebellions was that a Qolla leader would make a declaration naming himself as the new "Inka." In the case of the rebellion mentioned a moment ago, a Qolla leader from the northern Lake Titicaca region tried to foment a general uprising in the area south of Cuzco, and named himself "Pachakuti 'Inka." Pachakuti 'Inka, the ninth Inka, usurped the reign of his father; his name, Pachakuti, literally meant "cataclysm" (González Holguín, 1952, p. 270). By using this name, the Qolla leader was making his intentions to usurp Inca authority very clear. Even after the European arrival, a member of the Qari family of the Lupaca province, also Qolla in identity, declared himself to be "son of the sun," a title only the Inka could claim during the empire, and tried to unite the Lake Titicaca region under his rulership (Sitio del Cuzco, 1934, p. 121).

These ambitions are consistent with what we know about
Qolla ambitions before the Inca conquest. At that time
Zapana of Hatunqolla held a large territory, apparently the
result of his military conquests. Qari of the Lupaca
territory attempted to unseat Zapana because, in the words
of Cieza de León, in the Qolla region "there was only one
lord" (1967, cap. XLI, p. 139). Both the rivalry and
imperial ambitions were evident before the Inca conquest of
the region, and they surfaced again not only during the Inca
empire, but afterwards.

If only material remains were available for a study of
the Qollas under the Inca empire, then it would be reasonable
to claim that this group provided staunch support for Inca
rule. Historical information informs us that at the time of
the Inca conquest the Qollas were embarked on a similar path
of territorial expansion. It also documents Qolla attempts
to win their own independence. Insight from a consideration
of the historical sources suggests another interpretation
of the material remains. It appears that the material
expressions of identity with the symbols of Inca rule were
not necessarily an expression of loyalty. They may well have
been expressions of an identity with Inca goals by a people
who had not forgotten its own imperial ambitions.

Appendix

Principal Ceramic Pastes at Hatunqolla

Paste A:

This paste fires to a fairly bright orange, sometimes with a strong pinkish cast near the surface. It seems not to be as fine grained as the other principal pastes in evidence at Hatunqolla, and the breaks are characteristically uneven. Paste A has the visual consistency of cookie dough (Tollhouse variety). Unlike the other principal pastes, Paste A has a good quantity of temper, making it certain that the addition of temper was deliberate in nearly all cases. The temper consists mainly of clear quartzite particles, a smaller quantity of milky quartzite and a very small quantity of mica. Infrequently there are natural inclusions such as small, flat transparent particles of gray quartzite and fine sand. The quartzite is quite varied in size, and the visible grains are frequently as large as .5 mm. Their density is usually between 3 and 7 per sq. mm. The mica also varies a lot in size, but only the larger grains are noticeable. Two varieties of this paste are found at Hatunqolla. One is consistently oxidized to an orange color, while the other is not as well oxidized, a result of inadequate firing (low fired variety).

Paste C:

This paste may well be two different pastes.   It was
defined on the basis of both texture and temper.   Some
examples fire to a very clear cream color with no orange.
Most examples fire to a color between light and bright orange.
There is a great deal of difference in the intensity of the
color, and some differences in color value.   The cream paste
is more related to the local pre-Inca Sillustani style pastes.
The orange paste is apparently related to material showing
influence from the Cuzco-Inca style and is appropriately the
paste in which most of the Cuzco related material was fabricated. The consistency of Paste C is fine grained and can
be very fine grained when there is little visible temper.
When examples of Paste D and Paste C of the same degree of
fineness are compared, Paste C can be seen to have a more
even consistency, characterized by more even breaks.   The
temper consists of many milky quartzite particles, some
clear quartzite particles and a few thin shiny black particles. A large lump of rock composed of these three ingredients was lodged in a sherd found in Level 5, so it is highly
possible that this material was ground to produce the temper
for Paste C. The quantity of temper is like that described
for Paste D, except in slightly larger quantity. Again, the
size of the grains of quartzite is from .6 mm. down, with
most grains at .1 mm. or less. Usually there are from five to
ten visible grains per sq. mm. A fair number of examples of
Paste C are almost temperless and may form a class apart.
Since there are also minority pastes which fire to a cream

or orange color, these temperless sherds are much harder to
classify as Paste C. A variant of the cream fired Paste C
includes a number of coarse grains of mica.

Paste D:

This paste fires to a medium orange color with a slightly
pinkish cast and frequently appears to have a dull purplish
pink color all the way through the cross-section. This
coloring is probably due to a failure to totally oxidize the
carbon during firing. It is finer grained than Paste A and
the breaks are evener, though the consistency still resembles
cookie dough. The amount of temper varies from a moderate
amount to possibly none at all. Where little temper is used,
the paste grains themselves are quite small. There is a
small amount of evidence to suggest that the pinkish cast
is due to the addition of finely ground sandstone. Pink
sandstone, as well as white and yellow sandstone, occur as
natural inclusions in the paste. The only usual and obvious
addition is clear quartzite. The quartzite grains are not as
large as the grains of Paste A. Though some are as large
as .6 mm., most are .1 mm. or smaller. The quantity varies a
great deal, from one to eight grains per sq. mm., but again,
some examples seem almost temperless. Two variants of this
paste occur at Hatunqolla, one with a scattering of fine mica,
and another with a few coarse grains of mica. When fine mica
is added, it gives a shiny appearance to the surface,
and between 15 and 30 grains per sq. mm. can be counted on
the surface.

Bibliography

Acosta, José de

   1940   Historia natural y moral de las indias...[1590].
              Edición preparada por Edmundo O'Gorman. Fondo de
              Cultura Económica, México.

Araníbar, Carlos

   1967   Introducción. In, El Señorío de los Incas (2a.
              parte de la Crónica del Peru), pp. ix-xcvi.
              Fuentes e Investigaciones para la Historia del
              Perú, Instituto de Estudios Peruanos, Lima.

Bandelier, Adolph F.

   1910   The islands of Titicaca and Koati, illustrated.
              Hispanic Society of America, New York.

Bandera, Damian de la

   1968   Relación del origen e Gobierno que los Ingas
              tuvieron...[1557]. In, Biblioteca Peruana, primera
              serie, tomo III, pp. 491-510. Editores Técnicos
              Asociados, Lima.

Bertonio, Ludovico

   1879a   Arte de la lengua aymara [1603]. Publicada de
              nuevo por Julio Platzmann. Edición facsimilaria.
              B. G. Teubner, Leipzig.

Bertonio, Ludovico

  1879b   Vocabulario de la lengua aymara [1612]. Compuesto

             por el P. Ludovico Bertonio, publicado de nuevo por

             Julio Platzmann. Edición facsimilaria. B. G.

             Teubner, Leipzig. 2 vols.

Betanzos, Juan de

  1924   Suma y narración de los incas...[1551]. Colección

             de Libros y Documentos referentes a la Historia del

             Perú, tomo 8 (2a. serie), anotaciones y concordancias

             con las crónicas de indias por Horacio H. Urteaga,

             pp. 75-208. Lima.

Bingham, Hiram

  1930   Machu Picchu, a citadel of the Incas. Report of

             the explorations and excavations made in 1911, 1912

             and 1915 under the auspices of Yale University and

             the National Geographic Society. Yale University

             Press, New Haven.

Bouysse-Cassagne, Thérèse

  1975   Pertenencia étnica, status económico y lenguas en

             Charcas a fines del siglo XVI. In, Tasa de la

             visita general de Francisco de Toledo, introducción

             y versión paleográfica de Noble David Cook, pp.

             312-327. Universidad Nacional Mayor de San Marcos,

             Lima.

  1978   L'espace Aymara: urco et uma. Annales; Économies,

             Sociétés, Civilisations, no. 5-6, Septembre-Décembre,

             pp. 1057-1080. Librairie Armand Colin, Paris.

Cabello Valboa, Miguel

1951   Miscelánea antárctica, una historia del Perú antiguo
[1586]. Universidad Nacional Mayor de San Marcos,
Facultad de Letras, Instituto de Etnología, Lima.

Calancha, Antonio de la

1638   Coronica Moralizada del orden de San Avgvstin en el
Perv, con svcesos egenplares en esta monarqvia.
Barcelona.

Calancha, Antonio de la, and Torres, Bernardo de

1972   Crónicas augustinianas del Perú. Edición, introducción y notas por Manuel Merino. Biblioteca "Missionalia
Hispánica", tomo 17. C.S.I.C., Madrid. 2 vols.

Capoche, Luis

1959   Relación general de la villa imperial de Potosí, un
capítulo inédito en la historia del nuevo mundo
[1585]. Prólogo y notas de Lewis Hanke. Biblioteca
de Autores Españoles, desde la formación del lenguaje
hasta nuestros días (continuación), tomo 122, pp.
9-221. Ediciones Atlas, Madrid.

Cárdenas, Martín

1979   Manual de plantas económicas de Bolivia. Imprenta
Ichthus, Cochabamba.

Castro, Cristóbal de, and Ortega Morejón, Diego

1974   La relación de Chincha [1558]. Edición por Juan
Carlos Crespo. Historia y Cultura, 8, pp. 91-104.
Museo Nacional de Historia, Instituto Nacional de
Cultura, Lima.

Chamberlain, Alexander F.

1910　　　The Uran:　A New South American linguistic stock.
　　　　　American Anthropologist, new series, vol. 12, no. 3
　　　　　(July-Sept.), pp. 417-424.　Lancaster, Pennsylvania.

Chávez, Sergio Jorge

1975　　　The Arapa and Thunderbolt stelae:　A case of
　　　　　stylistic identity with implications for Pucara
　　　　　influences in the area of Tiahuanaco.　Ñawpa Pacha,
　　　　　13, pp. 3-26.　Institute of Andean Studies, Berkeley.

Cieza de León, Pedro de

1924　　　La crónica general del Perú [1550].　Anotada y
　　　　　concordada con las crónicas de Indias, por Horacio
　　　　　H. Urteaga.　Colección Urteaga, Historiadores
　　　　　clásicos del Perú, tomo 7.　Lima.

1967　　　El Señorío de los Incas (2a. parte de la Crónica
　　　　　del Perú)[1553].　Introducción de Carlos Araníbar.
　　　　　Fuentes e Investigaciones para la Historia del Perú,
　　　　　Instituto de Estudios Peruanos.　Lima.

Cobo, P. Bernabé

1964　　　Historia del nuevo mundo [1653].　Estudio preliminar
　　　　　y edición del P. Francisco Mateos de la misma
　　　　　compañía.　Biblioteca de Autores Españoles, desde la
　　　　　formación del lenguaje hasta nuestros días
　　　　　(continuación), tomos 91-92.　Ediciones Atlas, Madrid.

Cordero, Ariel; Casani, Rosa Maria de; Valencia, Vilma; and
Casani, Felix

1971　　　Hatunqolla.　Centro de Estudios y Reflexiones
　　　　　del Altiplano, Puno.

Cordero Miranda, Gregorio

1971   Reconocimiento arqueológico de Pucarani y sitios
adyacentes. Pumapunku, no. 3, segundo semestre,
julio-diciembre, pp. 7-27. H. Municipalidad de
La Paz, La Paz.

Crespo, Alberto

1972   El corregimiento de La Paz. 1548-1600. Empresa
Editora "Urquizo Ltda.," La Paz.

Diez de San Miguel, Garci

1964   Visita hecha a la provincia de Chucuito por
Garci Diez de San Miguel en el año 1567. Versión
paleográfica de la visita y una biografía del
visitador por Waldemar Espinoza Soriano. Documentos
Regionales para la Etnología y Etnohistoria Andinas,
Tomo I. Ediciones de la Casa de la Cultura del
Perú, Lima.

Eaton, George F.

1916   The collection of osteological material from
Machu Picchu. Memoirs of the Connecticut Academy
of Arts and Sciences, vol. V, May. New Haven.

Espinoza Soriano, Waldemar

1967   El primer informe etnológico sobre Cajamarca.
Año de 1540. Revista Peruana de Cultura, tomo 11-12,
pp. 5-41. Lima.

1969-1970 Los mitmas yungas de Collique en Cajamarca,
siglos XV, XVI, y XVII. Revista del Museo Nacional,
tomo XXXVI, pp. 9-57. Lima.

Falcón, Francisco

1867   Representación hecha por el Licenciado Falcón

            en concilio provincial, sobre los daños y molestias

            que se hacen á los indios [c. 1583]. Colección

            de Documentos Inéditos relativos al Descubrimiento,

            Conquista y Organización de las antiguas Posesiones

            españoles de América y Oceanía sacados de los

            Archivos del Reino, y muy especialmente del de

            Indias, por D. Luis Torres de Mendoza, tomo VII,

            pp. 451-495. Madrid.

Fernández Baca, Jenaro

1973   Motivos de ornamentación de la cerámica Inca-Cuzco.

            Tomo I. Librería Studium, Lima.

Flores Ochoa, Jorge A.

1972   El reino Lupaqa y el actual control vertical de

            la ecología. Historia y Cultura, 6, pp. 195-205.

            Lima.

Garcilaso de la Vega, "el Inca"

1959   Comentarios reales de los Incas [1604]. Estudio

            preliminar y notas de José Durand. Universidad

            Nacional Mayor de San Marcos, Patronato del Libro

            Universitario, Lima.

Gasparini, Graziano, and Margolies, Luise

1977   Arquitectura Inka. Centro de Investigaciones

            Historicas y Estéticas, Facultad de Arquitectura

            y Urbanismo, Universidad Central de Venezuela,

            Caracas.

González Holguín, Diego

1952   Vocabulario de la lengua general de todo el Peru
        llamada Qquicchua, o del Inca [1608]. Nueva
        edición, con un prólogo de Raul Porras Barrenechea.
        Imprenta Santa Maria, Lima.

Guaman Poma de Ayala, Felipe

1936   Nueva corónica y buen gobierno (codex péruvien
        illustré)[1615]. Travaux et Mémoires de l'Institut
        d'Ethnologie, XXIII. Paris.

Gutiérrez Flores, Pedro

1964   Padron de los mil indios ricos de la provincia
        de Chucuito y de los pueblos, parcialidades y
        ayllos que son y la cantidad de ganado de la
        tierra que cada uno tiene...[1574]. Versión
        paleográfica de Jennifer S. H. Brown. In, Visita
        hecha a la provincia de Chucuito por Garci Diez de
        San Miguel en el año 1567, versión paleográfica
        de Waldemar Espinoza Soriano, pp. 303-363.
        Ediciones de la Casa de la Cultura del Perú, Lima.

Hardoy, Jorge Enrique

1964   Ciudades precolombinas. Ediciones Infinito,
        Buenos Aires.

Helmer, Marie

1955-1956 La visitación de los yndios Chupachos; Inka et
        encomendero, 1549. Travaux de l'Institut Francais
        Andines, tomo V, volume unique, pp. 3-50.
        Lima.

Hyslop, John

1977a   Chullpas of the Lupaca zone of the Peruvian high
          plateau. Journal of Field Archaeology, vol. 4, no.
          2 (summer), pp. 149-170. Boston University, Boston.

1977b   Hilltop cities in Peru. Archaeology, vol. 30, no.
          4 (July), pp. 218-225. New York.

Jiménez de la Espada, Marcos

1885   Relaciones Geográficas de Indias...Perú.
          Tomo II. Publícalas el Ministerio de Fomento,
          Tipografía de Manuel G. Hernández, Madrid.

Julien, Catherine Jean

1978   Inca administration in the Titicaca basin as
          reflected at the provincial capital of Hatunqolla.
          Thesis (Ph.D), Department of Anthropology,
          University of California, Berkeley.

1979   Investigaciones recientes en la capital de los
          Qolla, Hatunqolla, Puno. Arqueologia Peruana,
          Seminario "Investigaciones Arqueologicas en el
          Peru 1976," Abril de 1976, organizado por la
          Universidad Nacional Mayor de San Marcos y con el
          auspicio de la Comision para Intercambio Educativo
          entre los Estados Unidos y el Peru, compilado por
          Ramiro Matos Mendieta, pp. 199-213. Lima.

1981   A late burial from Cerro Azoguini, Puno. Ñawpa
          Pacha 19, pp. 129-154. Berkeley.

1982   Inca decimal administration in the Lake Titicaca
          region. The Inca and Aztec States, 1400-1800;
          anthropology and history, Studies in Anthropology,
          pp. 119-151. Academic Press, New York and London.

ms.   Las tumbas de Sacsahuaman.

Kidder, Alfred II

1943 Some early sites in the northern Lake Titicaca
Basin. Papers of the Peabody Museum of American
Archaeology and Ethnology, Harvard University,
vol. XXVII, no. 1. Cambridge.

Kubler, George

1962 The art and architecture of ancient America;
Mexican, Maya, and Andean peoples. The Pelican
History of Art, Penguin Books, Baltimore.

La Barre, Weston

1941 The Uru of the Rio Desaguadero. American
Anthropologist, new series, vol. 43, no. 4, pt. 1
(Oct.-Dec.), pp. 493-522. Menasha.

Latcham, Ricardo E.

1938 Arqueología de la región atacameña. Universidad
de Chile, Santiago.

Lizárraga, Reginaldo de

1909 Descripción breve de toda la tierra del Perú,
Tucumán, Río de la Plata y Chile [1605]. Edición
por M. Serrano y Sanz. Historiadores de Indias,
tomo II. Nueva Biblioteca de Autores Españoles,
tomo 15, pp. 485-660. Bailly Bailliére é hijos,
Editores, Madrid.

Llanos, Luis A.

1936 Trabajos arqueológicos en el Departamento del
Cuzco. Revista del Museo Nacional, tomo V, no. 2,
II semestre, pp. 123-156. Lima.

Loredo, Rafael

1958   Los repartos. Bocetos para la nueva historia del
          Perú, Lima.

Lumbreras, Luis Guillermo

1974   The peoples and cultures of ancient Peru.   Trans-
          lated by Betty J. Meggers. Smithsonian Institution
          Press, Washington.

McBain, Heath

1961   The Adolph Bandelier archaeological collection
          from Pelechuco and Charassani, Bolivia, Imprenta
          de la Universidad Nacional del Litoral, Rosario.

Matienzo, Juan de

1967   Gobierno del Perú (1567). Edition et étude
          préliminaire par Guillermo Lohmann Villena.
          Travaux de l'Institut Francais d'Études Andines,
          tome XI. Lima.

Maúrtua, Victor M.

1906   Juicio de Límites entre el Perú y Bolivia,
          prueba Peruana presentada al Gobierno de la
          República Argentina. Imprenta de Henrich y Comp.,
          Barcelona. 14 vols.

Means, Phillip Ainsworth

1932   Fall of the Inca empire; and the Spanish rule in
          Peru: 1530-1780. Charles Scribner's Sons, New York.

Menzel, Dorothy

1976   Pottery style and society in ancient Peru; art as
          a mirror of history in the Ica Valley, 1350-1570.
          University of California Press, Berkeley.

Miranda, Cristóbal de

1906   Relación de los corregimientos y otros oficios
            que se proveen en los Reynos é provincias del
            Piru, en el distrito é gobernación del Vissorrey
            dellos [1583]. In, Juicio de Límites..., edited
            by Victor M. Maúrtua, tomo I, pp. 168-280. Imprenta
            de Henrich y Comp., Barcelona.

1925   Relación hecha por el Virrey D. Martín Enríquez
            de los oficios que se proveen en la gobernación de
            los reinos y provincias del Perú, 1583. In,
            Gobernantes del Peru, cartas y papeles, siglo XVI,
            Documentos del Archivo de Indias, publicación
            dirigida por D. Roberto Levillier, tomo IX, el
            Virrey Martín Enríquez, 1581-1583, pp. 114-230.
            Imprenta de Juan Pueyo, Madrid.

Molina, Cristóbal de

1943   Fabulas y ritos de los Incas [1575]. Los
            Pequeños Grandes Libros de Historia Americana,
            serie I, tomo IV, pp. 7-92. Lima.

Montesinos, Fernando de

1906   Anales del Perú [1644]. In, Juicio de Límites...,
            edited by Victor M. Maúrtua, tomos 13-14.
            Imprenta de Henrich y Comp., Barcelona.

Morales, Adolfo de

1977   Repartimiento de tierras por el Inca Huayna Capac
            (Testimonio de un documento de 1556). Universidad
            Boliviana Mayor de San Simón, Departamento de
            Arqueología, Museo Arqueológico, Cochabamba.

Mori, Juan de, and Malpartida, Hernando Alonso

1967   La visitación de los pueblos de indios [1549].

            In, Visita de la provincia de León de Huánuco en

            1562, tomo 1, visita de las cuatro waranqa de los

            Chupachu, Iñigo Ortíz de Zúñiga, pp. 289-310.

            Documentos para la Historia y Etnología de Huánuco

            y la Selva Central, tomo 1. Huánuco.

Morris, Craig, and Thompson, Donald E.

1970   Huánuco Viejo: An Inca administrative center.

            American Antiquity, vol. 35, no. 3 (July), pp.

            344-362. Salt Lake City.

Morúa, Martín de

1946   Historia del orígen y geneología real de los

            Incas del Peru [c. 1605]. Introducción, notas y

            arreglo por Constantino Bayle. Biblioteca

            "Missionalia Hispánica," vol. II. Consejo Superior

            de Investigaciones Científicas, Instituto Santo

            Toribio de Mogrovejo, Madrid.

Murra, John Victor

1964   Una apreciación etnológica de la visita. In,

            Visita hecha a la provincia de Chucuito por Garci

            Diez de San Miguel en el año 1567, versión paleográfica

            de la visita y una biografía del visitador por

            Waldemar Espinoza Soriano, Documentos Regionales

            para la Etnología y Etnohistoria Andinas, tomo I,

            pp. 421-444. Ediciones de la Casa de la Cultura

            del Perú, Lima.

Murra, John Victor

1968   An Aymara kingdom in 1567. Ethnohistory, vol. XV,
          no. 2, pp. 115-151. Seattle.

1972   El control "vertical" de un máximo de pisos
          ecológicos en la economía de las sociedades andinas.
          In, Visita de la Provincia de León de Huánuco en
          1562, tomo II, visita de los Yacha y Mitmaqkuna
          cuzqueños encomendados en Juan Sánchez Falcón,
          Iñigo Ortíz de Zúñiga, pp. 429-476. Universidad
          Nacional Hermilio Valdizán, Facultad de Letras y
          Educación, Huánuco.

1978a   Los límites y las limitaciones del "archipiélago
          vertical" en los Andes. Avances, Revista Boliviana
          de Estudios Históricos y Sociales, no. 1 (febrero),
          pp. 75-80. La Paz.

1978b   Los olleros del Inka: hacia una historia y
          arqueología del Qollasuyu. Historia, Problema y
          Promesa; homenaje a Jorge Basadre, pp. 415-423.
          Pontificia Universidad Católica del Perú, Lima.

Ortíz de Zúñiga, Iñigo

1967   Visita de la Provincia de León de Huánuco en
          1562, tomo 1, visita de las cuatro waranqa de los
          Chupachu. Edición a cargo de John V. Murra.
          Documentos para la Historia y Etnología de Huánuco
          y la Selva Central, tomo 1. Huánuco.

Ortíz de Zúñiga, Iñigo

1972   Visita de la Provincia de León de Huánuco en
            1562, tomo II, visita de los Yacha y Mitmaqkuna
            cuzqueños encomendados en Juan Sánchez Falcón.
            Edición a cargo de John V. Murra. Universidad
            Nacional Hermilio Valdizán, Facultad de Letras y
            Educación, Huánuco.

Pachacuti Yamqui Salcamaygua, Juan de Santa Cruz

1924   Relación de antiguedades deste reyno del pirú
            [c. 1600]. Colección de Libros y Documentos
            referentes a la Historia del Perú, anotaciones y
            concordancias con las crónicas de indias por
            Horacio H. Urteaga, tomo IX (2a. serie), pp.
            125-234. Lima.

Paredes Candia, Antonio

1966   La danza folklórica en Bolivia. Ediciones Isla,
            La Paz.

Pease G. Y., Franklin

1973   Cambios en el Reino Lupaqa (1567-1661). Historia
            y Cultura, 7, pp. 89-105. Lima.

Pizarro, Pedro

1944   Relación del descubrimiento y conquista de los
            reinos del Perú y del gobierno y orden que los
            naturales tenián, y tesoros que en ella se hallaron,
            y de las demás cosas que en él han sucedido hasta el
            día de la fecha [1571]. Editorial Futuro, Buenos
            Aires.

Polo de Ondegardo, Juan

1916   Relación de los fundamentos acerca del notable

            daño que resulta de no guardar a los indios sus

            fueros, junio 26 de 1571. Colección de Libros y

            Documentos referentes a la Historia del Perú, notas

            biográficas y concordancias de los textos por

            Horacio H. Urteaga, tomo III, pp. 45-188. Lima.

1917   Del linaje de los Ingas y como conquistaron

            [1571]. Colección de Libros y Documentos referentes

            a la Historia del Perú, notas biográficas y

            concordancias de los textos por Horacio H. Urteaga,

            tomo IV, pp. 45-94. Lima.

1940   Informe al Licenciado Briviesca de Muñatones sobre

            la perpetuidad de las encomiendas del Peru [1561].

            Revista Histórica, tomo 13, pp. 125-196. Lima.

Portugal, Maks

1957   Arqueología de La Paz. In, Arqueología Boliviana

            (Primera Mesa Redonda), publicación dirigida por

            Carlos Ponce Sanginés, pp. 343-401. Biblioteca

            Paceña, Alcaldía Municipal, La Paz.

Ramírez, Balthasar

1936   Description del Reyno del Piru del sitio temple.

            Prouincias, obispados.y ciudades. de los Naturales

            de sus lenguas y trage...[1597]. Quellen zur

            Kulturgeschichte des prakolumbischen Amerika,

            edited by Hermann Trimborn, pp. 1-122. Strecker und

            Schroder Verlag, Stuttgart.

Ramos Gavilán, Alonso

1976   Historia de Nuestra Señora de Copacabana.

            Segunda edición completa, según la impresion

            príncipe de 1621. Academía Boliviana de la Historia,

            La Paz.

Romero, Emilio

1928   Monografía del Departamento de Puno. Imp.

            Torres Aguirre, Lima.

Rowe, John Howland

1944   An introduction to the archaeology of Cuzco.

            Papers of the Peabody Museum of American Archaeology

            and Ethnology, vol. XXVII, no. 2. Harvard

            University, Cambridge.

1945   Absolute chronology in the Andean area. American

            Antiquity, vol. 10, no. 3 (January), pp. 265-284.

            Menasha.

1946   Inca Culture at the Time of the Spanish Conquest.

            Handbook of South American Indians, edited by

            Julian H. Steward, vol. 2, pp. 183-330. Bureau of

            American Ethnology, Bulletin 143. Smithsonian

            Institution, Washington.

1948   The kingdom of Chimor. Acta Americana, vol. VI,

            nos. 1-2, pp. 26-59. México.

1950   Sound patterns in three Inca dialects.

            International Journal of American Linguistics, vol.

            16, no. 3 (July), pp. 137-148. Indiana University,

            Bloomington.

Rowe, John Howland

1957   The Incas under Spanish colonial institutions.
            Hispanic American Historical Review, vol. XXXVII,
            no. 2 (May), pp. 155-199. Durham.

1960   The origins of creator worship among the Incas.
            Culture in History: Essays in Honor of Paul Radin,
            edited by Stanley Diamond, pp. 408-429. Columbia
            University Press, New York.

1962   Stages and periods in archaeological interpreta-
            tion. Southwestern Journal of Anthropology,
            vol. 18, no. 1 (Spring), pp. 40-54. Albuquerque.

Ruiz Estrada, Arturo

1973a   Informe de Sillustani. Presentado a Gen. Enrique
            Falconí Mejía, June 8, 1973, Puno.

1973b   Las ruinas de Sillustani. Tesis de doctorado,
            Programa de Antropología, Universidad Nacional
            Mayor de San Marcos, Lima.

Rydén, Stig

1947   Archaeological researches in the highlands of
            Bolivia. Göteborg.

Sánchez Albornóz, Nicolás

1973   El indio en el alto Perú a fines del siglo XVII.
            Seminario de Historia Rural Andina, Lima.

Sancho de la Hoz, Pedro

1938   Relación para S. M. de lo sucedido en la conquista
            y pacificación de estas provincias de la Nueva
            Castilla y de la calidad de la tierra...[1534].
            Biblioteca de la Cultura Peruana, primera serie, no.
            2, pp. 117-185. Desclée, De Brouwer, Paris.

Santillán, Hernando de

1968   Relación del origen, descendencia, política y
            gobierno de los incas [1563]. Biblioteca Peruana,
            primera serie, tomo III, pp. 375-463. Editores
            Técnicos Asociados, Lima.

Sarmiento de Gamboa, Pedro

1906   Geschichte des Inkareiches von Pedro Sarmiento de
            Gamboa [1572]. Herausgegeben von Richard
            Pietschmann. Abhandlungen der Königlichen
            Gesellschaft der Wissenschaften zu Göttingen,
            Philologisch-Historische Klasse, Neue Folge, Band
            VI, No. 4. Weidmannsche Buchhandlung, Berlin.

Schmidt, Max

1929   Kunst und Kultur von Peru. Propyläen-Verlag,
            Berlin.

{Segovia, Bartolomé de}

1943   Relación de muchas cosas acaecidas en el Peru
            [1553]. Los Pequeños Grandes Libros de Historia
            Americana, serie I, tomo IV, pp. 3-88. Lima.

Shepard, Anna Osler

1965   Ceramics for the archaeologist. Carnegie
            Institution of Washington, publication 609.
            Washington.

Sitio del Cuzco

1934   Relación del sitio del Cuzco y principio de las
            guerras civiles del Perú hasta la muerte de Diego
            de Almagro, 1535-1539 [1539]. Colección de
            Libros y Documentos referentes a la Historia del

Peru, anotaciones y concordancias con las crónicas
de indias por Horacio H. Urteaga, tomo X (2a. serie),
pp. 1-133. Lima.

Stark, Louisa

1972   Machaj-juyai: secret language of the Callahuayas.
Papers in Andean Linguistics, vol. I, pp. 199-227.
Madison.

Tapia Bueno, Walter

1975   Sillustani. Editorial "Qolla Cultura," Puno.

Toledo, Francisco de

1975   Tasa de la visita general de Francisco de Toledo
[1570-1573]. Introducción y versión paleográfica
de Noble David Cook. Universidad Nacional Mayor de
San Marcos, Lima.

Tschopik, Harry

1946   The Aymara. Handbook of South American Indians,
edited by Julian H. Steward, vol. 2, pp. 501-573.
Bureau of American Ethnology, Bulletin 143,
Smithsonian Insitution, Washington.

Tschopik, Marion Hutchinson

1946   Some notes on the archaeology of the Department of
Puno. Papers of the Peabody Museum of American
Archaeology and Ethnology, vol. XXVII, no. 3.
Harvard University, Cambridge.

Ubbelohde-Doering, Heinrich

1941   Auf dem Königstrassen der Inka. Reisen und
Forschungen in Peru. Verlag Ernst Wasmuth, Berlin.

Vaca de Castro, Cristóbal

  1908   Ordenanzas de tambos, distancias de unos a otros,
                modo de cargar los indios y obligaciones de las
                justicias respectivas hechas en la ciudad del
                Cuzco en 31 de Mayo de 1543. Revista Histórica,
                tomo III, pp. 427-492. Instituto Histórico del
                Perú, Lima.

Valcárcel, Luis Eduardo

  1934a   Sajsawaman redescubierto. Revista del Museo
                Nacional, tomo III, no. 1-2, pp. 3-36. Lima.

  1934b   Los trabajos arqueológicos del Cuzco. II.
                Sajsawaman Redescubierto. (1) Revista del Museo
                Nacional, tomo III, no. 3, pp. 211-234. Lima.

  1935   Los trabajos arqueológicos en el Departamento del
                Cuzco. Sajsawaman Redescubierto. (III) Revista
                del Museo Nacional, tomo IV, no. 2, I semestre,
                pp. 1-24. Lima.

Vellard, Jean

  1960   Notes et documents bibliographiques sur les
                ourous. Travaux de l'Institut Français d'Études
                Andines, tome 8, pp. 29-41. Lima.

Key to Illustrations

Excavation provenience for illustrated ceramics is given by pit and level in abbreviated form. For example, 1A:9 is Pit 1A, Level 9. Four different reductions have been used in producing the plates which contain ceramics. Plate 25 (fig. 99) has been reduced approximately 75%; Plates 20-22, 26 and 43 have been reduced by about 68%; Plates 23-24, 27 and 42 have been reduced about 56%; and the remainder have been reduced by about 47%.

PLATE 7. Fig 1: 1A:9. Fig. 2: 1A:9. Fig. 3: 1A:9. Fig. 4: 1A:10b, 1-SW:8c. Fig. 5: 1A:9. Fig. 6: 1-SW:8c, 1-SW:10c.

PLATE 8. Fig. 7: 1A:10b. Fig. 8: 1A:9. Fig. 9: 1A:9; illustration shows a broad white band painted over a black stripe (painted in outline) and a light red base. Fig. 10: 1A:9; see comment for Fig. 9. Fig. 11: 1A:9. Fig. 12: 1-SW:10c. Fig. 13: 1A:9.

PLATE 9. Fig. 14: 1A:10a. Fig. 15: 1A:10b; orange-red line design is painted on a cream slipped surface (not illustrated). Fig. 16: 1A:10a; see comment for Fig. 9 above. Fig. 17: 1A:9; see comment for Fig. 9 above. Fig. 18: 1A:10b.

Fig. 19: 1A:10b; see comment for Fig. 9 above. Fig. 20:
1A:9; see comment for Fig. 9 above. Fig. 21: 1A:9.

PLATE 10. Fig. 22: 1A:10a. Fig. 23: 1A:10b. Fig. 24:
1A:9. Fig. 25: 1A:9. Fig. 26: 1A:11c. Fig. 27: 1A:10a.

PLATE 11. Fig. 28: 1-SW:10c; interior is unpigmented,
exterior was slipped with a light red but damaged over a
good part of the surface. Fig. 29: 1-SW:10c. Fig. 30:
1A:7b-c. Fig. 31: 1A:8a. Fig. 32: 1A:8a.

PLATE 12. Fig. 33: 1A:8a. Fig. 34: $1A:7a_I$. Fig. 35:
1A:7b-c. Fig. 36: 1A:8a. Fig. 37: 1A:7c.

PLATE 13. Fig. 38: 1A:8a. Fig. 39: 1A:7. Fig. 40:
$1A:7b_I$. Fig. 41: 1A:7c. Fig. 42: 1A:8a. Fig. 43: 1A:8a.
Fig. 44: 1A:8a.

PLATE 14. Fig. 45: 1A:7a. Fig. 46: 1A:8b. Fig. 47:
1A:7. Fig. 48: 1A:7a. Fig. 49: $1A:7b_I$. Fig. 50: 1A:8a.

PLATE 15. Fig. 51: 1A:8a. Fig. 52: 1A:7a. Fig. 53:
1A:7a. Fig. 54: 1A:7a. Fig. 55: 1A:8a. Fig. 56: 1A:8a.

PLATE 16. Fig. 57: 1A:7a. Fig. 58: 1A:7. Fig. 59:
1A:8b. Fig. 60: 1A:8a. Fig. 61: 1A:8a.

PLATE 17. Fig. 62: 1A:8a. Fig. 63: 1A:8a. Fig. 64:
1A:8a. Fig. 65: 1A:8a. Fig. 66: 1A:8a. Fig. 67: 1A:8b.

PLATE 18. Fig. 68: 1A:7. Fig. 69: 1A:8b. Fig. 70:
1A:8a. Fig. 71: 1A:8a. Fig. 72: 1A:8a.

PLATE 19. Fig. 73: 1A:7a. Fig. 74: 1A:8a. Fig. 75:
1A:8a. Fig. 76: 1A:8a. Fig. 77: 1A:8a.

PLATE 20. Fig. 78: 1A:8a. Fig. 79: 1A:7a, 1A:6;
smoking is superimposed on the blue-red surface of the
neck.

PLATE 21. Fig. 80: 1A:7a$_I$. Fig. 81: 1A:7a. Fig. 82: 1A:7. Fig. 83: 1A:7a. Fig. 84: profile outline of Azoguini jar.

PLATE 22. Fig. 85: 1A:8a; smoked surface may not be smoked black, but pigmented. Fig. 86: 1A:7$_I$; see comment for Fig. 85. Fig. 87: 1A:8a; see comment for Fig. 85.

PLATE 23. Fig. 88: 1A:7a. Fig. 89: 1A:8b. Fig. 90: 1A:7. Fig. 91: 1A:7a. Fig. 92: 1A:8b.

PLATE 24. Fig. 93: 1A:8b. Fig. 94: 1A:7a. Fig. 95: 1A:8b, 1A:7b$_I$; see comment to Fig. 85 above. Fig. 96: 1A:8a. Fig. 97: 1A:7a$_I$. Fig. 98: 1A:7a.

PLATE 25. Fig. 99: 1A:7a, 1A:7a$_I$, 1A:7c, 1A:8a.

PLATE 26. Fig. 100: 1A:7$_I$; interior of the neck has a surface treatment like Fig. 85 above. Fig. 101: 1A:8a. Fig. 102: 1A:7a. Fig. 103: 1A:7a$_I$.

PLATE 27. Fig. 104: 1A:8a, 1A:7c.

PLATE 28. Fig. 105: 1A:8a. Fig. 106: 1A:8a. Fig. 107: 1A:7a. Fig. 108: 1A:7a. Fig. 109: 1A:8a. Fig. 110: 1A:8a.

PLATE 29. Fig. 111: 1A:7, 1A:2t, Roadcut 2:6/3a. Fig. 112: 1A:8a, 1A:7a. Fig. 113: 1A:8b, 1A:10a.

PLATE 30. Fig. 114: 1A:8a. Fig. 115: 1A:8b; exterior surface has a firing ghost. Fig. 116: 1A:7a. Fig. 117: 1A:7b-c. Fig. 118: 1A:8b.

PLATE 31. Fig. 119: 1A:7a. Fig. 120: 1A:7b$_I$. Fig. 121: 1A:8a, 1A:2t. Fig. 122: 1A:7a$_I$.

PLATE 32. Fig. 123: 1:3(2f); the black is faded where it occurs over a white surface. Fig. 124: 1A:3. Fig. 125: Testpit 4:4. Fig. 126: Testpit 4:6. Fig. 127: 1A:5.

PLATE 33. Fig. 128: 1A:5. Fig. 129: Testpit 4:4.
Fig. 130: 1A:5. Fig. 131: Testpit 4:6. Fig. 132: 1A:5;
the black is faded where it occurs over the cream slipped or
unpigmented surface. Fig. 133: Testpit 4:7.

PLATE 34. Fig. 134: 1A:5. Fig. 135: 1A:5. Fig. 136:
Testpit 4:4. Fig. 137: Testpit 4:4.

PLATE 35. Fig. 138: Testpit 4:4. Fig. 139: 1A:5.
Fig. 140: Testpit 4:7. Fig. 141: Testpit 4:3.

PLATE 36. Fig. 142: Testpit 4:2. Fig. 143: Testpit 4:4.
Fig. 144: Testpit 4:6. Fig. 145: 1A:5. Fig. 146: 1:3(2f).
Fig. 147: 1A:3.

PLATE 37. Fig. 148: Testpit 4:4. Fig. 149: Testpit 4:7.
Fig. 150: Testpit 4:4. Fig. 151: Testpit 4:5. Fig. 152:
profile drawing of Azoguini bowl.

PLATE 38. Fig. 153: 1A:4. Fig. 154: Testpit 4:6.
Fig. 155: Testpit 4:4. Fig. 156: Testpit 4:2. Fig. 157:
Testpit 4:2. Fig. 158: Testpit 4:7.

PLATE 39. Fig. 159: Testpit 4:2. Fig. 160: 1A:5;
smoking occurs over an unpigmented surface. Fig. 161: 1A:5.
Fig. 162: 1A:5. Fig. 163: 1A:5. Fig. 164: 1A:5.

PLATE 40. Fig. 165: 1A:4. Fig. 166: 1A:5; the design
on the exterior base was incised into the surface before
firing. Fig. 167: Testpit 4:4.

PLATE 41. Fig. 168: 1A:5. Fig. 169: Testpit 4:6.
Fig. 170: 1A:5. Fig. 171: 1A:5.

PLATE 42. Fig. 172: 1:2. Fig. 173: 1:2. Fig. 174: 1:2.

PLATE 43. Fig. 175: 1:2. Fig. 176: 1:2.

Plates

Plate 1

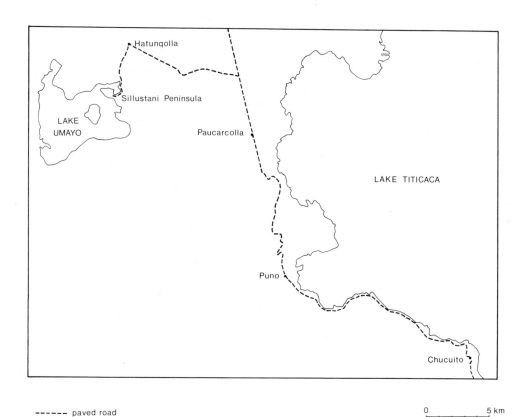

------ paved road

0 _____ 5 km

PLATE 1. Detail of the Puno area.

Plate 2

2a

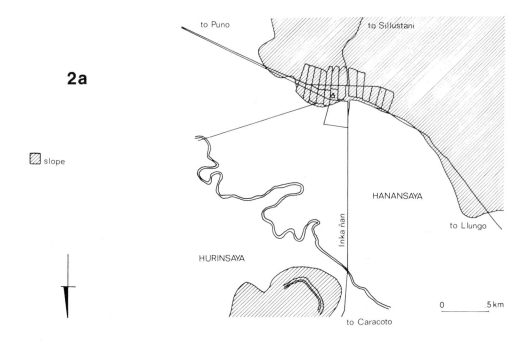

to Puno   to Sillustani

◨ slope

HANANSAYA

Inka ñan

to Llungo

HURINSAYA

to Caracoto

0   5 km

2b

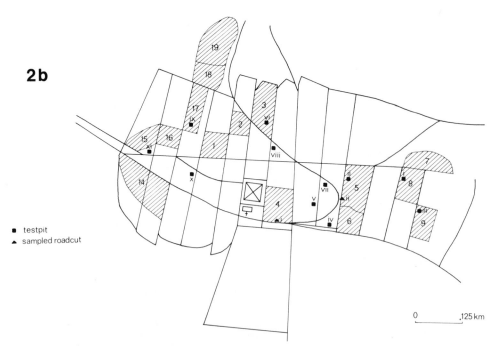

■ testpit
▲ sampled roadcut

0   .125 km

PLATE 2. 2a: Grid plan of Hatunqolla, roadways and saya division. 2b: Areas of surface collection and test excavation at Hatunqolla.

Plate 3

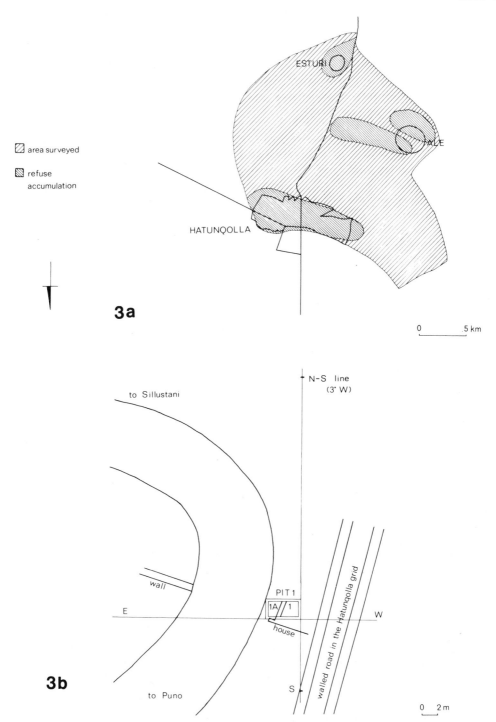

area surveyed

refuse accumulation

ESTURI

ALE

HATUNQOLLA

3a

0   .5 km

to Sillustani

N-S line
(3° W)

wall

PIT 1

1A / 1

E   W

house

to Puno

S

walled road in the Hatunqolla grid

3b

0   2m

PLATE 3.   3a: Archaeological sites in the vicinity of
Hatunqolla.   3b: Pit 1/1A in relation to 1971 roadway.

Plate 4

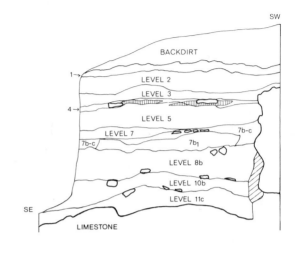

PIT 1A

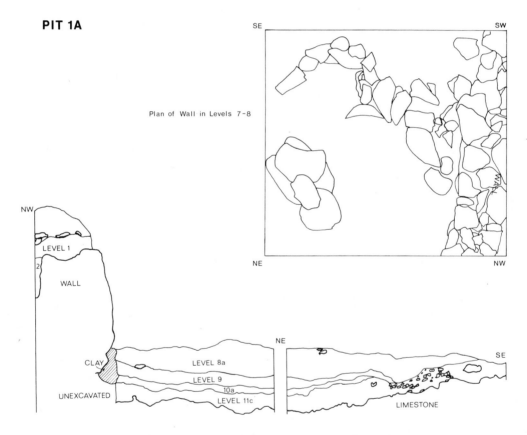

Plan of Wall in Levels 7-8

PLATES 4-5. Profiles and floor plans of Pit 1/1a. Note: Pit 1A was extended directly from Pit 1 without leaving a balk.

Plate 5

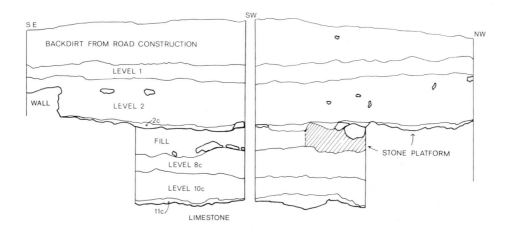

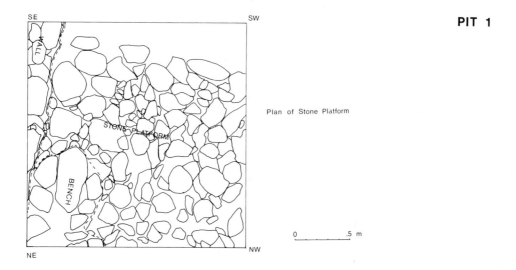

PIT 1

Plan of Stone Platform

0 _____ .5 m

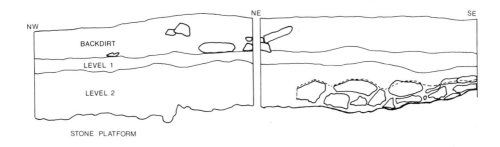

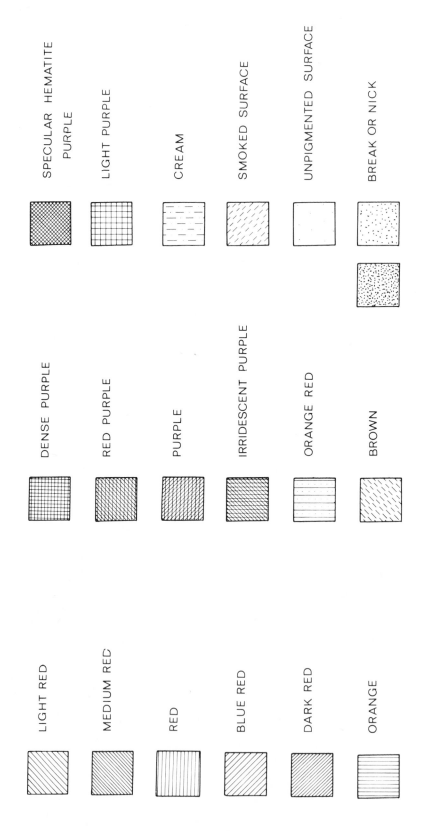

PLATE 6. Color key used in illustrating Hatunqolla ceramics.

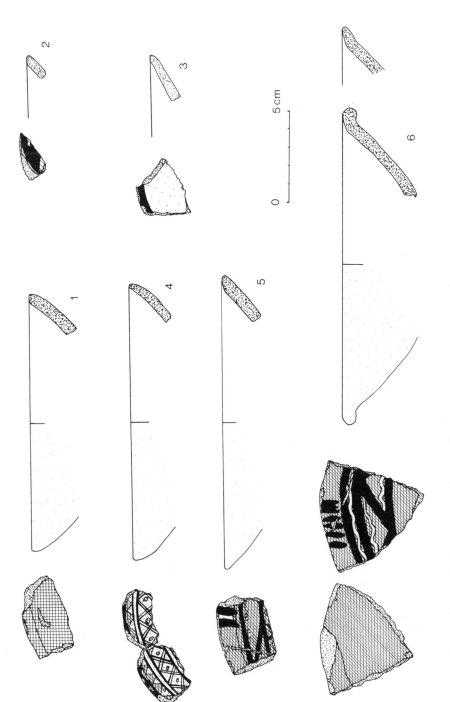

5 cm

0

PLATE 7. Figs. 1-6: Ceramics of Phase 1.

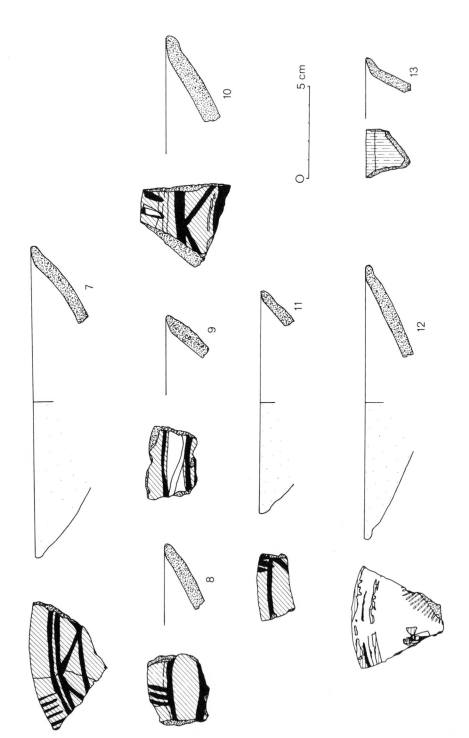

PLATE 8. Figs. 7-13: Ceramics of Phase 1.

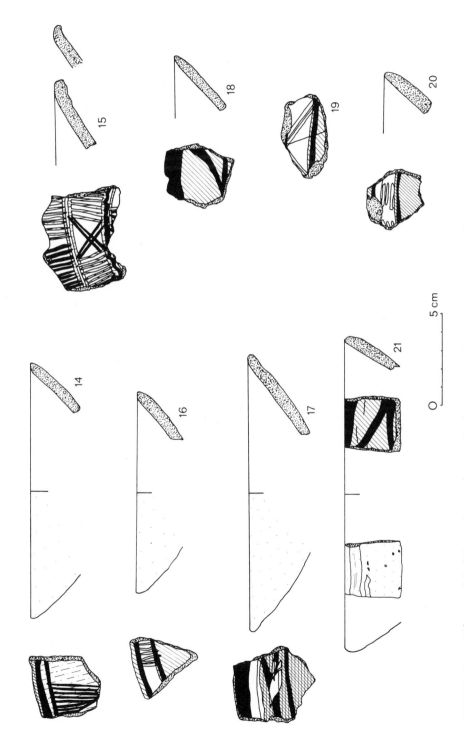

PLATE 9. Figs. 14-21: Ceramics of Phase 1.

0 ⌊_____⌋ 5 cm

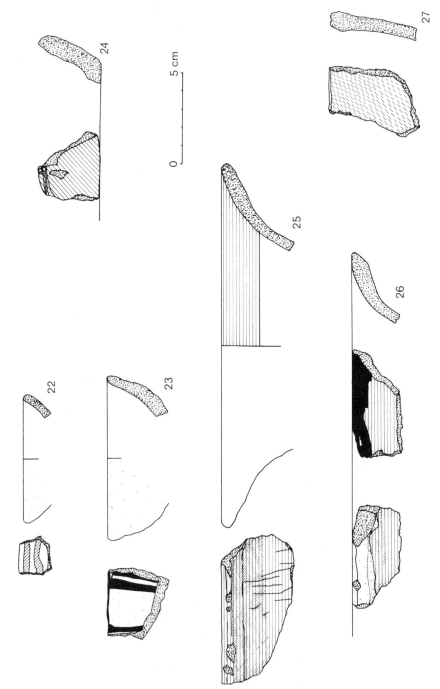

PLATE 10. Figs. 22-27: Ceramics of Phase 1.

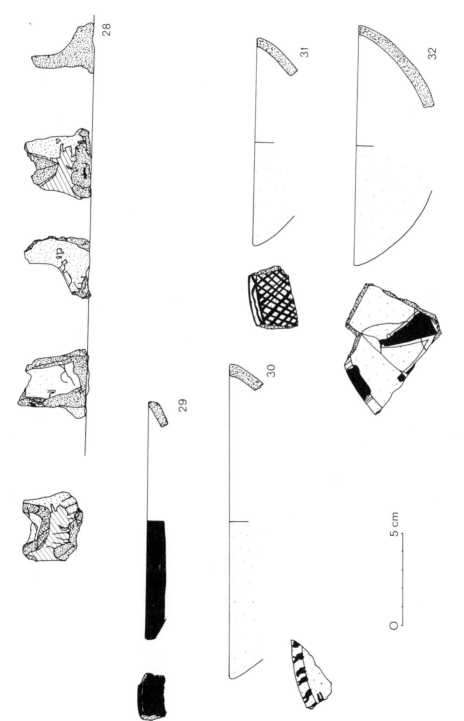

PLATE 11. Figs. 28-29: Ceramics of Phase 1. Figs. 30-32: Ceramics of Phase 2.

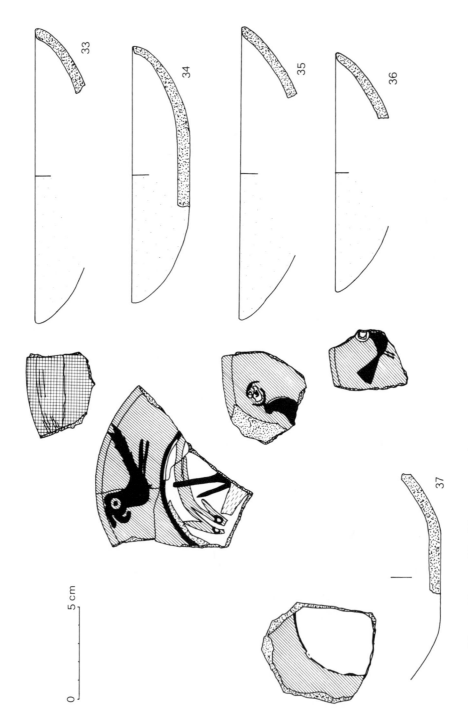

PLATE 12. Figs. 33–36: Ceramics of Phase 2.

0 ___ 5 cm

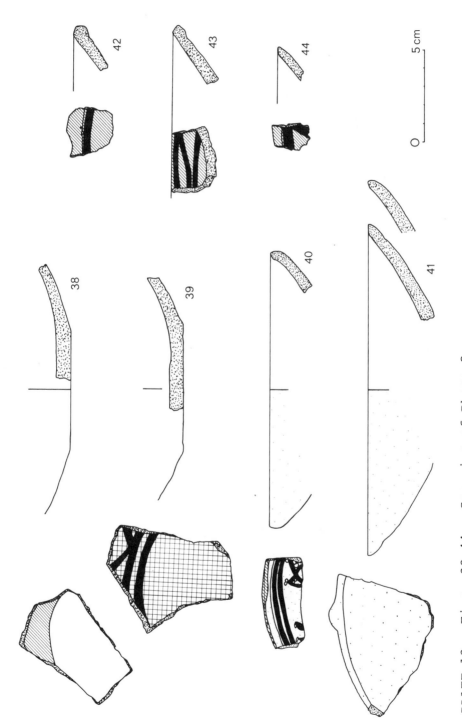

PLATE 13. Figs. 38-44: Ceramics of Phase 2.

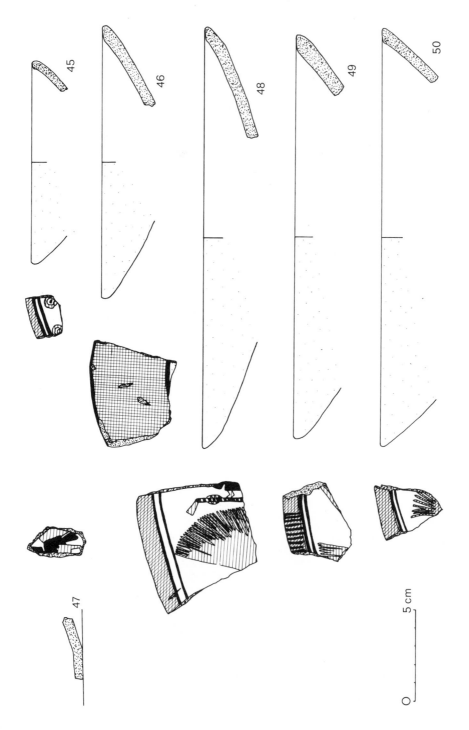

PLATE 14. Figs. 45-50: Ceramics of Phase 2.

0   5 cm

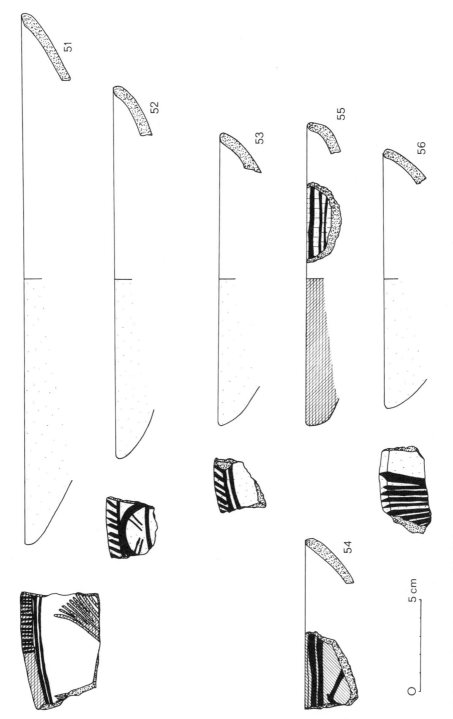

PLATE 15. Figs. 51-56: Ceramics of Phase 2.

0   5 cm

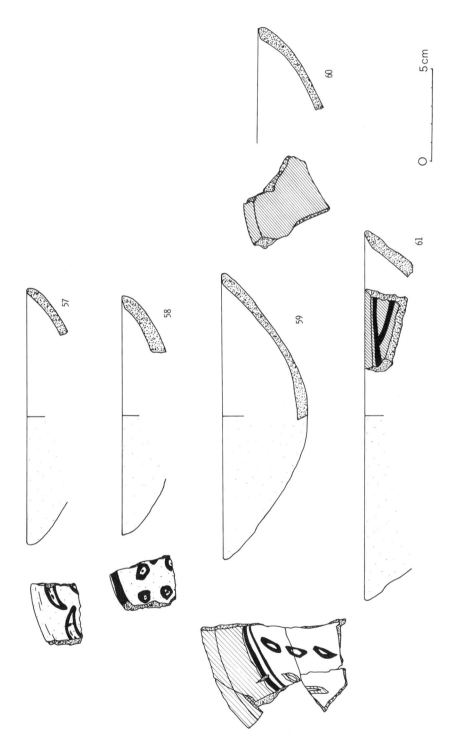

PLATE 16. Figs. 57-61: Ceramics of Phase 2.

5 cm

0

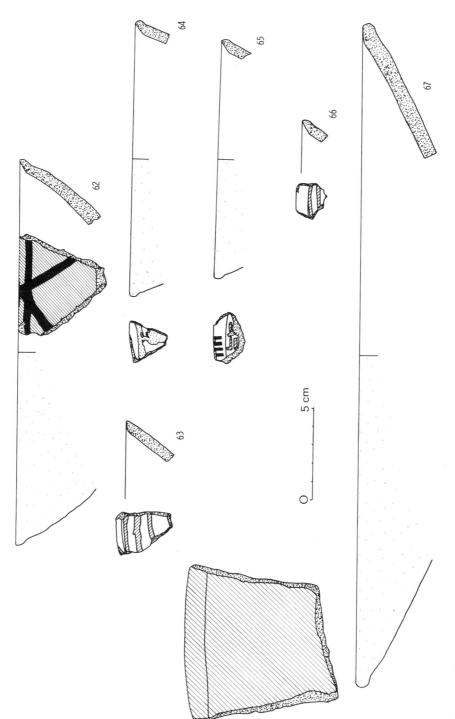

PLATE 17. Figs. 62-67: Ceramics of Phase 2.

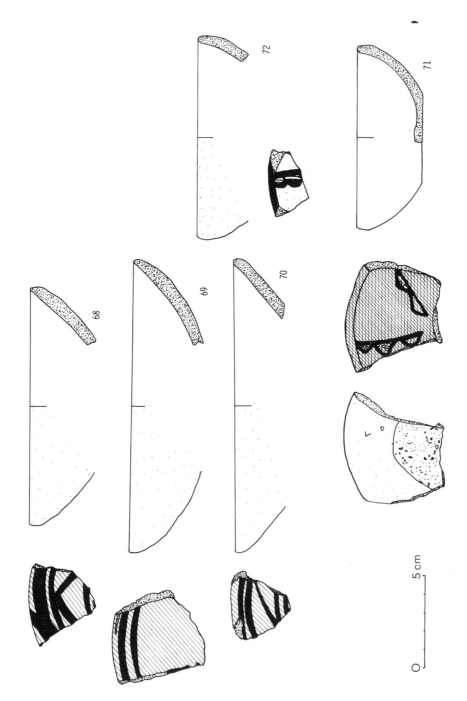

PLATE 18. Figs. 68-72: Ceramics of Phase 2.

0 ___ 5 cm

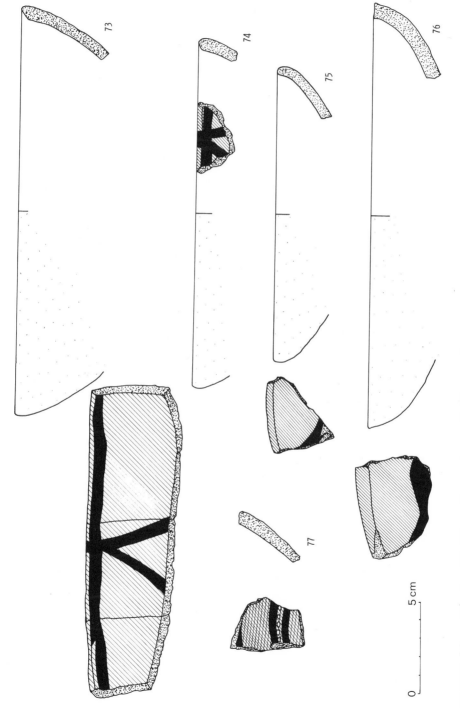

PLATE 19. Figs. 73-77: Ceramics of Phase 2.

0   5 cm

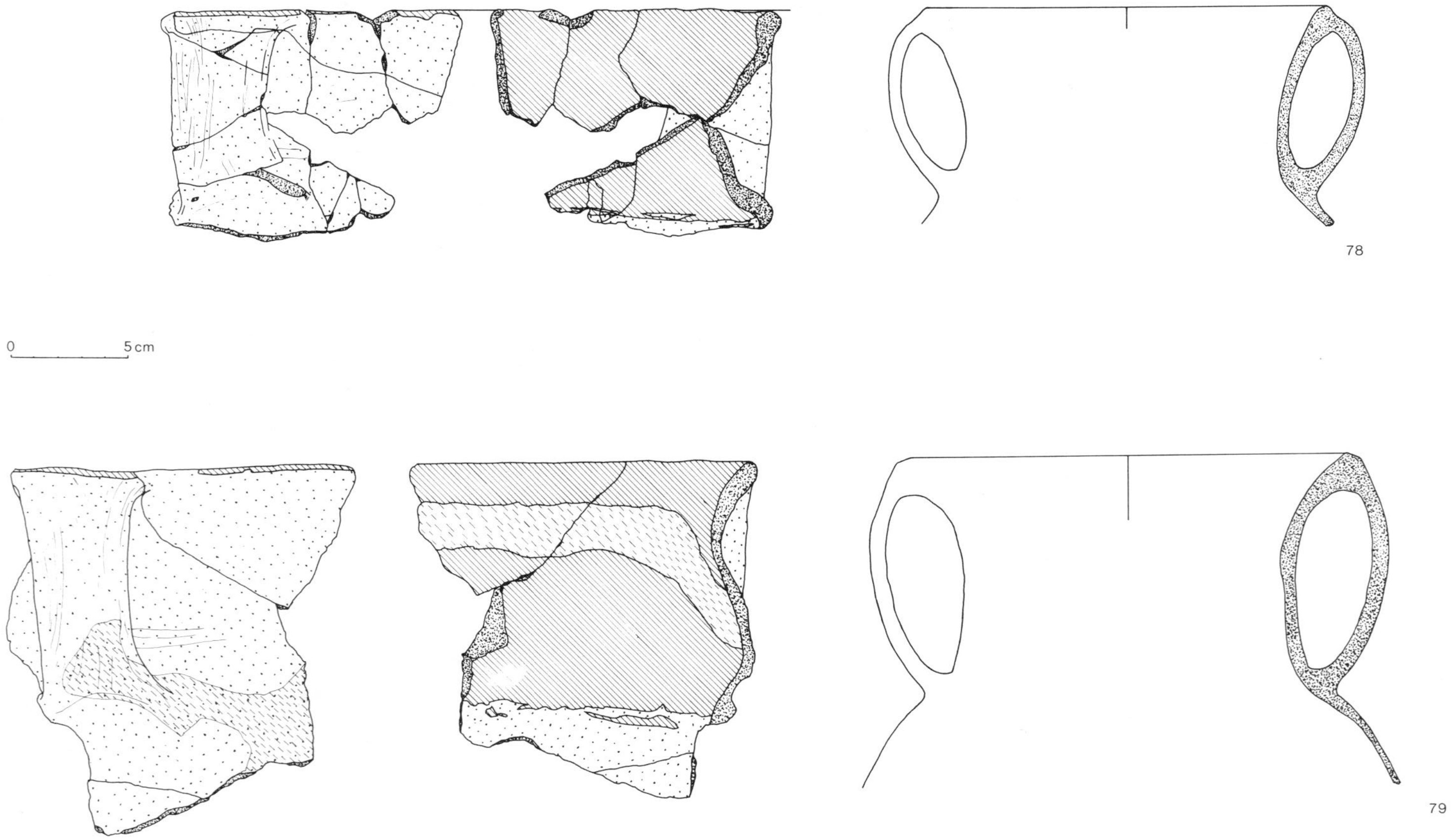

78

79

5 cm

0

PLATE 20. Figs. 78-79: Ceramics of Phase 2.

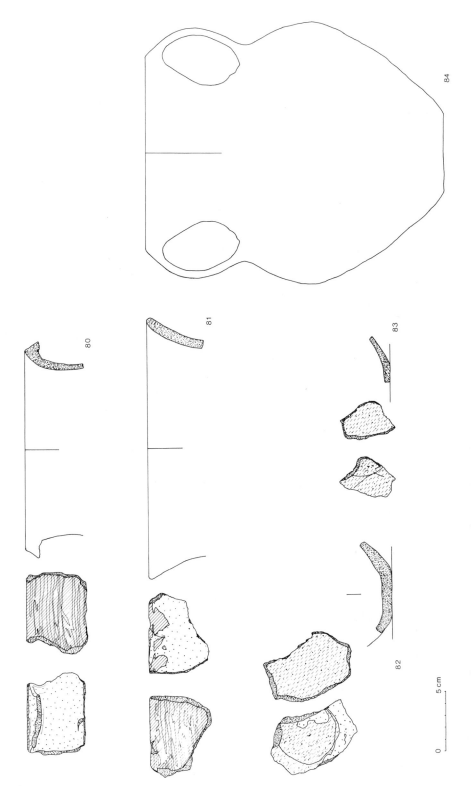

PLATE 21. Figs. 80-84: Ceramics of Phase 2.

0   5 cm

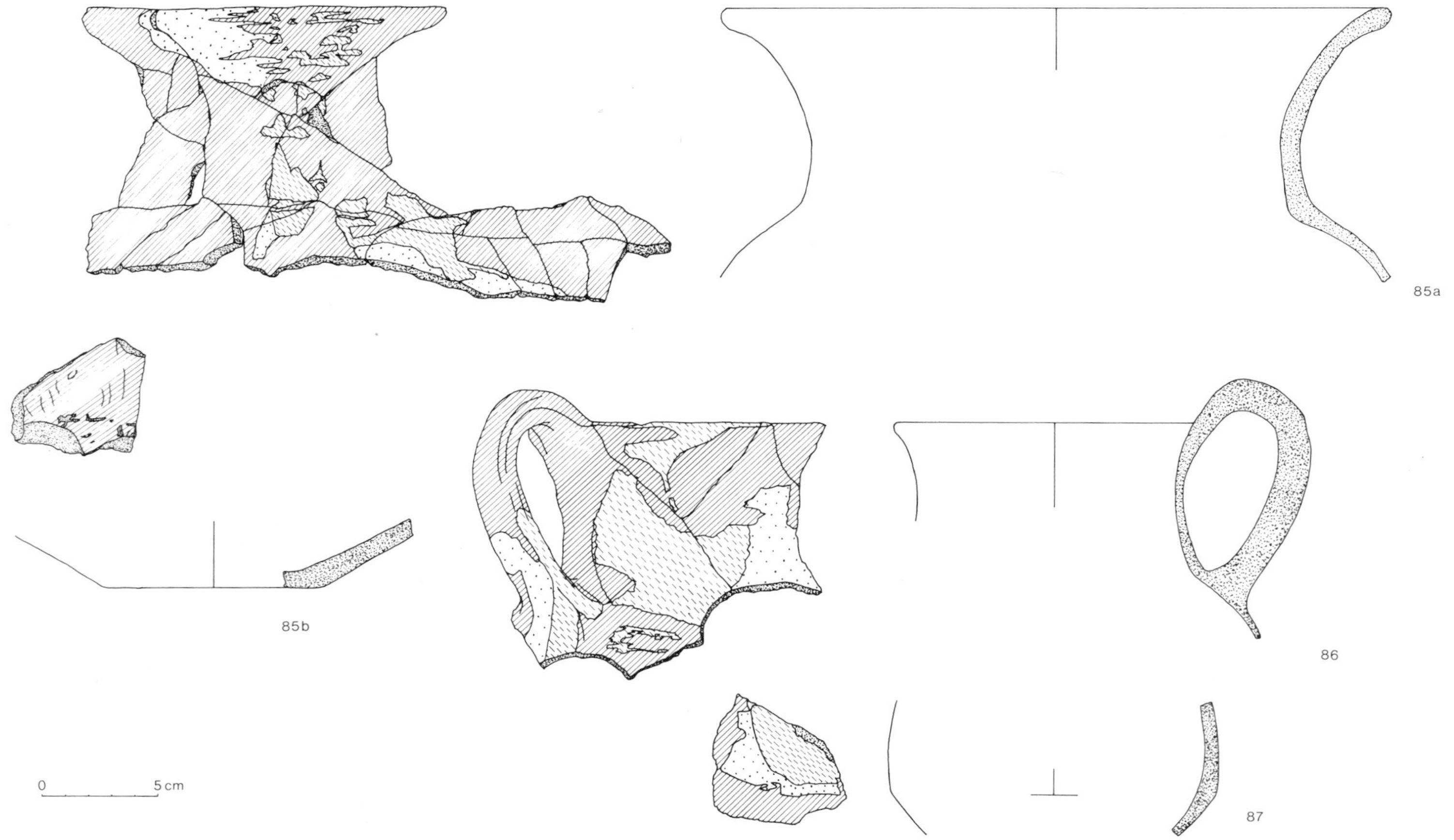

85a

86

87

85b

0 ___ 5 cm

PLATE 22. Figs. 85–87: Ceramics of Phase 2.

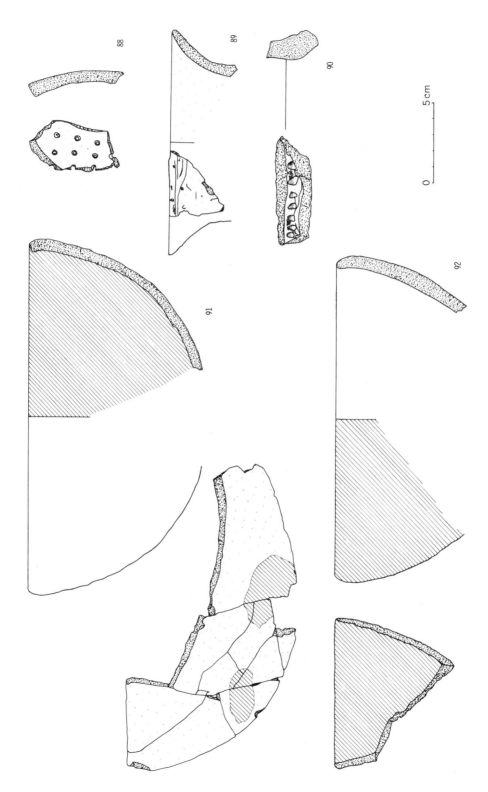

PLATE 23. Figs. 88-92: Ceramics of Phase 2.

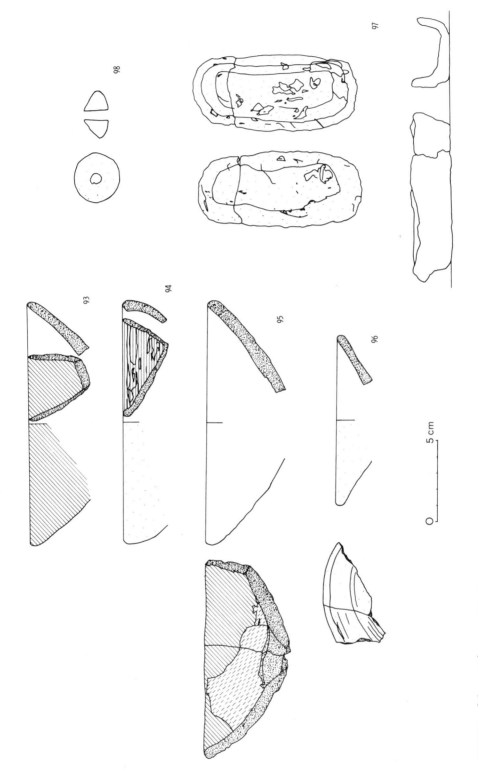

PLATE 24. Figs. 93-98: Ceramics of Phase 2.

5 cm

Plate 25

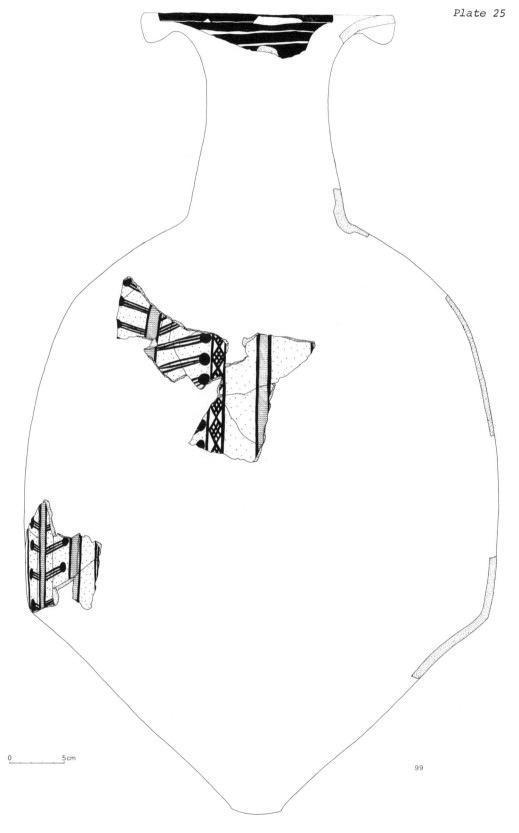

0 _____ 5cm

99

Plate 25. Fig. 99: Ceramic vessel of Phase 2.

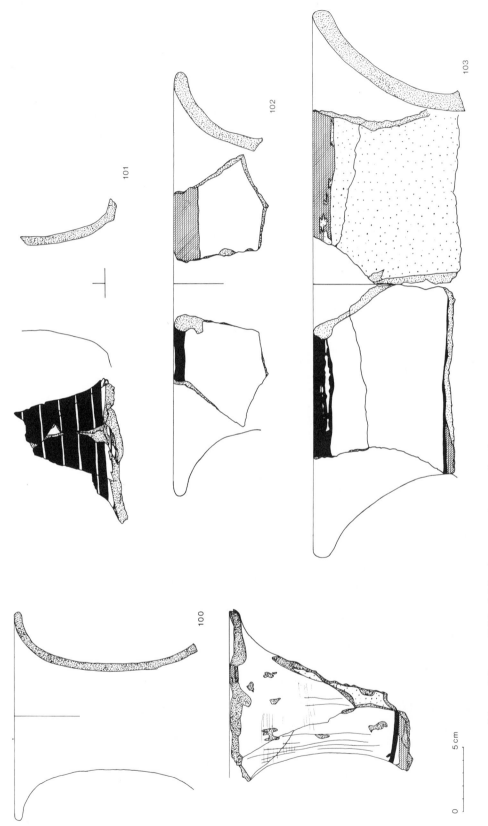

PLATE 26. Figs. 100-103: Ceramics of Phase 2.

0   5 cm

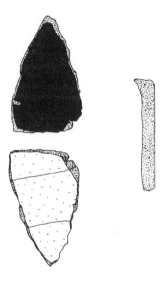

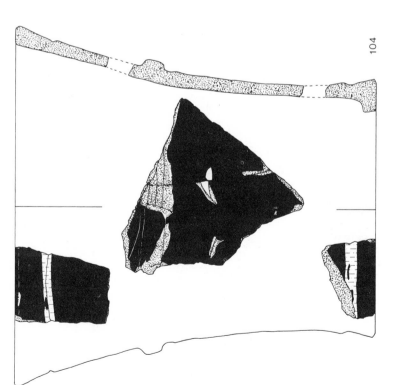

104

5 cm

0

PLATE 27. Fig. 104: Ceramic vessel of Phase 2.

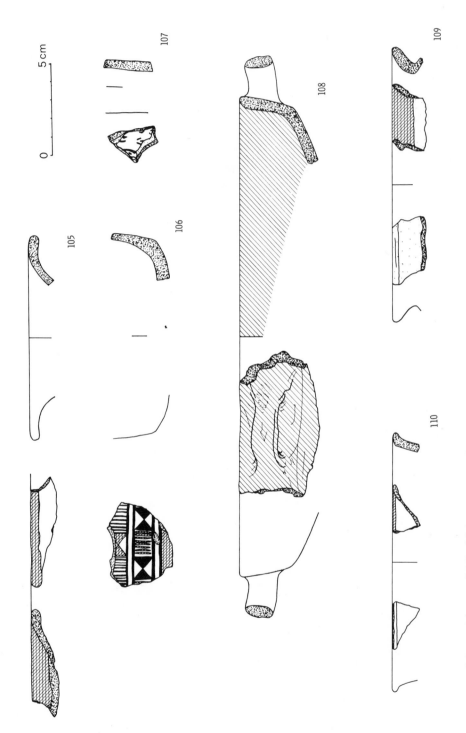

PLATE 28. Figs. 105-110: Ceramics of Phase 2.

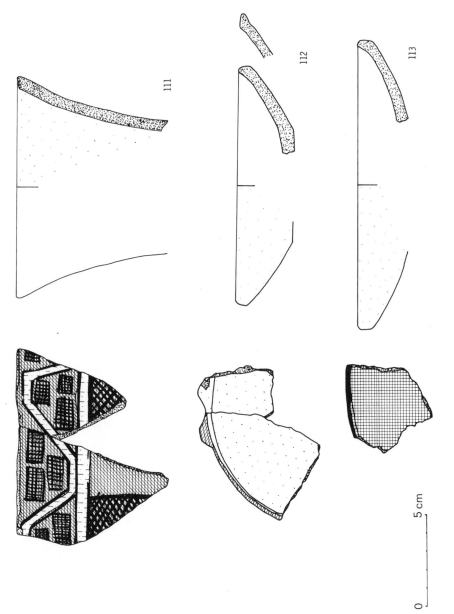

111

112

113

PLATE 29. Figs. 111-113: Ceramics of Phase 2.

0   5 cm

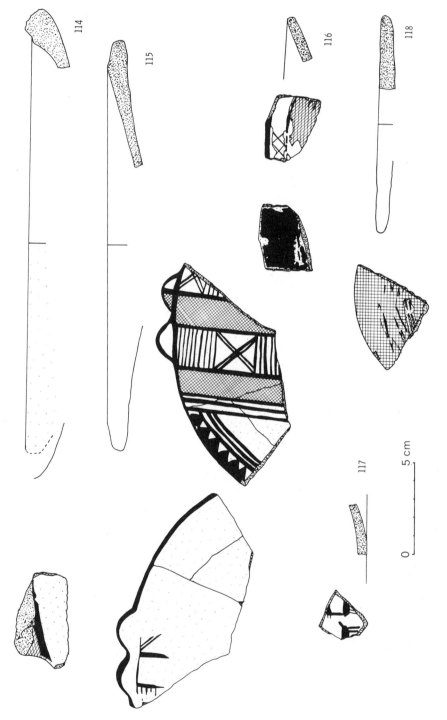

PLATE 30. Figs. 114–118: Ceramics of Phase 2.

0   5 cm

114

115

116

118

117

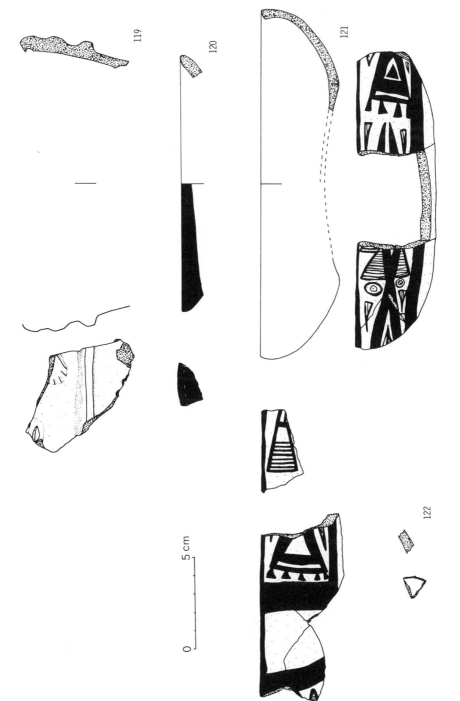

119

120

121

5 cm

0

122

PLATE 31. Figs. 119-122: Ceramics of Phase 2.

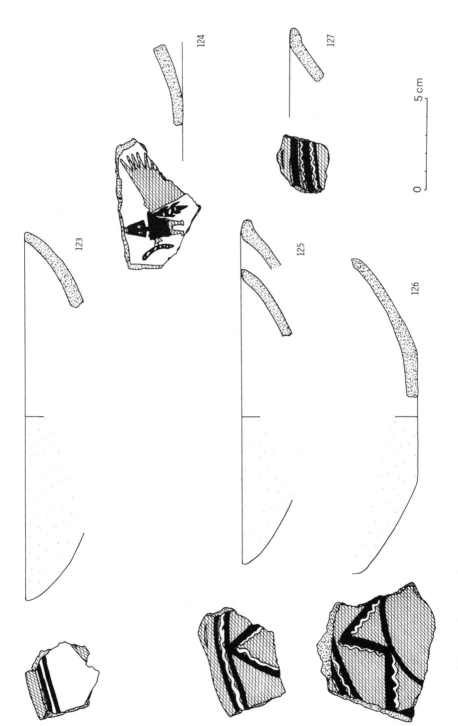

PLATE 32.   Figs. 123-127:   Ceramics of Phase 3.

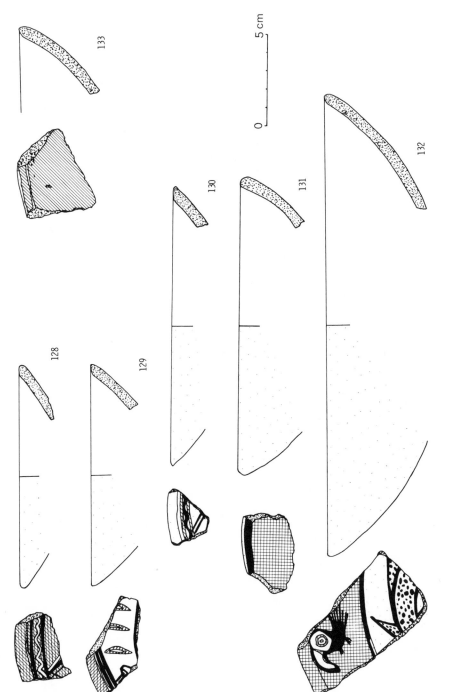

PLATE 33. Figs. 128–133: Ceramics of Phase 3.

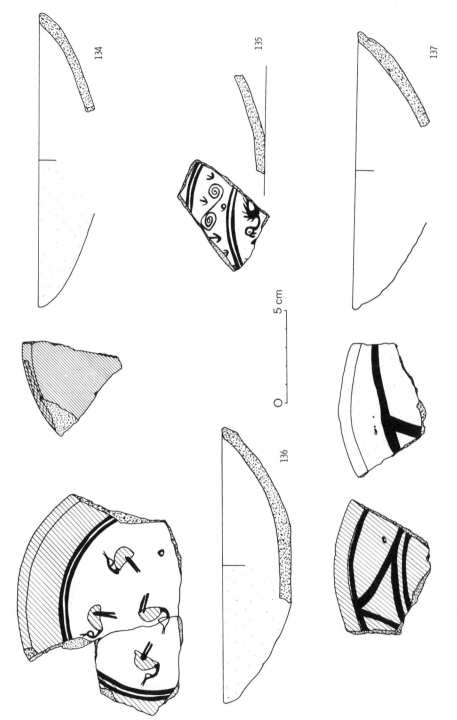

PLATE 34. Figs. 134–137: Ceramics of Phase 3.

5 cm

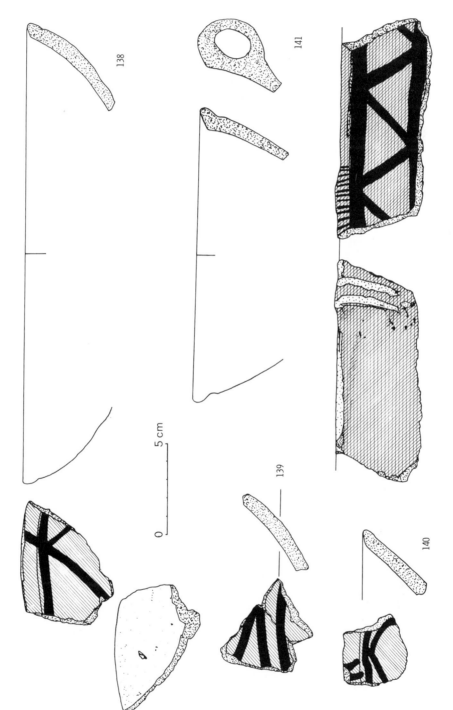

0   5 cm

138

139

140

141

PLATE 35. Figs. 138-141: Ceramics of Phase 3.

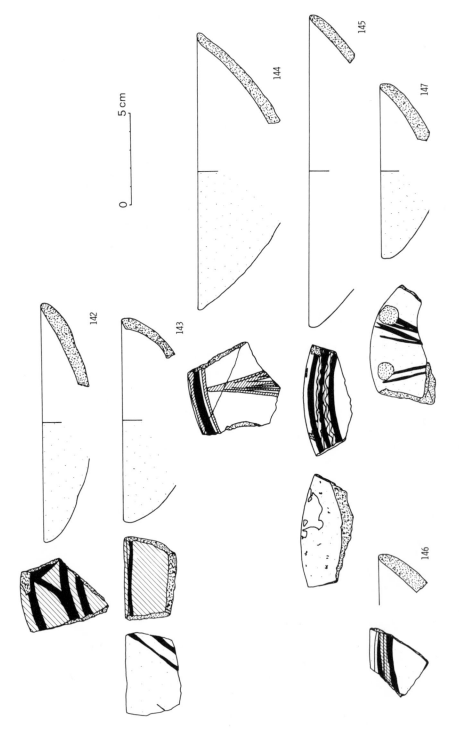

PLATE 36. Figs. 142-147: Ceramics of Phase 3.

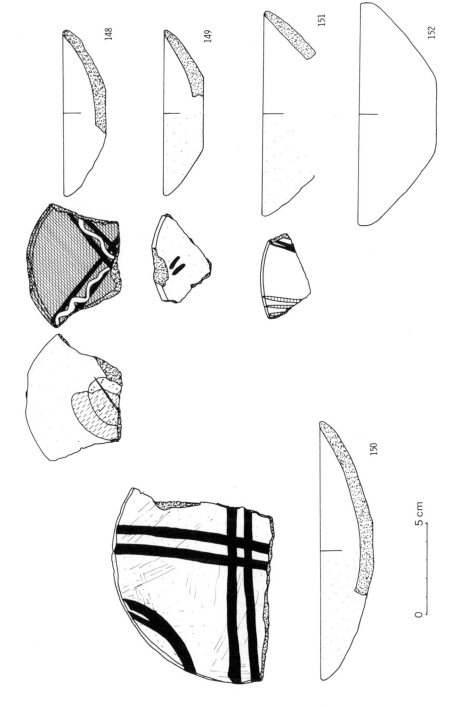

PLATE 37. Figs. 148–152: Ceramics of Phase 3.

0   5 cm

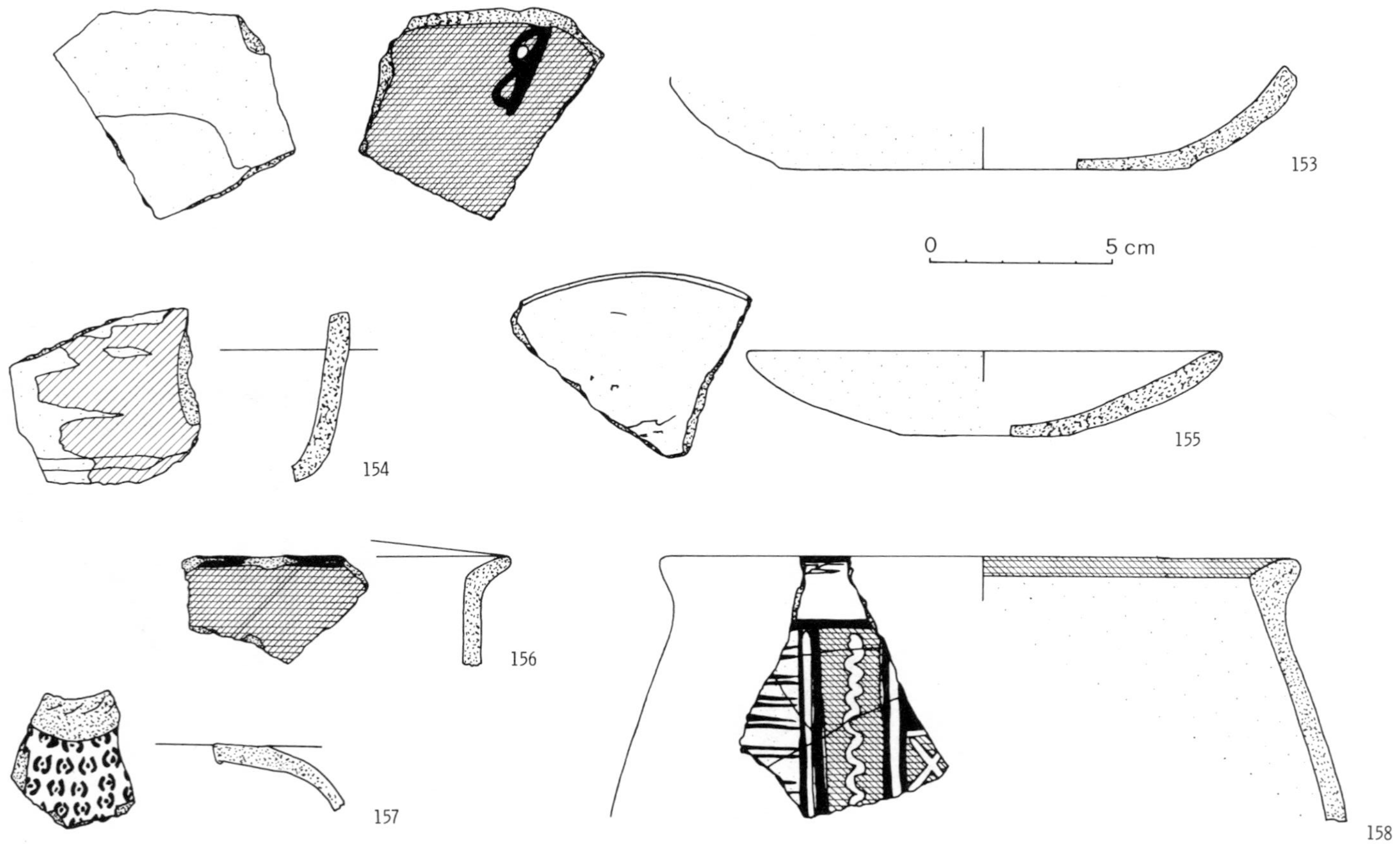

153

155

158

5 cm

0

154

156

157

PLATE 38. Figs. 153-158: Ceramics of Phase 3.

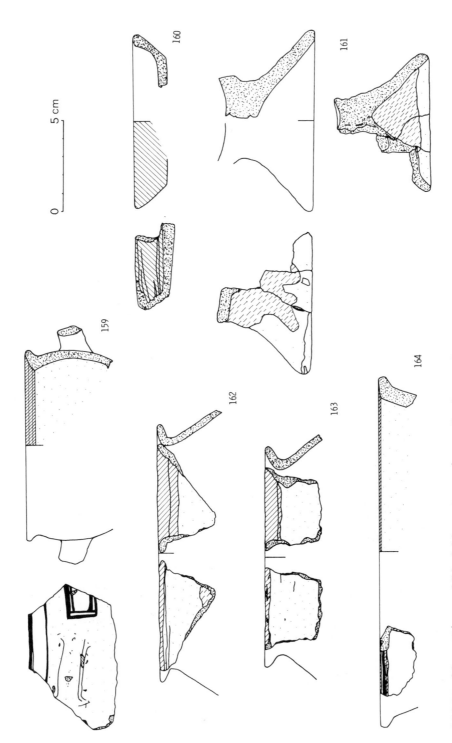

PLATE 39. Figs. 159-164: Ceramics of Phase 3.

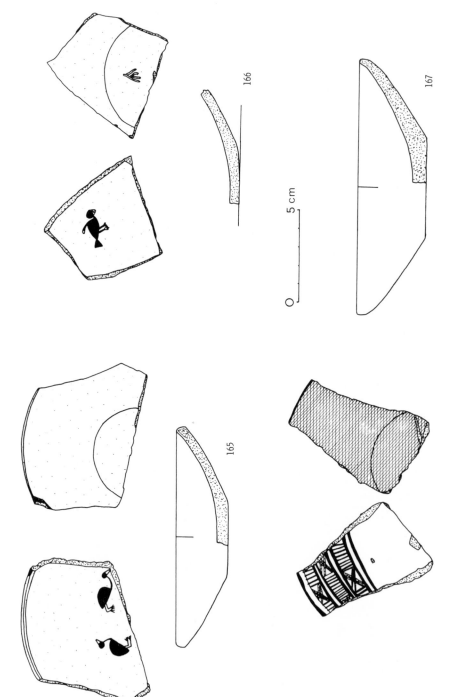

PLATE 40. Figs. 165–167: Ceramics of Phase 3.

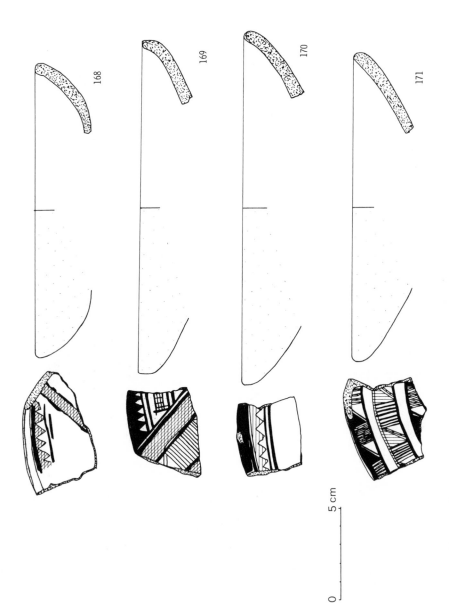

PLATE 41.   Figs. 168-171:   Ceramics of Phase 3.

5 cm

0

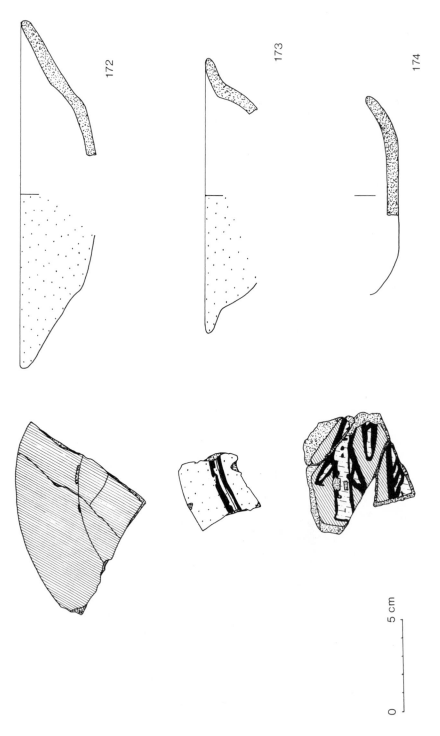

PLATE 42. Figs. 172-174: Ceramics of Phase 4.

0   5 cm

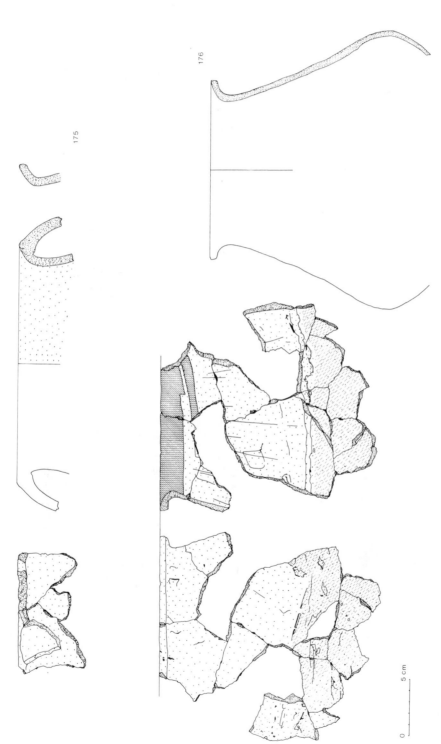

175

176

PLATE 43. Figs. 175-176: Ceramics of Phase 4.

0   5 cm

PLATE 44.   Fig. 177a-b: Ceramics of Phase 1.   5 cm. scale.

PLATE 45.   Fig. 178a-c: Ceramics of Phase 1.   5 cm. scale.

PLATE 46. Fig. 179a–e: Ceramics of Phase 1. 5 cm. scale.

PLATE 47. Fig. 180a–j: Ceramics of Phase 1. 5 cm. scale.

PLATE 48. Fig. 181a-h: Ceramics of Phase 2. 5 cm. scale.

PLATE 49. Fig. 182a-f: Ceramics of Phase 2. 5 cm. scale.

PLATE 50.   Fig. 183a-e: Ceramics of Phase 2.   5 cm. scale.

PLATE 51.   Fig. 184a-d: Ceramics of Phase 2.   5 cm. scale.

Text within image: HATUNQOLLA PPu 7-1 PIT 1A LEVEL 5

PLATE 52. Fig. 185a-j: Ceramics of Phase 3. 5 cm. scale.

Text within image: HATUNQOLLA PPu 7-1 PIT 1A LEVEL 5

PLATE 53. Fig. 186a-f: Ceramics of Phase 3. 5 cm. scale.

PLATE 54.   Fig. 187a-e: Ceramics of Phase 3.   5 cm. scale.

PLATE 55.   Fig. 188a-d: Ceramics of Phase 3.   5 cm. scale.

Plate 56

PLATE 56. Fig. 189a-i: Ceramics of Phase 4. 5 cm. scale.

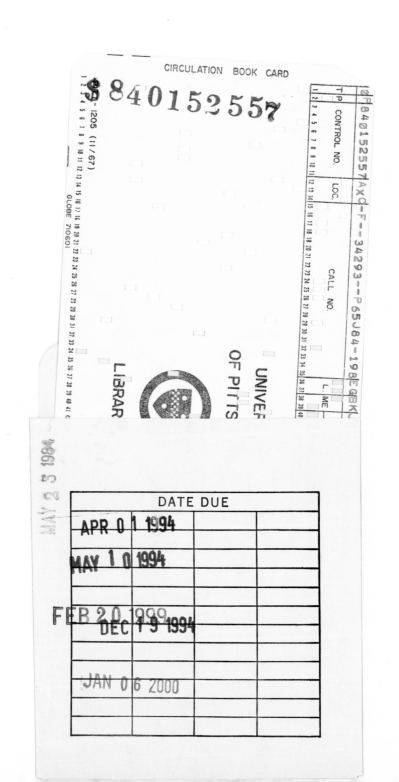